Original Teachings of
CH'AN BUDDHISM

Selected from *The Transmission of the Lamp*

Original CH'AN

Teachings of BUDDHISM

Selected from
The Transmission of the Lamp

TRANSLATED WITH INTRODUCTIONS BY
CHANG CHUNG-YUAN

FIRST PRINTING

Copyright © 1969 by Chang Chung-Yuan

All rights reserved under International and Pan-American Copyright Conventions. Published in the United States by Pantheon Books, a division of Random House, Inc., New York, and simultaneously in Canada by Random House of Canada Limited, Toronto.

Library of Congress Catalog Card Number: 75-79799

Original Edition Published:
Pantheon Books
New York, 1969.

Designed by Kenneth Miyamoto

Contents

Foreword   vii

PART I

INTRODUCTION *Metaphysical and Logical Approaches in Early Ch'an Teachings*   3

NIU-T'OU FA-YUNG *No-mind Is Not Different from Mind*   17

YUNG-CHIA HSÜAN-CHIO *Dialectic as a Self-conscious Movement*   27

PART II

INTRODUCTION *Interfusion of Universality and Particularity*   41

TUNG-SHAN LIANG-CHIEH *"He Is the Same as Me, Yet I Am Not He!"*   58

TS'AO-SHAN PÊN-CHI *"Purity Is in the Impure"*   71

PART III

INTRODUCTION *Liberation from Subjectivity and Objectivity*   85

HUANG-PO HSI-YÜN *To Roar Like a Tiger*   102

MU-CHOU TAO-TSUNG *"Before a Donkey and After a Horse"*   107

LIN-CHI I-HSÜAN *"Here I Will Bury You Alive"*   116

PART IV

INTRODUCTION *Illogical and Unconventional Approaches to Ch'an*   129

KIANGSI TAO-I *"The Mind Is the Buddha"*   148

Contents

NAN-CH'ÜAN P'U-YÜAN *"To Be a Buffalo Down the Hill"*	153
CHAO-CHOU TS'UNG-SHEN *"You See the Logs, But Not the Chao-chou Bridge"*	164
P'ANG YÜN *Inner Harmony in Daily Activity*	174

PART V

INTRODUCTION *Inner Experience Illustrated in Three-Way Interplay*	185
KUEI-SHAN LING-YU *Great Action and Great Potentiality*	200
YANG-SHAN HUI-CHI *"An Excellent Swordsman"*	209
HSIANG-YEN CHIH-HSIEN *Enlightened by One Stroke*	219

PART VI

INTRODUCTION *The Six Phenomena and the Void*	229
FA-YEN WÊN-I *"One Got It, the Other Missed"*	238
YUNG-MING YEN-SHOU *"From the Womb of a Cow an Elephant Is Born"*	250

PART VII

INTRODUCTION *"The Swiftness and Steepness"—a Forceful Means to Enlightenment*	259
HSÜEH-FÊNG I-TS'UN *"Not To Blind Any Man's Eye"*	275
YÜN-MÊN WÊN-YEN *"The Mountain Is Steep; the Clouds Are Low"*	283
TUNG-SHAN SHOU-CH'U *"Living Words and Dead Words"*	296
Final Remarks	302
A CHART OF THE EMINENT CH'AN MASTERS (594–990) Selected from *The Transmission of the Lamp*	305
Bibliography	313
Index	321

Foreword

There is a story of an art lover from the Far East who went to a museum in New York to see Picasso's famous "Guernica" when that canvas was first acquired. This eager Easterner trudged through the entire museum, up and down stairs, through all the galleries, but could not find the picture he had come to see. Disappointed, he decided to leave, but on his way out, by the entrance where he had first come in, he finally discovered the painting he had been seeking. Then his disappointment gave way to astonishment. Could this huge, grotesque canvas truly be the masterpiece of a world-renowned painter? No matter how long he stared, or how carefully he examined and considered it, he still found it difficult to understand why this work was so highly valued by recognized experts and men of taste in the Western world. This earnest admirer of art from an alien culture truly wished to become initiated into the best in modern Western aesthetics, but his ignorance of its philosophy stood in his way. He had found the painting physically, yet it still eluded him because he could not appreciate it, sincerely though he wished to.

Foreword

For many Westerners the understanding of Chinese Ch'an Buddhism (or Zen Buddhism, as it is called in Japanese) presents similar problems. First of all, there is the question of finding it, since much of the literature has not yet been translated, particularly the ancient Chinese texts that we are making available, in part, in this volume. But there is another barrier, of the sort that is presented to the uninitiated by Picasso's artistry. Chinese Ch'an Buddhism, when we first approach it, may seem strange and unfamiliar. Yet the work of the Ch'an Buddhists is a historic milestone in the development of the mind and personality of man, though its significance has been little appreciated in the West until recent years, when some of the treasures of Ch'an literature have been interpreted and made available to its admirers and students. This work is an effort to enlarge that understanding.

In 1934, Carl Gustav Jung, in his foreword to Daisetz T. Suzuki's *An Introduction to Zen Buddhism*,[1] described Ch'an as a process transforming the limited ego-form self into the unlimited non-ego-form self. When one embraces an insight into the nature of one's self, emancipation from the illusory conception of self takes place and total consciousness emerges. This new, total consciousness is distinguished from the ego-form consciousness in that the latter is always conscious of something, whereas the former takes no object but itself. It is as if the subject character of the ego has disappeared, leaving this total consciousness conscious of itself. It is free from attachment to things, creatures, and circumstances. By this turning inward, man glimpses a total exhibition of potential nature. This realization may be illustrated by the words of Hsüan-sha Shih-pei. A disciple once asked him how he could enter Ch'an. He answered, "Do you hear the murmuring of the stream?" "Yes." "Therein you may enter."

Jung explains that this "hearing" is obviously something quite different from ordinary hearing. William Barrett, who uses the same story in his introduction to Suzuki's *Zen Buddhism*, calls this consciousness Radical Intuitionism.[2] Intuition is an activity, but one without either subject or object. It is our most unified state of consciousness, or pure experience. When it is in action, artists gain new inspiration, scientists make new breakthroughs and discoveries, and religious devotees acquire new vision. But this faculty is not limited to the genius; it may be manifested as well in the daily activities of the common man and even by the innocent child. All thought is systematic, but at the base of any system there must be a unifying intuition. Intuition is beyond all thought, yet it is the ground from which all thought takes form. As Kitarō Nishida, late professor at Kyoto University, has said: "At the base of thought there is always concealed a certain mystical element; even a geometric axiom is a thing of this kind. Usually we say that thought can explain but intuition cannot, yet explanation means nothing more than being able to reduce to an even more basic intuition."[3]

Basic intuition is not abstract knowledge, and neither is it blind emotion. It is the profound unity which is identified as the real self. Jung calls it the unlimited non-ego-form self. The Ch'an Buddhist calls it enlightenment. That is why, as William Barrett puts it: "Zen [Ch'an] expresses itself concretely because Zen is above all interested in facts, not theories, in realities and not those pallid counters for reality which we know as concepts. Fact may suggest to the Western mind something merely quantitative, or statistical —therefore also a lifeless and abstract thing. Zen wants, rather, the facts as living and concrete. In this sense, Zen may be described as Radical Intuitionism—if the Westerner wishes a handle by which to lay hold of it. This does not mean a philosophy of intuition like Bergson's, though it agrees with Bergson that the conceptualizing intellect does not reach reality; rather it is radical intuition in the act itself. Radical Intuitionism means that Zen holds that thinking and sensing live, move, and have their being within the vital medium of intuition."[4]

Barrett goes on to compare the mind of Plato with the mind of Buddha. In the philosophy of Plato, who founded the Western intellectual tradition, one proceeds from the lower world of the senses to the lofty realm of thought, of fixed and unchanging ideas. Buddhist philosophy, on the other hand, leads beyond the world of the intellect to the one real world that was always there, living and palpable, unabstracted. Ch'an grew from this tradition, which

Foreword

so sharply diverges from that of the West.* But Ch'an is not content with mere doctrine, or exposition. Ch'an must be lived, must be experienced concretely every single moment of the day.

In reviewing the development of Chinese Buddhist thought, we see that the Radical Intuitionism of Ch'an did not occur immediately, but after centuries of logical, metaphysical, and psychological exploration. For example, the San-lun School was deeply involved in logical exposition of the relationship between affirmation and negation, or being and non-being, and set forth a dialectic system by which one was supposed to be able to achieve enlightenment. The Hua-yen School took a metaphysical approach in their exploration of the interfusion of particularity and universality, or the One and the Many. The Mere-Ideation School adopted a psychological approach, and categorized divergent mental states in an effort to transform ordinary consciousness into pure consciousness. These schools paved the way for the development of Ch'an. By the seventh century, Chinese thinkers were ready to go beyond logic, beyond metaphysics, and beyond psychology to a more direct confrontation of reality. It was then that Ch'an emerged. It flourished all over China, up until the thirteenth century, and in Japan it continues to flourish even to this day.

For Ch'an Buddhists, intellection was a hindrance to the achievement of enlightenment. The logical and metaphysical approach depended heavily upon intellectual effort, but these efforts often resulted in mere knowledge about reality, failing to reveal reality itself. Nature, they felt, is not an external imposition or a mechanical system, but an expression of the same dynamic process that manifests itself in the highest level of total consciousness. Total consciousness is pure activity and is the fountain of creative potentiality. It is an invisible but all-pervading and far-reaching universal self which is considered the Source of All Things, or, as the Ch'an Buddhist puts it, the "original face before one is born."

* However, a totally new spirit in the world of philosophy seems quite likely to emerge in the West. Contemporary science, mathematics, and the arts are presently in a state of transition. Discoveries have been made that prove conclusively that all so-called "facts" are relative, and that the very nature of knowledge itself is paradoxical.

Foreword

For the Ch'an Buddhist, being and non-being, life and death, right and wrong, are mutually identified; they all emerge from this original face. Man is real insofar as he is rooted in this ground; he is not real as an isolated individual. Therefore the goal of man is to reach this ground of life, and it is here that he attains the highest level of consciousness. It is here that absolute reality unfolds itself, that light emerges from darkness, that freedom casts off the last of its bonds and limitations. The man who attains this is called by the Ch'an Buddhist *chu*, or "Master of His Own." When one is truly his own master, his actions are spontaneous and he draws freely upon his own endowments and potentialities. His life and his actions emerge directly from the center of his own being.

Therefore, self-realization is the essential principle in the teachings of Ch'an. Ta-chu Hui-hai, an eighth-century Buddhist, once went to visit the great master Ma-tsu (Kiangsi Tao-i). The Master asked him, "Why do you come here?" Ta-chu replied, "I come seeking enlightenment." The Master said, "Why should you leave your home to wander about and neglect your own precious treasure? There is nothing I can give you. Why do you seek enlightenment from me?" The visitor pressed him for the truth: "But what is my treasure?" The Master answered, "It is he who has just asked the question. It contains everything and lacks nothing. There is no need to seek it outside yourself."[5]

The type of exchange described above, a dialogue between master and student, is the *kung-an*, or *koan* in Japanese. Dr. Suzuki describes the method of *kung-an* as follows:

> The method of the *koan* exercise . . . is to blot out by sheer force of the will all the discursive traces of intellection whereby students of Zen prepare their consciousness to be the proper ground for intuitive knowledge to burst out. They march through a forest of ideas thickly crowding up into their minds; and when, thoroughly exhausted in their struggles, they give themselves up, the state of consciousness . . . after which they have so earnestly but rather blindly been seeking unexpectedly prevails.
>
> This last giving-up is what I would term a state of passivity in our religious experience. Without this giving-up, whether

Foreword

intellectually or conatively or emotionally, or in whatever way we may designate this psychological process, there is generally no experience of a final reality.[6]

To pursue the study of Ch'an through this *kung-an* training is no easy matter. Of Ta-hui Tsung-kao (1089–1163), who became a strong advocate of *kung-an*, it is said that when he was a student under Master Yüan-wu K'ê-ch'in (1063–1135) he was given the following *kung-an* to meditate upon: "The eastern mountain sails on the river." He made forty-nine attempts to come up with the right answer and failed utterly.

Another case, involving one of Tung-shan Liang-chieh's disciples, may help us realize how difficult it can be to fathom the riddles of the *kung-an*. This elderly monk had tried ninety-six times to give the correct answer to a *kung-an* of Tung-shan's but failed each time, only to succeed on his ninety-seventh attempt. His achievement made one of his brother monks anxious to learn the correct answer from him. The younger man attended upon the older for three years in the hope of getting his secret from him, but he learned nothing. Eventually the old man fell ill. His companion said to him, "I have been with you for three years hoping you would tell me the answer you gave the Master, but you have never been kind enough to do so. Now, since I have failed to get it from you honestly, I will get it in the worst way!" Thereupon he drew a sword and brandished it at the old monk: "If you refuse me the answer now, I will kill you!" The old monk replied, "Wait! I will tell you! It is this: Even if I gave it to you, you would have no place for it." Suddenly repentant, the young monk made a deep bow.

These two extreme examples of the study of *kung-an* give us some idea of how difficult it is to abandon habits of intellectual pursuit and open the mind to another and deeper awareness.

The opening of another's mind through one's own inner light is called "the transmission of the lamp," the lamp signifying the mind-light, enlightenment, transmitted by the master to his disciples. This inner illumination, transmitted from generation to generation, is the chief characteristic of the teachings of Ch'an.

FOREWORD

The Transmission of the Lamp, from which the texts in this book are taken, consists mainly of more than a thousand *kung-an*, expressions of the inner experience and illumination of enlightened men, from the ancient patriarchs and masters to the disciples of Fa-yen Wên-i in the tenth century. Compiled by Tao-yüan in the year 1004, it is the earliest of the historical records of Ch'an Buddhism and is also the first and best source for the study of Ch'an.[7] Its thirty volumes record the sayings of over six hundred masters and the names of more than a thousand others. The present work comprises translations of the fascicles of nineteen masters,* representing the Five Schools of Ch'an Buddhism as well as the earliest known Ch'an teachings. Because these dialogues of irrelevant questions and answers may be new to the reader, I have written an interpretative introduction for each group of masters.

The original Chinese scripts that I used for my translation are reprints from the Yüan edition, printed in Japan in 1308. Another Yüan edition was preserved at the T'ien-ning Temple of Ch'ang-chou, in China, and reprinted in 1919. The Japanese edition was given to me by Dr. Suzuki; the Chinese edition was my own possession. These two editions are identical. There are three other editions: one in *Szu-pu Chung-k'an* (Part 3, Section 1), another in *Taishō shinshū daizōkyō* (*Buddhist Canon Published in the Taishō Era*: No. 2076, Vol. 51), and a third in *Chung-hua Ta-ts'ang Ching* (*Chinese Buddhist Canon*: Vol. 33, Section 9). The scripts are primarily the same, with only occasional variations from the script used in this translation. I have written an article in Chinese comparing the scripts, which will be published with the original texts by Ta Chio Szu (Temple of Great Enlightenment) in New York.

Since the thirteenth century,[8] when Ch'an teaching disappeared in China, Japanese masters and scholars have carried on the tradition, and some Ch'an texts lost in China have been preserved in monasteries in Kyoto and elsewhere in Japan. As a Chinese stu-

---

* Sixteen more fascicles have been translated by the author, but are not included here.

xiii

Foreword

dent of Ch'an, I should like to express my gratitude to the Japanese masters and scholars who have carried on the teaching of Ch'an and enabled people in the present-day world to learn this tradition.

I particularly benefitted from study under the late Dr. Daisetz T. Suzuki, while he was in America from 1951 to 1958. I also sought his guidance in this translation of *The Lamp* while I was in Japan from 1960 to 1963. During my work on this project, my thoughts have often turned to the various times I approached him with a difficult textual or interpretative point and waited for his brilliant and often very witty replies. When I was in Kamakura in early 1963, before returning to America, Dr. Suzuki gave me his final approval of my selection of the fascicles from *The Lamp* and of my translations.

In the spring of 1962, while I was in Kyoto, Mr. Richard De Martino arranged a dinner-party meeting between myself and Dr. Joseph Mitsuo Kitagawa of the University of Chicago. Dr. Kitagawa brought a message to me from Dr. Hu Shih in Taiwan, who was ill at the time and unable to write to me himself. The message was that Dr. Hu Shih had read my manuscript with approval and encouraged me to go on with my work.

While I was in Japan, I sent the fascicle of Niu-t'ou Fa-yung to Dr. Derk Bodde of the University of Pennsylvania and to Mr. C. T. Shen of the China Institute, founder of the Temple of Great Enlightenment in New York. This fascicle involves the Mādhyamika philosophy and was originally written in five-word-line rhymed verse. Both Dr. Bodde and Mr. Shen were impressed with my translation. Mr. Shen has read all of the fascicles in my manuscript, and has given me his continuous encouragement and help for publication.

During my first six months of work in Tokyo, I often had the opportunity to discuss difficult textual problems with Rōshi Asahina Sogen, the leading Rinzai Zen master in Japan. The following two years I spent in Kyoto, where Rōshi Yamada Mumon, president of Hanazono University, was very kind, often letting me stay in his temple and learn from him. The late Rōshi Hashimoto of Hokeiji and Rōshi Fujimoto Rindo of Shorinji, both leading masters of Sōtō Zen, showed enthusiasm for my translation and gave me the benefit of their thoughts on many questions. The long letters and fine comments on my work that I received from Rōshi Hashimoto are precious relics of a noble scholar and a true friend.

Professor Iriya Yoshitaka of the Research Institute for Humanistic Studies went over some of the fascicles that I had studied and gave me special help with the intricacies of the T'ang language. Professor Masao Abe of Kyoto University and Reverend Kobori Sohaku of Daitokuji read some of the fascicles and made helpful comments. Professor Pa Hu-t'ien and Mr. Nan Huai-ching in Taiwan read several fascicles and made valuable emendations. The late Mrs. Ruth F. Sasaki of the First Zen Institute of America in Kyoto kindly gave me access to the fine collections in her library and discussed difficult problems of Ch'an with me. The librarians of the Department of Philosophy at Kyoto University and at Otani University also gave me access to their collections. Mr. R. Akizuki, cotranslator with Dr. Suzuki of the Chao-chou dialogue from Chinese into Japanese, Mr. Ryosho Tanaka of Komazawa University in Tokyo, and Miss Kaikiko Yokagawa of Otani University in Kyoto helped me gather important books and documents and served valiantly as my interpreters when I had interviews with Zen masters in the Japanese temples. I should also like to thank Miss Cynthia Scheff for her aid in reading and revising the manuscript.

The translation of these significant sections of *The Transmission of the Lamp* was first suggested to me by Professor Herbert W. Schneider and Bollingen Foundation in America with the consent of Professor Daisetz T. Suzuki in Japan. The work was sponsored by Bollingen Foundation in New York and the Blaisdell Institute in Claremont, California, through whose assistance I was able to spend two and a half years in Japan, concentrating my study on Ch'an Buddhism and preparing my first draft of the translation. My revised drafts and the interpretative sections were made possible through the assistance of the Institute of Asian Studies, St. John's University, and of the Temple of Great Enlightenment in New York.

Finally, I wish to express my grateful appreciation to all those

Foreword

individuals and organizations who sponsored this exploration of the ancient texts of Ch'an.

NOTES

1. Daisetz T. Suzuki, *An Introduction to Zen Buddhism*, p. 14.
2. Daisetz T. Suzuki, *Zen Buddhism*, ed. William Barrett, p. xv.
3. Kitarō Nishida, *A Study of Good*, trans. V. H. Viglielmo, p. 35.
4. Suzuki, *Zen Buddhism*, p. xv.
5. *Ching-tê Record of the Transmission of the Lamp*, comp. Tao-yüan, Chüan 6 (*chüan* means "volume" in Chinese).
6. Daisetz T. Suzuki, *Essays in Zen Buddhism*, Series II, p. 312.
7. See Suzuki, *Essays in Zen Buddhism*, Series I, p. 166, and Series II, p. 77. See also the Chart of Eminent Ch'an Masters, pages 305–11 below: it lists nine other source materials, all of which were compiled after *The Lamp*. After careful examination, I have found *The Lamp* to be the best of all. It is because of its superior quality that Dr. Suzuki suggested to Bollingen Foundation that it be translated.
8. It is common knowledge that traditional Ch'an teaching disappeared from China after the thirteenth century. This fact is acknowledged by Hu Shih, Daisetz T. Suzuki, and other Zen scholars. In Part VI of my book, I discuss the reason for this disappearance, with reference to Yung-ming Yen-shou's mingling of Pure Land practice with Zen.

Part I

Introduction
*Metaphysical and Logical Approaches
in Early Ch'an Teachings*

Niu-t'ou Fa-yung (594–657)
No-mind Is Not Different from Mind

Yung-chia Hsüan-chio (665–713)
Dialectic as a Self-conscious Movement

Metaphysical and Logical Approaches in Early Ch'an Teachings

At the beginning of its history Chinese Ch'an Buddhism was closely associated with the *Laṅkāvatāra Sūtra*.[1] As we read the fascicle of Bodhidharma in *The Transmission of the Lamp*, we find that when the First Patriarch was transmitting the Dharma to his disciple Hui-k'ê, he handed him the four volumes of the *Laṅkāvatāra*, telling him that this sūtra was the key to Buddhahood and that he should enlighten the coming generations according to what was said in it. However, in the process of transmission Ch'an teaching gradually became detached from this sūtra, turning instead to the *Prajñāpāramitā Sūtra*[2] for its fundamental tenets.

In the *Platform Sūtra* by Hui-nêng, the Sixth Patriarch, the teachings of the Prajñāpāramitā philosophy are frequently mentioned and discussed. The *Diamond Sūtra*, which he particularly mastered, belongs to the *Prajñāpāramitā* group. It is interesting to compare the fascicle of Hui-nêng in *The Lamp* with the teachings of Master Fa-yung of the Niu-t'ou Mountain. Even before he was converted to Ch'an Buddhism, Fa-yung had read the *Mahāprajñāpāramitā Sūtra* with deep understanding. Later, when he was abbot in the Niu-t'ou Mountain, he was invited to lecture on that sūtra in the monastery of Chien-ch'u in Tan-yang. His sermons on Ch'an, recorded in *The Lamp*, are based on the philosophy of Prajñāpāramitā.

The *Prajñāpāramitā Sūtra* is generally considered a systematic presentation of the doctrine of Mādhyamika.[3] T. R. V. Murti has this to say:

> The conception of Prajñāpāramitā is the distinctive feature of the Mādhyamika system. It dominates every part of its philosophy—its metaphysics, ethics and religion. Prajñā is the non-dual knowledge (Jñānam advayam). . . . The dialectic reaches its fruition through three "moments," the antinomical conflict of opposed views of the real advanced by speculative systems (dṛṣṭivāda); their criticism, which exposes their hollowness (śūnyatā); and intuition of the Real in which the duality of "is" and "is not" is totally resolved (prajñā). It is the Absolute beyond Reason. Implicit in the process, Prajñā guides the entire dialectical movement.[4]

This "Absolute beyond Reason" is the Ultimate Reality of all things. For the Buddhist, it is the Buddha-nature within all beings. The Mādhyamika maintains that when all particular existence is reduced to *śūnyatā*, or Emptiness, by the dialectic process of negation of negation, Supreme Enlightenment takes place and *prajñāpāramitā*, or "non-dual knowledge," is fulfilled. Niu-t'ou Fa-yung applied the basic principle of the Mādhyamika in his teachings of Ch'an. According to tradition, Niu-t'ou Fa-yung was not considered one of the orthodox Ch'an masters, such as those belonging to either the Nan-yo or Ch'ing-yüan centers, or later, to the Lin-chi or Ts'ao-tung schools. Neverethless, his fascicle, so well written in Chinese verse—mostly five words to a line—presents rather systematically the essence of early Ch'an teachings. It gives us the philosophical background from which blossomed forth the Buddhist ideas of later centuries. What is recorded in Master Fa-yung's fascicle is really a condensed form of the Prajñāpāramitā philosophy which he applied to his teachings.

Prajñā means the highest intuition which views things in their aspect of *śūnyatā*. *Śūnyatā* is neither relativity nor nothingness, but Ultimate Reality, or the Absolute. When the Mādhyamika Buddhist says that all things are empty, he is not expressing a nihilistic view, but speaking of Ultimate Reality, which cannot be placed in any modern logical system. When a Buddhist says that Emptiness is within the Five Aggregates, or *skandhas*,[5] he means that in all concrete things there is the Absolute, which is limitless. Thus *śūnyatā* is the immanent and universal reality of all things. To reach this universal reality, the Mādhyamika Buddhist advocates the process of negation. This is the main theme of the Prajñāpāramitā philosophy and the goal of the early patriarchs and Ch'an masters, Fa-yung being one of them. We have Fa-yung's own words:

> All talk has nothing to do with one's Original Nature, which can only be reached through *śūnyatā*. No-thought is the Absolute Reality, in which the mind ceases to act. When one is free from thoughts, one's nature has reached the Absolute.
> The Ultimate Essence of things is what is most important. But in the realm of illusion it becomes different from what it is. The nature of Reality is invisible and cannot be understood by our conscious mind.

What does the Master mean by "Original Nature" and "Ultimate Essence"? All of these refer to *śūnyatā*. Thus the aim of the Ch'an Buddhist is the same as that of the Prajñāpāramitā philosopher. According to the Prajñāpāramitā, *śūnyatā* can be achieved by a series of negations which lead to Supreme Enlightenment. So long as there is the conscious intention of attaining something, a real obstacle is in the way. In order to attain Ch'an, one has to remove all obstacles completely. In the *Prajñāpāramitā-hridaya Sūtra*, we learn of one Avalokiteśvara who took Buddha's advice to negate everything that could be conceived of as an object of thought. This is also the Ch'an approach maintained by the early patriarchs and masters. In fact, it was the first lesson in Ch'an that Fa-yung received from Tao-hsin, the Fourth Patriarch:

> All the hindrances to the attainment of *bodhi* [wisdom] which arise from passions that generate karma are originally nonexistent. Every cause and effect is but a dream. There is no

triple world which one leaves, and no *bodhi* to search for. The inner reality and outer appearance of man and ten thousand things are identical. The great Tao is formless and boundless. It is free from thought and anxiety.

Freedom from thought and anxiety is picturesquely described by a later master: It is like a pail of water when the bottom has fallen away. When nothing retains the water and it has all dropped, the negation is indeed complete.

Negation does not lead to nothingness, however, but reaches *śūnyatā*. When duality is removed, *prajñā*-intuition is realized. Here the knower and the known coincide, subjectivity and objectivity are mutually identified. In the *Prajñāpāramitā Sūtra* this is called non-duality, or non-differentiation, or *prajñāpāramitā*. Thus when Fa-yung was asked how he knew the cause of the emergence of any mental attitude and how to stop it, he answered:

> When a mental attitude and the external world emerge, the natures of both are non-existent. Originally there is no knower of the cause of the emergence. The capacity of mind and the known are identical. When their origin is illumined, all that is in emergence no longer emerges. Emergence itself ceases. . . . When a mental attitude and the external world are not created, it is the Void. . . .

The inner experience of the Void is the foundation of the spiritual structure of Buddhism. It is the insight into the depth of the mind, the wonder of Ch'an. To achieve this wonder, we must go beyond even negation. We must follow the process of negation of negation if we want to be led to the hidden source of our being. The Prajñāpāramitā dialectics differ from those of earlier Indian thinkers and of Western dialectic philosophers, for even when thesis and antithesis are logically synthesized, there still remains an intellectual concept that cannot become one's inner experience. Therefore, when the question is put to modern scientific philosophers: "All things return to One. Where does the One return to?" they cannot give an answer. How well Master Fa-yung mastered the dialectics of the Prajñāpāramitā is evident from the following subtle remarks he made in answer to the question: "Where does the One return to?"

> The moment when the mind is in action is the moment at which no-mind acts. To talk about names and manifestations is useless, but a direct approach easily reaches it. No-mind is that which is in action; it is that constant action which does not act. The no-mind of which I speak is not separate from the mind.

Thus, no-mind is the mind and the mind is no-mind. Or we may say that no-mind and the mind are one and the same. When we deal with worldly affairs we do not disturb the world of Reality. When we contemplate the world of Reality, we do not avoid the worldly affairs.

The Mādhyamika doctrine was brought to China at the end of the fourth century by Kumārajīva and became known in China as the San-lun, or "Three Treatises." In its idea of the "double truth," it gave reinforcement to the San-lun School, whose emphasis was on the achievement of *śūnyatā* through negation. (This will be discussed in detail when we come to the teachings of Yung-chia Hsüan-chio.) We know from his sermons that Fa-yung was a true exponent of the Mādhyamika philosophy, which played such an important role in the development of Ch'an Buddhism. We also know that he was a disciple of Tai-ming, the leading master of the T'ien-t'ai School in the Monastery of Feng-lu. After Tai-ming's death, he went to study under Yen-kuan, who recognized Fa-yung as a great scholar of the "eightfold negation," by which he meant the Mādhyamika philosophy. This shows that Fa-yung was known as an exponent of the Mādhyamika even before his conversion to Ch'an. At the time he was aware of the T'ien-t'ai doctrine of the Middle Way, as set forth by its founder. In Fa-yung's discussion of this doctrine with one of his disciples he defines it thus:

> Do not abide in the extremity of the Void, but illumine the non-being in the being. It is neither out of the Void nor out of being. Void and being are not conceived of as two. This is called the Middle Way.

7

Metaphysical and Logical Approaches in Early Ch'an Teachings

To understand Fa-yung's position in the historical development of Buddhism, it is necessary to understand the circumstances of his conversion to Ch'an. As *The Lamp* tells us, Fa-yung was meditating in a rock cave on the Niu-t'ou Mountain when he was approached by Tao-hsin, the Fourth Patriarch, who addressed to him the question, "Who is he that contemplates and what is the Mind that is contemplated?" When he heard this, Fa-yung was suddenly awakened.

In the sermons of later Ch'an masters there are many allusions to the flower offerings made by birds to Fa-yung on the mountain before his interview with the Patriarch. Nan-ch'üan P'u-yüan (748–834) and Tung-shan Liang-chieh (807–869) tried to explain why these offerings had ceased after the interview. They both concluded that prior to that time, Fa-yung's achievement was not yet complete. But after his enlightenment, as Tung-shan expressed it, "his entire being was gone." By this he meant that Fa-yung, as host of the birds, no longer existed to receive their offerings. In other words, when the subject is no more, the object does not emerge. The miracle of the flower offerings naturally would cease after Fa-yung had thoroughly grasped the essence of Ch'an.

Although Fa-yung had learned the Mādhyamika philosophy before his conversion, his meditation practice had been one-sided. As he later pointed out to one of his disciples:

> There is another type of man who contemplates the Void. . . . He intentionally searches for the Void through abiding in stillness. His understanding is just the opposite of the Truth. He thinks that the Truth is achieved by the calculating mind. Eventually what he understands is not Ultimate Truth. He also says that the cessation of the activity of the mind is brought about by intellectual knowledge. This is because he does not understand his original nature; his search for the Void only wears him out. The result is that he will abide forever in darkness of mind without realizing that what he grasps are only manifestations.

After Fa-yung had become a Ch'an master, there was also a great change in his way of living. Instead of sitting in the rock cave

METAPHYSICAL AND LOGICAL APPROACHES

ignoring his visitors, he went down the mountain, asking for alms and carrying rice for three hundred people to the temple. This complete change can be attributed only to his understanding of the Ch'an doctrine as it differs from the pure negation of the San-lun School. Both these approaches can be traced back to the Mādhyamika. It is only in their emphasis that they differ.

However, there was often criticism of Fa-yung's teachings. Huang-po Hsi-yün (d. 849), the famous teacher of Lin-chi I-hsüan, once commented: "The great master Niu-t'ou Fa-yung, a disciple of the Fourth Patriarch, expounded Ch'an in every way, but he still did not know the secret of making the further leap to the Ultimate." What is this further leap to the Ultimate of which Huang-po speaks? It is what differentiates the teachings of the early Ch'an patriarchs and masters from those of the later Ch'an masters after Ma-tsu (Kiangsi Tao-i). We know that the early masters, opposing the pure negation of the San-lun School, leaned heavily upon intellectual knowledge and philosophical understanding. However, one may learn the theories of a great school of philosophy, but one does not thereby become enlightened. Whatever the great philosophy of Prajñāpāramitā and the system of Mādhyamika may have accomplished, they had their limitations. Man's mind can be opened up no more by mere reasoning or philosophical speculation than by the conscious search for *śūnyatā*. Since the days of Ma-tsu, the direct approach has been strongly recommended and *kung-an* (*koan* in Japanese) and *wên-ta* (*mondō*) as well as Ho (*Kwatz*) and striking have been applied. All of these led to the further leap to Ultimate Reality, and a new page was therewith turned in the history of Ch'an Buddhism. Niu-t'ou Fa-yung lived one hundred years before Ma-tsu, and in his age Ch'an teachings were still limited to philosophical exposition, which rarely led to the further leap. However, it is worthwhile to examine carefully this fascicle of Niu-t'ou Fa-yung, because in it the influence of the Middle Way philosophy on Ch'an Buddhism is systematically presented.

The Middle Way philosophy involves both *prajñā* and *śūnyatā*, which cannot be considered apart from one another. They are, in fact, two aspects of one inseparable reality. However, generally speaking, a distinction is drawn in that *śūnyatā* is reached by a process of manifold negation, while *prajñā* is realized by an immediate and intuitive identification. This is particularly evident in the teachings of Ch'an's pioneers, such as Niu-t'ou Fa-yung and Yung-chia Hsüan-chio. Their emphasis differs in that Niu-t'ou stresses *prajñā*, while Yung-chia concentrates on *śūnyatā*. Although Yung-chia's teaching aims at the achievement of *prajñā*, the process that he engaged in was dialectic negation to the Absolute Void. Epistemologically, *prajñā* is Ultimate Reality, of which nothing may be predicated. The realization of this ultimate reality, however, may be suggested in Yung-chia's own words: "What clear seeing! Yet there is nothing to see. Neither a man nor a Buddha."[6] One may wonder, as later Ch'an masters did, what it was that he saw so clearly, since there was nothing to see. The answer here is that the highest intuition is described as self-realization, or the highest consciousness, conscious of itself. Ontologically, Ultimate Reality is *śūnyatā*, the Absolute Void.

Since the highest inner consciousness is the Absolute Void, it is reached through the negation of things, of man, even of Buddha. Yung-chia's approach to Ch'an fundamentally follows the doctrine of manifold negation implicit in this method. The idea of incessant denial as contained in the eightfold negation of the San-lun School serves as a basic principle of his teachings. In this school, however, there is another path to *śūnyatā*. This consists in freeing oneself from what are called the four alternatives: (1) being, (2) non-being, (3) both being and non-being, and (4) neither being nor non-being. The first two are the primary alternatives; the second two, as is apparent, are derived from them.

In his *Collected Works*,[7] Yung-chia explains the importance of freedom from the four alternatives: "When mind is either being or non-being, it falls into the trap of affirmation. When mind is neither being nor non-being, it falls into the trap of negation." Either affirmation or negation, then, is a "trap" from which one must free oneself in order to reach *śūnyatā*.

Basing himself upon the Middle Way dialectic, Chi-tsang (549–623), the great philosopher of the San-lun School, had developed an even more refined approach called the Double Truth on Three Levels. The double truth consists of a common truth and a higher truth. On the first level, when the common truth is denied, it becomes a higher truth. Chi-tsang said that the common man sees things as really existent—being—and knows nothing about their non-existence. The Buddhists said that all things are non-existent. On the first level non-existence, or non-being, which is a denial of existence or being, is the higher truth. On the second level both being and non-being are the common truth. The denial of this, *neither* being nor non-being, is the higher truth. On the third level, according to Chi-tsang, both being and non-being, and neither being nor non-being, are the common truth. The higher truth of this is: both not being and not non-being, and neither not being nor not non-being.[8]

When Yung-chia defined the mind he said, "It is neither being nor non-being, and simultaneously it is neither not being nor not non-being." This corresponds to the higher truth of the third level as set forth by Chi-tsang. Yung-chia applies the third level of the dialectic as a means of reaching Ultimate Reality. He explains: "If you are attached to being and non-being, you will become one-sided, because you will not understand that the form of being is not the reality of being, and that the form of non-being is not the true non-being."[9] Here he maintains that the assertion of either being or non-being is inadequate; and the negation of both non-being and not non-being is also wrong. One cannot approach Ch'an one-sidedly, because Ch'an takes no sides. Instead, the dialectic must be applied until the absolute reality of the third level is reached. At this point, as Yung-chia illustrates from his own experience, "Not only are the means of expression destroyed, but the roots of mental activity itself are cut out."[10] When one reaches such a state, according to Yung-chia, one achieves Ch'an.

Yung-chia was not influenced only by the San-lun School; his teaching is deeply involved in T'ien-t'ai philosophy as well. He studied Buddhism with Tso-ch'i Fa-lang (673–754), under T'ien-kung Hui-wei,[11] and became well versed in all of the basic principles of the T'ien-t'ai School. One of the most essential contributions of

Metaphysical and Logical Approaches in Early Ch'an Teachings

T'ien-t'ai to Buddhist philosophy is the theory of the threefold truth identified as one. The threefold truth embodies the real, the unreal, and the middle. The real refers to the Void, which nullifies all differentiated elements. The unreal refers to the common truth, through which all differentiated elements are established. The middle does not denote a position between the two; rather it transcends both the real and the unreal and simultaneously embraces both.

The T'ien-t'ai School, as we have seen, set forth the threefold truth identified as one, and then taught a threefold contemplation through which to achieve this understanding. From the threefold contemplation one gains three kinds of "eyes": the dharma-eye, the wisdom-eye, and the Buddha-eye. Yung-chia comments on this: "All the thousands of manifestations vary from one another, and to that which sees these differentiations the name of dharma-eye is given. Silence never varies, and that which sees this is called the wisdom-eye. When one is free from both non-differentiated reality, and differentiated materiality, one has attained the vision of the Buddha-eye. Therefore the three truths are identified as one. Thus the ultimate reality of things is absolutely pure."[12] This clearly identifies Yung-chia's application of the metaphysical structure of T'ien-t'ai to his search for the ultimate reality of Ch'an.

Yung-chia adopted T'ien-t'ai philosophy to his own teachings, but he was by no means limited to these principles. To be sure, he accepted what T'ien-t'ai called the "perfect mutual solution among the three aspects of truth—the real, the unreal, and the middle." This is commonly stated in the formula: "Three are one; one is three." Yung-chia, however, goes on to negate this concept. He says:

> When one searches out the ultimate in all its subtlety, it is neither three nor one. Thus, the three which is not three is called three; and the one which is not one is called one. When three is derived from one, it is not the real three, so how can it be called three? When one is derived from three, it is not the real one, so how can it be called one? When one is not one, it is not necessarily three, nor is the three that is not three neces-

sarily one. However, you cannot deny the existence of one, even though one cannot exist without three; nor can three be denied even though three cannot exist without one. The one that does not exist is originally not three. The three that does not exist is originally not one. Both one and three are originally non-existent, and even this nothingness is non-existent. The non-existence of nothingness is the primal nothingness, and so it is the ultimate in all its subtlety.[13]

Yung-chia's purpose here is to negate in every possible way the established relationship between the three and the one, and ultimately their very existence. Here it must be understood that he is not in any way criticizing the T'ien-t'ai doctrine but is actually carrying it to its logical extreme. If he were simply to accept it without at once denying it, this would be one-sided. His acceptance and simultaneous denial of this principle is the real Mādhyamika approach, leading to what the T'ien-t'ai School called *chen-k'ung miao-yu,* or "real void and subtle reality."

According to Yung-chia, when we say that something is real, it is not a relative reality. When we say that it is void, it is not a relative void. What is real is void; what is void is real. This identification of the void and the real is achieved by the absolute mind, which is free of all dichotomy. It is the emergence of constant consciousness which is conscious of itself. And yet it is not different from the ordinary mind. Ch'an Master Ta-ning Tao-kuan of the eleventh century has this to say: "No-thought is the source. No-abiding is the ground. Subtle reality is the action. The real void is the substance. Therefore we may say that everywhere on the earth the real void abides. All things in the universe are activities of the subtle reality."

Ta-ning Tao-kuan further explains: "Who is capable of embracing this? The four seasons follow each other in succession. The sun and the moon shine constantly. Truth suffers no fundamental alteration, and the Tao is not confined to a single place. Therefore free yourself to yield to whatever happens to you. Rise and fall with it. Here you may be simultaneously a common man and a sage."[14]

When the real void is the substance, and the subtle reality is in

Metaphysical and Logical Approaches in Early Ch'an Teachings

action, one pursues ordinary daily activities—and at the same time transcends them. One thus embraces both freedom and wisdom. Yung-chia says: "When wisdom emerges, freedom is achieved. Yet in this freedom there is nothing from which to be free. When this freedom is achieved, wisdom is produced. Yet in this production of wisdom nothing is produced."[15] Here we see a true synthesis of T'ien-t'ai and Ch'an in Yung-chia's teachings.

In point of fact, the teachings of Hui-ssu (514–577) and Chih-i (531–597), the founders of the T'ien-t'ai School, are recorded in *The Transmission of the Lamp*, Chüan (Volume) 27. *The Lamp* is the prime sourcebook of Ch'an, and the fact that Hui-ssu's and Chih-i's teachings are recorded side by side with those of other Ch'an masters shows how close the early philosophy of T'ien-t'ai was to Ch'an. The late Daisetz T. Suzuki is on record as saying: "In my view the Tendai [T'ien-t'ai] is a variation of Ch'an, and its first promulgators may justly be classed as Ch'an Masters, though not of the pedigree to which belong Shih-t'ou, Yüeh-shan, Ma-tsu, Lin-chi, etc."[16]

We have presented the approaches of Yung-chia as representative of the logical teaching of Ch'an. Yung-chia died in 713, the same year as Hui-nêng, the Sixth Patriarch. At that time Ma-tsu, founder of the unconventional and illogical teaching of Ch'an, was only four years old. Ch'an study at that time was in many ways still primitive. Many of its pioneer thinkers were still deeply involved in the entanglements of metaphysics and logical exposition. Although Yung-chia's aim, in his own words, was "to destroy the means of expression and cut out the roots of mental activity," he remained quite dependent upon such "means of expression" and his mental activity grew deeper and deeper, of its kind, and was hardly to be cut out. Later masters were able to directly experience absolute freedom primarily because they set up no means of expression to destroy and had no roots of mental activity to cut out. Yung-chia moved in the framework of a fixed logic from which he was never able entirely to free himself. In other words, he was preoccupied with dichotomizing concepts of affirmation and negation. The later masters adopted a completely different approach. They used startling and graphic irrationalities instead of setting up elaborate logical formulas and destroying them. In their dialogues the power of paradox opens up an impassable chasm, over which one must leap, beyond logic.

Once Chao-chou, grandson-in-dharma of Ma-tsu, was asked what he would say to a man who possessed nothing. Chao-chou replied, "Throw it away!"[17] If a man has nothing, what can he throw away? The paradox completely confounds our intellectual faculty.

Lin-chi, another dharma descendant of Ma-tsu, once said to his assembly, "A man is on the highway, yet he has not left his home. Another man, who has left his home, is not on the highway. Which of these two should be respected?"[18] Lin-chi's question cannot be answered logically. His disciples thus were urged to the very edge of the chasm and impelled to leap over. In Ch'an history we have many such famous statements which have repeatedly served as vehicles for the leap, such as: "You are not allowed to travel at night, but you must arrive before daybreak." "The bridge flows, the water does not." "Let the poor farmer's cow be taken away and the hungry man's food be snatched from him." These *kung-an* were all used on various occasions to open new areas of vision and to perpetuate the teaching of the primordial intuition as originated by Ma-tsu.

Of all the Ch'an masters recorded in *The Transmission of the Lamp,* Yung-chia is the only one who advocated a logical process for the attainment of enlightenment. As we have seen, he carried logical analysis to the very brink of the chasm, but it fell short of making the final leap. For Yung-chia himself, perhaps, the method was adequate, for he was an extraordinarily intuitive genius endowed with an inherent capacity for enlightenment. His approach, however, had its limitations. Logic, after all, cannot be made nonlogic—and this was the effort he was engaged in. His teaching easily fell into the trap of intellectual complexity and confusion, instead of enlightenment. Still, his exhaustive exposition of Middle Way logic paved the way for the subsequent development of non-logical means in the teaching of Ch'an.

Metaphysical and Logical Approaches in Early Ch'an Teachings

Previously, I mentioned that Yung-chia's teaching stresses *śūnyatā*, while Niu-t'ou Fa-yung's emphasizes *prajñā*. Now we realize that Niu-t'ou's philosophical speculations and Yung-chia's logical analysis both have their limitations. Because Yung-chia utterly exhausted the possibilities of logic, the illogical approach of the later masters emerged. From Niu-t'ou's philosophical speculations on the search for *prajñā* grew the later unconventional and direct approach. We have already illustrated the limitations of Yung-chia's logic. Here is an illustration of the way in which Ch'an masters taught *prajñā*, a way that is radically different from Niu-t'ou's teaching:

Chao-chou Ts'ung-shen went to visit T'ou-tzu Ta-t'ung and asked, "What is the substance of *prajñā?*" T'ou-tzu repeated, "What is the substance of *prajñā?*" Thereupon Chao-chou laughed heartily and left. Next morning, when T'ou-tzu saw Chao-chou sweeping the yard, he stepped forward, and asked, "What is the substance of *prajñā?*" As soon as Chao-chou heard this, he threw down his broom, and laughing heartily, went away.

To understand Chao-chou's radical departure, it is necessary to familiarize oneself with Niu-t'ou's teaching of *prajñā*, because therein is contained the essence from which grew the later teaching, as exemplified in the quotation above.

NIU-T'OU FA-YUNG
(594–657)

No-mind Is Not Different from Mind

(*From* The Transmission of the Lamp, *Chüan 4*)

CH'AN Master Fa-yung, the founder of the School of the Niu-t'ou Mountain, was a native of Yen-ling in Jun-chou.[19] His original surname was Wei. When he was nineteen years old, he was thoroughly acquainted with both the Confucian classics and the literature of Chinese history. Subsequently he read the *Mahāprajñāpāramitā Sūtra*,[20] and gained a deep understanding of the real void. One day, sighing with regret, he said that Confucianism was the teaching for worldly affairs and did not leap to Ultimate Reality, but that the *prajñā* doctrine of Buddhism was the ferryboat that takes us to the other shore, away from mundane affairs. Hence he decided to become a devotee of Buddhism. He shaved his head and went into Mount Mao.[21] Later he stayed in a rock cave in a cliff north of the Yu-hsi Monastery in the Niu-t'ou Mountain, and this was the setting of the legendary flower offerings brought to Fa-yung by a hundred birds.

In the middle of the Chen-kuan period [627–649] of the T'ang Dynasty, the Fourth Patriarch, Tao-hsin,[22] observed the Niu-t'ou Mountain from a distance and conjectured that some outstanding Buddhist must be living there. Therefore he went to the mountain to make a search. Upon his arrival he asked a monk of the temple whether a man of Tao was staying there. The monk answered that those who became monks were all men of Tao. The Patriarch went on, "But which one is the man of Tao?" The monk made no reply. Thereupon another monk directed him: "Ten li^{23} from here, deep in the mountain, there lives a man called Lazy Yung. He never stands up or joins his hands to greet approaching people. Is this not a man of Tao?" Having learned this, the Patriarch immediately went there, as directed.

On his arrival he saw Fa-yung sitting, quiet and self-possessed, paying no attention to his visitor. The Patriarch asked him:

"What are you doing here?"

"I am contemplating Mind."

"Who is he that contemplates and what is the Mind that is contemplated?" Fa-yung did not answer, but immediately stood up and made a deep bow. Then he asked his visitor:

"Where have you stayed before?"

"I never remain in any one place, but wander either east or west."

"Do you know the Ch'an master Tao-hsin?"

"Why do you mention him?"

"I have always greatly admired him, and I intend to visit him that I may pay my respects to him."

"Tao-hsin is my humble name."

"Why have you come here?"

"To look for you. Do you have a place where I can stay?"

Fa-yung took his visitor to another hut behind the cave. On their way the Patriarch saw wild animals, a tiger and a wolf, and he held up his hands as if frightened. Fa-yung remarked:

"There is still this in you."

"What did you see?" replied the visitor. Fa-yung made no answer. A moment later the Patriarch traced the character *fu*, or Buddha, on the rock where Fa-yung sat. When the latter saw this, he was taken aback. The Patriarch said to him:

"There is still this in you."

Fa-yung failed to grasp the meaning of the remark and earnestly implored the Patriarch to instruct him in the ultimate essence of Buddhism. The Fourth Patriarch expounded thus:

"All systems of Buddhist teaching[24] center in Mind, where immeasurable treasures originate. All its supernatural faculties[25] and their transformations revealed in discipline, meditation, and wisdom are sufficiently contained in one's mind and they never depart therefrom. All the hindrances to the attainment of *bodhi*[26] which arise from passions that generate karma[27] are originally non-existent. Every cause and effect is but a dream. There is no Triple World[28] which one leaves, and no *bodhi* to search for. The inner reality and outer appearance of man and a thousand things are identical. The Great Tao is formless and boundless. It is free from thought and anxiety. You have now understood this Buddhist teaching. There is nothing lacking in you, and you yourself are no different from Buddha. There is no way of achieving Buddhahood other than letting your mind be free to be itself. You should not contemplate nor should you purify your mind. Let there be no craving and hatred, and have no anxiety or fear. Be boundless and absolutely free from all conditions. Be free to go in any direction you like. Do not act to do good, nor to pursue evil. Whether you walk or stay, sit or lie down, and whatever you see happen to you, all are the wonderful activity of the Great Enlightened One. It is all joy, free from anxiety—it is called Buddha."

Fa-yung asked, "Since Mind is sufficient and complete in itself, then what is Buddha, and what is Mind?"

The Fourth Patriarch answered, "To deny this mind, one need not look for Buddha; to look for Buddha, one should not deny this mind."

Fa-yung continued, "As you do not permit contemplation, what do you do when mental attitude[29] emerges?"

The Patriarch replied, "The origin of mental attitude is neither good nor bad; its emergence is due to your mind. If your mind were free from formulation or conception, how could illusions occur? When illusions do not occur, the real mind will be free to be aware of everything. You just follow the mind as it is. Do not look for ways to deal with it. This is called the ever abiding essence of things

Metaphysical and Logical Approaches in Early Ch'an Teachings

[*dharmakāya*]. Do not deviate from it! I have had the teachings of sudden enlightenment from the Third Patriarch, Sêng-ts'an, and now I am giving them to you. Keep in mind what I have said. Stay in this mountain, and later on there will be five wise men to succeed you as teachers of Ch'an." After this transmission of Ch'an to Fa-yung, the Fourth Patriarch returned to Mount Shuang-fêng and remained there for the rest of his life.

Having had the teachings from the Fourth Patriarch, Master Fa-yung began to preach, and his teachings flourished widely. In the middle of the Yung-hui period [650–655] of T'ang there was a shortage of food for his disciples and the residents of the temple. Every day the Master went to Tan-yang,[30] eighty *li* from his mountain, to beg alms.[31] He left the temple every morning and came back in the evening carrying one picul and eight pecks of rice on his back. This provided two meals a day for three hundred monks in the temple. In the third year of the Yung-hui period the magistrate Hsiao Yüan-shan invited him to lecture on the *Mahāprajñā-pāramitā Sūtra* at the Monastery of Chien-ch'u. A great crowd came to listen. When he came to the section, "Extinction and Quiescence," an earthquake occurred. After finishing his lectures, he returned to Mount Niu-t'ou.

Prince Po-ling asked the Master, "When a mental attitude arises owing to the external world,[32] you say that this emergence is not due to it. Then how do you know the cause of the emergence and when to stop it?"

The Master answered, "When a mental attitude and the external world emerge, the natures of both are non-existent. Originally there is no knower of the cause of the emergence. The capacity of mind[33] and the known are identical. When their origin is illumined, all that is in emergence no longer emerges. Emergence itself ceases. When there is no illumination, the knowledge of causation is produced. The illuminated mind does not go after causation; it is just as it was before the emergence. When a mental attitude and the external world are not created, it is the Void, which is primarily free from thoughts. Through ideas and sensations,[34] words and thoughts are produced. The teaching of the truth is not the Truth. What is the use of the instruction of Buddhism?"

NIU-T'OU FA-YUNG

The Prince then asked, "The external world cannot be seen when the eyes are closed. However, thoughts in mind then grow more and more. Since the external world has nothing to do with mind, how does this mental attitude arise?"

The Master replied, "The external world cannot be seen when the eyes are closed. But as the mind is in action, thoughts increase. Thus the illusory consciousness is created which is the false action of the mind. What are produced are simply namable concepts. When one understands that the external world has nothing to do with one's real self, and if one acts accordingly, then one will return to one's original nature. Just as when birds fly away the real sky is revealed."

The Prince said, "You say the internal condition is produced from nowhere, and that through one's consciousness clear knowledge emerges; yet when the first internal condition fades away, one's consciousness transforms itself into the second condition. If we assume that one state of mind leads to another, it means that what was the first consciousness later becomes the object of the second consciousness. If one accepts this sequence of transformation, one cannot be non-attached to birth and death."

The Master replied, "The external world and the mind of consciousness, one following the other, cannot really produce the internal condition. Through 'One Thought'[35] all of them naturally disappear in contemplation. Who can tell whether the mind is in action or non-action? In this state of knowing, primarily nothing is known. Knowledge in which something is known falls short of this. One should look into one's original nature and not search outside. Then there is no need for the first condition to fade away, nor for continuing thought to be present. How can one seek the moon by observing its shadow? How can one catch a bird by tracing its tracks? So it is with the search for the original nature of the mind. What one can discover is like that which can be seen in a dream. It is like the ice that cannot last anywhere during the summer. If you run away from the Void, you can never be free from it; if you search for the Void, you can never reach it. Let me ask you this: 'When there is an image occupying a mirror-mind, where can you find mind?'"

Metaphysical and Logical Approaches in Early Ch'an Teachings

The Prince asked, "When the mind is in action, would it be better for it to be brought to quiescence?"

The Master replied, "The moment when the mind is in action is the moment at which no-mind acts. To talk about names and manifestations is useless, but a direct approach easily reaches it. No-mind is that which is in action; it is that constant action which does not act. The no-mind of which I speak is not separate from the mind."

The Prince said, "The wise man uses subtle words to identify the mind. However, words and mind are different. To say that the mind and words are one is completely wrong."

The Master replied, "Subtle words are used as a means to Truth in order to correct misunderstandings, thus fulfilling the teachings of Mahāyāna Buddhism. When one's words have nothing to do with original nature, it would be better for one to be transformed through *śūnyatā*. No-thought is the absolute reality in which the mind ceases to act. When one is free from thoughts, one's nature is not altered. Production and extinction are then not unnatural. They occur like echoes from the valley, or reflections from the mirror."

The Prince said, "A Buddhist ascetic is aware of the existence of internal conditions, but because of the awakening, internal conditions become non-existent. Thus previous knowledge, the later awakening, and the internal conditions constitute a threefold mind."

The Master replied, "The internal conditions and mental activity cannot be identified with awakening. After the awakening there is no-thought. Because of the awakening, internal conditions disappear. During the awakening, internal conditions do not arise. Thus a previous knowledge, a later awakening, and internal conditions are merely names, lately made, for that which no longer exists."

The Prince said, "When one remains in concentration without regressing one is conceived of as having achieved *samādhi*,[36] which cannot be defiled by any karma. However, one can fail to realize that 'basic ignorance'[37] may enter stealthily so that *samādhi* is lost."

The Master answered, "I have also heard that there are those who falsely take concentration for enlightenment[38] and fail to follow the 'Threefold Contemplation.'[39] Even without regression, progress made by concentration is still a delusion. Because the mind is bound by concentration, concentration itself becomes the hindrance of good karmas. If there is even a tiny spot of impurity in the mind, this imperfection is conceived of as ignorance. Hence it continues on and on, and the senses of hearing and of seeing are gradually manifested. Their emergence resembles the movement of ripples when the breeze blows, and then the return to serenity when the breeze ceases. Any further description will frighten and astonish lesser minds. When the mind is free from thoughts, the 'lion roar'[40] is achieved; when one's nature is the Void, frost and hail are dispersed; when the stars are scattered, the foul weeds are cleared; when the sky is limitless, the voyaging birds drop away. Then the five *gati*[41] cease to revolve, and the four devils[42] fear to be active. The power of no-thought is like the burning flame or the swift stroke of a sharp sword."

The Prince said, "Through the awakening of mind the existence of all things is known. All things, however, are what they originally are. If the existence of things is only the reflection of mind, then there is only the reflecting mind, but not the things that the mind reflects."

The Master answered, "Through the awakening of mind the existence of things is known. The existence of all things is itself not reliable. If the existence of things is only the reflection of mind, then nothing exists outside the mind."

The Prince said, "If one acts casually without discrimination, the illumination of mind will not be revealed. Furthermore, one is afraid that one's mind may become ignorant, and one strives to cultivate it. However, one can hardly get rid of intellectual hindrance."[43]

The Master replied, "To have what one cannot have and to search for what cannot be sought. Non-discrimination is real discrimination. From the depth of darkness illumination is revealed. Those who calculate are ignorant; they depend upon their own effort of cultivation. Their difficulties are not limited to intellectual hindrance. Their approach to Buddha is in trouble."

The Prince said, "In the fluctuating process of following the Middle Way[44] one can hardly maintain one's tranquillity. Unless one strives for cultivation, one will not realize this difficulty."

The Master replied, "In the process of the Middle Way, one looks for the real essence. It is neither easy nor difficult to obtain it. One should first contemplate Mind within the mind; secondly, one should search for that Wisdom hidden in the wisdom; third, one should illuminate the searcher himself; fourth, one should penetrate into that which is neither good nor bad; fifth, one should be free from the enslavement of names; sixth, one should realize the identity of the real and the unreal; seventh, one should be aware of the origin of things; eighth, one should achieve great compassion without effort; ninth, one should permeate both the Void and the Five Aggregates;[45] and lastly, one should let wisdom turn like the clouds into a fertile rain, which falls everywhere.[46]

"When the utmost void is reached, enlightenment is still not obtained. But in ignorance Original Wisdom emerges. The manifestation of the three karmas, deed, word, and thought, is only a mirror image; and they are illusionists who claim to transform them. Do not abide in the extremity of the Void, but illumine the non-being in the being. It is neither out of the Void nor out of being. Void and being are not conceived of as two. This is called the Middle Way. The Middle Way cannot be expressed in words. It is that tranquillity which lacks a place in which to be tranquil. How can we determine it by cultivating the mind?"

The Prince said, "There is another type of man who knows the nature of the Void. He advocates that concentration and confusion are one, and maintains that non-being is within being. He tries to prove that activity is tranquil and tranquillity active. His mind is in action to find the Truth, and yet he says that action is non-action. He claims that knowledge is full of means leading to Truth, and that his words and Truth are one. Things are what they are and their reality is identified, and this cannot be understood by the conscious mind. Although he knows that enlightenment cannot be achieved by the conscious mind, he maintains that thought after thought is extinguished. One can hardly understand this approach to the teaching of Buddhism. Perhaps it can never be understood. Those whose minds function in this way will never be transformed by the teaching of Buddha."

The Master replied, "There is another type of man who contemplates the Void as I mentioned previously. He intentionally searches for the Void through abiding in stillness. His understanding is just the opposite of the Truth. He thinks that Truth is achieved by the calculating mind. Eventually what he understands is not Ultimate Truth. He also says that the cessation of the activity of the mind is brought about by intellectual knowledge. This is because he does not understand his original nature; his search for the Void only wears him out. The result is that he will abide forever in darkness of mind without realizing that what he grasps are only manifestations. Even Buddha, whose teaching brought such illumination that the earth shook,[47] couldn't do anything for this man."

The Prince said, "The type of man I was discussing before may feel as if his mind were covered with a gauzelike garment."

The Master replied, "When one contemplates mind with gauze-covered faculties, it is only a mind of delusion, which is not worthy of being contemplated. Furthermore, the one who contemplates does not exist. How can we obtain the truth[48] through words?"

The Prince said, "I have been disciplining my mind for a long time, in pursuit of that which is most fundamental. Since my approach is wrong, I have taken my subsequent experience of primal delusion as the Ultimate Reality. Unless I have a great wise teacher to help me, this truth will not be made clear to my mind. May I beg you, the great master, to open for me the essential gate of Truth? Please guide me, your devotee, so that I shall not again deviate from the correct path."

The Master replied, "The ultimate essence of things is what is most fundamental. But in the realm of illusion it becomes different from what it is. The nature of Reality is invisible, and cannot be understood by our rational mind. Today I met someone confused by Tao, but sympathetic toward all people. Because of the doubt in his mind he raises all kinds of questions. Grasp the Ultimate Truth and you will be absolutely illumined within. When you thoroughly understand the subtle path of life and death, you will not fear slander nor seek praise. I, as an old monk, have replied to many different questions that you raised. Let my teachings on the Ultimate Truth and its manifestations be my gift to you for your visit here. To discover the remedies with which to save people, you must act in accordance with the nature of things."

In the first year of the Hsien-ching period [656–660], the magistrate Hsiao Yüan-shan invited Fa-yung to move to the Chien-ch'u Monastery to stay, and the Master could not refuse. Therefore he bestowed the dharma-seal upon his head monk, Chih-yen, and ordered that it be handed down to the generations to follow. When he was leaving the mountains, he told his disciples that he would not be coming back. Birds and animals cried for months. In front of the temple four great paulownia trees suddenly withered away in the middle of the summer.

Master Fa-yung died at the Chien-ch'u Monastery on the twenty-third day of the first month of the second year of the Hsien-ching period [657]. He was then sixty-four years old. This was forty-one years after he had been ordained. Four days later he was buried in Mount Chi-lung. More than ten thousand people took part in his funeral service. His old residence in the Niu-t'ou Mountain, the springs of Chin-yüan, Hu-p'ao, and Hsi-chang, the Chin-kuei and other pools, and the rock cave in which he meditated are all still well kept even to this day.

YUNG-CHIA HSÜAN-CHIO
(665–713)

Dialectic as a Self-conscious Movement

(*From* The Transmission of the Lamp, *Chüan* 5)

CH'AN Master Yung-chia Hsüan-chio of Wên-chou[49] was a native of Yung-chia. His original surname was Tai. When he was still young, he left his home to become a Buddhist monk. He studied all the sūtras, vinayas, and śāstras,[50] being particularly well versed in the profound and subtle teaching of cessation and contemplation maintained by the T'ien-t'ai School. Even in the practice of the four awe-inspiring deportments of walking, standing, sitting, and lying down, he was deep in the contemplation of Ch'an. Encouraged by Ch'an Master Hsüan-lang of Tso-ch'i, he set out one day with Ch'an Master Hsüan-ts'ê of Tung-yang to visit the Sixth Patriarch in Ts'ao-ch'i.[51]

When he arrived there, he shook his staff and held a vase in his hand; he walked around the Patriarch three times and then stood still. The Patriarch said to him:

"A Buddhist monk is he who follows the three thousand regulations and performs the eighty thousand detailed duties.[52] Where do you come from, sir? Why should you have such great self-pride?"

"Life and death are a serious matter," replied Yung-chia, "and death follows life with terrible speed."

Metaphysical and Logical Approaches in Early Ch'an Teachings

"Why don't you attain no-birth and free yourself from this speed?" inquired the Patriarch.

"Attainment is no-birth, and basic freedom is never speedy," replied Yung-chia.

"That's so! That's so!" exclaimed the Patriarch.

At this everyone in the assembly was astonished, and it was not until then that Yung-chia observed the rule of bowing to the Patriarch.

A little while later he came to the Patriarch to bid him goodbye.

"Are you not leaving too soon?" asked the Patriarch.

"Basically, motion does not move. How can you say that I am leaving too soon?" challenged Yung-chia.

"Who is he who is aware of no-movement?" asked the Patriarch.

"You, Master, are making this discrimination," replied Yung-chia.

"You have grasped very well the meaning of no-birth."

"How can no-birth have meaning?"

"If it has no meaning, who can differentiate it?"

"Even though one may differentiate it, it is still meaningless."

The Patriarch exclaimed, "Good! Good! Please stay here for at least one night."

Therefore, the people of that time called Yung-chia's visit "Enlightenment from One Night's Lodging."

The following day Master Hsüan-ts'ê remained in Ts'ao-ch'i, but Yung-chia went down the hill back to Wên-chou.

Students from many places gathered around Yung-chia, and he was called the Great Master Chen-chio, or True Enlightenment. He composed the *Odes on Enlightenment,* and also set forth his ideas on the cultivation of Ch'an, in a step-by-step exposition. Wei-ching, the governor of Ching-chou, compiled and arranged these manuscripts in ten sections with a preface and entitled them the *Collected Works of Ch'an Master Yung-chia.* This book was widely read throughout the country.

The following is an outline of the *Collected Works of Ch'an Master Yung-chia:*

Section I. *Longing for the Tao and Deportment*

He who wishes to follow the Tao must first be strongly determined to achieve it, and then must model his conduct after his masters. Deportment displays what is within one. Therefore, in searching for the Tao it is first necessary to study deportment.

Section II. *Guarding Against Self-Pride and Extravagance*

One may set out strongly determined to achieve Tao and study deportment; but if one's actions, words, and thoughts are proud and extravagant, one's mind becomes disturbed and deluded. How, then, can one attain *samādhi?* Hence, this section deals with the elimination of self-pride and extravagance.

Section III. *The Purification of the Three Karmas—Thoughts, Words, and Actions*

The previous section sets forth fundamental instructions for the pursuit of Tao. The third section illustrates the way in which the three karmas may be pursued by proper discipline. It teaches how to avoid physical and mental disturbances by self-examination.

Section IV. *Śamatha, or Tranquillity of Mind*

After having mastered the teaching set forth in the previous section, the next step is gradual self-cultivation through the discipline of "The Five Stages of the Emergence of Thought"[53] and "The Six Procedures for Achieving Śamatha."[54] In this way one achieves *prajñā*, the great wisdom, through the practice of meditation. This fourth section includes a hymn celebrating the achievement of *śamatha*.

Section V. *Vipaśyanā, or Perfect Insight*

Without discipline, there is no Ch'an. And without Ch'an, there can be no enlightenment. The cultivation of *samādhi* has already been discussed in section II. When *samādhi*, or concentration, reaches the innermost depths, *prajñā*, or wisdom, is attained. The fifth section is a hymn of *vipaśyanā*.

Section VI. *A Hymn of Upekṣā, or Equilibrium*

When concentration alone is stressed, the mind stagnates. When wisdom alone is stressed, the mind becomes overactive. Therefore, the sixth section is a hymn to equilibrium, which illustrates the proper identification of *samādhi* with *prajñā*. A perfect balance between *samādhi* and *prajñā* must be attained so that one's mind may be free from the two extremes of stagnation and overactivity.

Section VII. *The Gradual Attainment of the Three Vehicles*

When *samādhi* and *prajñā* are identified within tranquillity, illumination constantly takes place. When the Threefold Contemplation is identified as one, confusion is transformed into perfect illumination. Although one achieves self-realization at this point, one's sense of compassion for others has not necessarily been awakened, for there are different depths of awakening. This seventh section deals with the gradual attainment of the Three Vehicles.[55]

Section VIII. *The Identification of Events and Reality*

In searching through the Three Vehicles, one may at last experience the Ultimate Reality. There is no reality that cannot be pursued. The pursuit of the Ultimate Reality must be based upon the particular event. When the event is thoroughly perceived, its ultimate reality has been realized. Therefore, the eighth section teaches that events and their ultimate reality are identical. It is through a thorough understanding of this truth that one frees oneself of wrong views.

Section IX. *A Letter to a Friend*

When events and Ultimate Reality interfuse, the mind becomes transparent. One sympathizes with one's friend, who has not yet achieved enlightenment but has wasted time in a vain search. Therefore, the ninth section contains a letter of advice.

Section X. *The Vow To Save All Beings*

Offering advice to one's friends demonstrates compassion for others, but this compassion is still limited to a few individuals and is not widely diffused enough. Thus, the tenth section concerns the vow to save *all* beings.

The following are the ten steps of contemplation:

The first is to discuss "suchness"; the second is to reveal the substance of contemplation; the third is to talk about mutual identification; the fourth is to warn against the danger of self-conceit; the fifth is to prohibit indolence; the sixth is to reveal once more the substance of contemplation; the seventh is to clarify the relationship between negation and affirmation; the eighth is to clarify the meaning of contemplation; the ninth is to reveal contemplation in whatever one says; the tenth is to identify the mystic source.

The first way is to discuss "suchness." Mind and nature invisibly penetrate one into the other. The source of motion and that of motionlessness are the same. *Bhūtatathatā*, or reality, is free from thoughts and yet it is no different from the calculating mind. Illusory thoughts come forth in disorder; yet when we trace them back to their source, they are nothing but silence. Their spiritual origin is formless, but our discrimination causes a thousand manifestations to occur. These thousand manifestations vary from each other, and when we perceive their differences, we have the dharma-eye.[56] Silence never varies, and when we see this, we have the wisdom-eye.[57] When we have freed ourselves from both non-differentiated reality and differentiated materiality, we have attained the vision of the Buddha-eye.[58] Therefore, the three truths[59] are identified as one; thus the ultimate reality of being is absolutely pure. The three aspects of wisdom are the simultaneous revelations of one mind; the light of *prajñā* is eternally illuminating. At the moment when objective conditions and subjective wisdom are silently identified, liberation takes place in all conditions.[60] The symbol *yi* is neither vertical nor horizontal. It indicates that the perfect Tao is grasped only through silent identification. Therefore, the nature of the three virtues[61] apparently cannot be differentiated. A mind which is deep and boundless has neither doubts nor thoughts. This is the essence of the Tao, yet it is not the way to approach it. To see that the mind is the Tao is to follow the stream and reach the source.

The second way reveals the object of contemplation, wherein one realizes that One Thought is both void and no-void, yet neither void nor no-void.

The third way speaks of mutual identification. When mind and void are identified, there is neither anxiety nor delight, even after one has been criticized or praised. When body and void are identified there is neither suffering nor joy, whether one is treated with cruelty or with kindness. When material things[62] are identified with the void, where is the loss or gain, bestowed or taken away? When one's mind identifies void and no-void, one is free from the ties of love that come from thinking of others. By showing compassion to all, one saves others from their suffering. When the body is identified with void and no-void, the inner quiescence is similar to that of lifeless wood, while the outer appearance inspires respect. When one identifies material things with void and no-void, one is eternally free from craving, yet one has enough to be able to help others. When one identifies the mind as either void or no-void, both not void and not no-void, then one begins to understand the meaning of Reality and gains the vision that Buddha had. When the body is identified with either void or no-void, both not void and not no-void, then one's thought becomes purified, and one enters *samādhi*. When one identifies material things with both void and no-void, both not void and not no-void, then the Hall of Buddha[63] becomes the Pure Land for the transformation of Buddhas and Bodhisattvas.

The fourth way warns of the danger of self-conceit, which, if not overcome, jeopardizes all identification.

The fifth way prohibits indolence. In crossing the sea, one depends entirely upon a boat, without which one cannot cross over. This is also true of cultivation of the mind. It depends entirely upon contemplation. Without contemplation the mind cannot be illuminated. If the mind is not illuminated, mutual identification cannot be expected to take place. One should carefully consider the obstacles that self-indulgence creates.

The sixth way reveals the object of contemplation again. One now understands that One Thought is void and no-void, not being and not non-being, but does not yet realize that whenever a thought occurs it is immediately void and no-void, not non-being and not not-non-being.

The seventh way explains why one should understand the relationship between affirmation and negation. Mind is neither being nor non-being, and simultaneously it is neither not being nor not non-being. When mind is either being or non-being, it falls into the trap of affirmation. When it is neither being nor non-being, it falls into the trap of negation. Thus, it merely asserts that both affirmation and negation are wrong, but it does not assert that both non-affirmation and non-negation are right. Now to use both negations [the negation of affirmation and the negation of negation] in order to deny both affirmations [the affirmation of negation and the affirmation of affirmation] is to say that when affirmation is denied and becomes non-affirmation, it is still negation. Conversely, if one uses both negations to deny both negations—that is, when negation is denied and turned into negation of negation—the result is affirmation. Thus, what we have is the assertion of the rightness of non-affirmation and non-negation; but it is neither not negation nor not non-negation, neither not affirmation nor not non-affirmation.

The subtlety of the relation between negation and affirmation is refined and difficult to perceive. Let your spirit be pure and your thoughts quiescent, and search for this subtlety carefully.

The eighth way is to clarify the meaning of interpretation. The perfect truth is inexpressible, but through words its meaning is revealed. Neither its meaning nor its source is identical with contemplation. However, it is through contemplation that the source is realized. If the true meaning is not revealed, it is because the words have been poorly interpreted. If the source is not yet realized, then the contemplation has not been deep enough. Through deep contemplation, the source is realized; through adequate interpretation, the meaning is revealed. When the meaning has been revealed and the source realized, words and contemplation do not necessarily remain.

The ninth way is to transmit the fruits of contemplation in whatever one says, for it is through words that the object of one's contemplation is revealed. Thus, source and meaning are seen to be the same. When words express contemplation, the two become fused. Then articulation and absolute reality are one. When articulation and reality are one, the state of contemplation may be revealed in words. When the state of contemplation is expressed verbally, it is absolute reality. When absolute reality is no different from this verbal expression, it is the source. The essence is one and the same; only its names vary. Applying the terms "words" and "contemplation" is a mere game.

The tenth way is to identify the mystic source. Those whose minds have been awakened will never be trapped by contemplation, and thus fail to grasp the meaning of words. Those who are well versed in the doctrine of Buddhism will never be impeded by words and thus fail to understand reality. When reality is understood, the obstacle of words is broken, for what more can words discuss? When meaning is revealed, the action of the mind is extinguished, for what more can contemplation do? That which cannot be contemplated and expressed by words is indeed the essence of Tao.

On the seventeenth day of the tenth month in the second year of the Hsien-t'ien period [713], the Master entered *nirvāna*[64] by sitting quietly. On the thirteenth day of the eleventh month, his body was enshrined in the pagoda to the south of Mount Hsi. His posthumous name, bestowed on him by the Royal Court, was Great Master of Formlessness. His pagoda was called Pure Illumination. In the middle of the Shun-hua period [990–994] of the Sung Dynasty, the Emperor T'ai-tsung[65] issued an imperial mandate to Wên-chou to repair the shrine and the pagoda.

NOTES

1. The *Laṅkāvatāra Sūtra* is attributed to Śākyamuni, who is said to have delivered it on the Laṅkā Mountain in Ceylon. It is one of the most important texts of Mahāyāna Buddhism, containing the doctrines of Mind-Only, *tathagātagarbha*, and *ālayavijñāna* (all-conserving consciousness). Four Chinese translations were made between A.D. 420 and 704, three of which survive. An English translation by Daisetz T. Suzuki was published in 1932 by George Routledge and Sons, London.

2. *Prajñā* is the highest of the six *pāramitās*, or ways "to reach the other shore," which include charity, moral conduct, patience, devotion, contempla-

NOTES

tion, and wisdom (*prajñā*). *Prajñāpāramitā*, therefore, is the highest wisdom for reaching the other shore. It revolutionized Buddhism in all its philosophical and religious aspects by the basic concept of *śūnyata*, or Emptiness. *Astasāhasrikā* is believed to be the oldest and most basic Prajñāpāramitā text; it was translated into Chinese as early as A.D. 172 by Lokaraksha. Kumārajīva's translation was finished early in the fifth century. In the latter half of the seventh century, Hsüan-tsang completed his grand translation of the *Mahāprajñāpāramitā Sūtra* in six hundred fascicles. The *Prajñāpāramitā-hridaya Sūtra* is a very short text on the Prajñāpāramitā, consisting of only 262 Chinese characters in the Hsüan-tsang translation. This short text is commonly used for chanting in Buddhist temples.

3. Mādhyamika is the doctrine of the Middle Way, known as San-lun in China and Sanron in Japan. In the fifth century Nāgārjuna's *Mādhyamika Śāstra* was translated and expounded by Kumārajīva (d. A.D. 409). San-lun means "Three Treatises"; these are: (1) the Middle Way, or *Mādhyamika Śāstra*; (2) the Twelve Gates, or *Dvādaśanikāya Śāstra*; (3) the One Hundred Verses, or *Śata Śāstra*. The first two śāstras were written by Nāgārjuna. The third is by Aryadeva, a disciple of Nāgārjuna. However, in the early Ch'an Buddhist literature the text of the *Prajñāpāramitā Śāstra*, by Nāgārjuna, was added to the San-lun, forming the Shih-lun, or "Four Treatises."

4. T. R. V. Murti, *The Central Philosophy of Buddhism*, p. 226–27.

5. According to Buddhist philosophy, each individual existence is composed of the Five Skandhas (Chinese: *yin*), or Aggregates: *rūpa*, or material element; *vedanā*, or sensation; *samjñā*, or perception; *saṁskāra*, or formative principle; *vijñāna*, or consciousness.

6. Yung-chia, *Odes on Enlightenment*, in *Taishō shinshū daizōkyō*, No. 2014, Vol. 48, p. 396.

7. *Collected Works of Ch'an Master Yung-chia Hsüan-chio*, in *Taishō shinshū daizōkyō*, No. 2013, Vol. 48, p. 391.

8. Chi-tsang, *Essay on the Double Truth*, in *Taishō shinshū daizōkyō*, No. 1854, Vol. 45, pp. 77–115.

The Double Truth on Three Levels may be schematized as follows:

common truth	higher truth
1) being	1) non-being
2) both being and non-being	2) neither being nor non-being
3) both being and non-being and neither being nor non-being	3) both not being and not non-being and neither not being nor not non-being

9. *Collected Works of Ch'an Master Yung-chia*, p. 393.

10. *Ibid.*

11. According to *General Records of Buddhas and Patriarchs*, Chüan 7, p. 188, T'ien-kung Hui-wei was the Seventh Patriarch of the T'ien-t'ai School, and Tso-ch'i Fa-lang the Eighth.

12. *Collected Works of Ch'an Master Yung-chia*, p. 391.

13. *Ibid.*, p. 392.

14. *Supplement to the Transmission of the Lamp*, in *Taishō shinshū daizōkyō*, No. 2077, Vol. 51, p. 508.

Metaphysical and Logical Approaches in Early Ch'an Teachings

15. *Collected Works of Ch'an Master Yung-chia*, p. 391.
16. Daisetz T. Suzuki, *Essays in Zen Buddhism*; Series I, p. 203.
17. *The Dialogues of Ch'an Master Chao-chou*, p. 64b.
18. *Recorded Dialogues of Ch'an Master Lin-chi*, in *Taishō shinshū daizōkyō*, No. 1985, Vol. 48, p. 495.
19. Now, Chen-chiang (Chinkiang), in Kiangsu Province on the south bank of the Yangtze River.
20. The *Mahāprajñāpāramitā Sūtra*, one of the oldest Buddhist canonical books, contains six hundred fascicles. Its fundamental purpose was the achievement of *śūnyatā* through detachment from all existence with its multiplicities. An Indian creation, it was translated into Chinese by Kumārajīva, Hsüan-tsang, and many others.
21. Mount Mao is southeast of Chu-yung in Kiangsu Province. Fa-yung studied here under the San-lun master Kuei. Next he was a student of the T'ien-t'ai doctrine at Feng-lu; then he went to Yu-hsi Monastery in the Niu-t'ou Mountain, south of Nanking in Kiangsu Province.
22. 580–651. See *The Lamp*, Chüan 3.
23. The *li* is about one-third of the Western mile.
24. *Dharmaparyāya* (Chinese *fa-men*) means the doctrine or system of teaching given by Buddha.
25. *Bala-abhijñā* (Chinese *shen-t'ung*) means the supernatural faculties generally believed to be the endowment of the Bodhisattva.
26. *Bodhi* means the enlightened and illuminated mind.
27. Karma generally means a deed or action which causes its proper result. A thought or emotion is conceived of as a karma. There are two kinds of hindrance to the attainment of *bodhi:* the hindrance of knowledge and that of passion.
28. Trailokya or Triloka, called the Three Realms in Chinese: *kāmadhātu* is the realm of sensuous desire; *rūpadhātu*, the realm of form; and *arūpadhātu*, the formless realm of pure spirit.
29. The Chinese *ching* covers a threefold meaning: *gocara*, or mental attitude toward the external world; *artha*, or sense field; and *visaya*, or external world.
30. A town south of Chen-chiang in Kiangsu Province.
31. Begging alms is one of the twelve *dhūtas* prescribing the outward conduct of the monk.
32. *Rūpa* (Chinese *shih*) means form, outward appearance, or material element.
33. *Laṅkāvatāra Sūtra:* "The capacity of mind of no-mind I call *hsin-liang*, or the capacity of mind."
34. *Samjñā* (Chinese *hsiang*) means perception or ideation; *vedanā* (Chinese *shou*) means sensation. Both are elements of the Five Aggregates, or Skandhas.
35. "One Thought" is often regarded as the thoughtless thought which indicates the absolute state of mind.
36. *Samādhi* expresses the idea of sudden enlightenment maintained by the *Avataṁsaka Sūtra*.
37. "Basic ignorance" is conceived of as remaining invisible passions which rise up and disappear in the realm of quiescence.
38. Capacity of mind of no-mind; see note 33 above.

NOTES

39. The "Threefold Contemplation" was originated by the T'ien-t'ai School. It is the contemplation of real; of unreal; and of the Middle, which is both real and unreal, and is neither real nor unreal.

40. Siṁhanāda, or "lion roar," symbolizes the power of the highest achievement of meditation. The roar of the lion makes all animals tremble and even arrests birds in their flight and fish in the water.

41. The five *gati*: hell, hungry ghosts, animals, human beings, devas.

42. *Skandha māra* is the evil spirit that works through physical and mental forms; *kleśa māra*, the evil spirit of passions that trouble mind and body; *mrtyu māra*, the evil spirit of death, *devaputra māra*, the lord of the sixth heaven of desire.

43. *Jñeyāvarana*, or intellectual hindrance, is one of the two hindrances to the attainment of *bodhi*. The other is *kleśāvarana*, conative hindrance, or the hindrance of passion.

44. According to the teaching of the Middle Way, the extremes of being and non-being are removed. There is neither a real existence nor a real void. Real and unreal are the outcome of causal relation. Thus, existence is at the same time non-existence; non-existence is in turn existence. Therefore, "When discrimination is done away with, the Middle Way, or *śūnyatā*, is reached."

45. See note 5 above.

46. This symbolizes Buddha's teaching, which permeates all sentient beings and awakens them, which wonder is derived from the *Lotus Sūtra*.

47. According to tradition, when Buddha expounded the philosophy of ultimate reality of all things in the *Mahāyāna Sūtra*, illumination took place and the earth trembled.

48. In the *Doctrine of the Mean*, one of the Confucian classics, *ts'ung-yung-chung-tao* means to obtain the truth naturally and easily. *Ts'ung-yung* is an abbreviation of this expression.

49. Wenchow, now Yung-chia (Yungkia) in Chekiang Province.

50. The sūtras are collections of sermons, chiefly those given by the Buddha. The śāstras are Buddhist philosophical discourses. The vinayas are works dealing with monastic discipline.

51. Ts'ao-ch'i, in northern Kwangtung Province, is where Hui-nêng, the Sixth Patriarch of Ch'an, founded his school.

52. The three thousand regulations govern the proper way of walking, standing, sitting, and lying down. The eighty thousand detailed duties are rules concerning the four awe-inspiring deportments and many other aspects of the monk's behavior.

53. The Five Stages of the Emergence of Thought:
    1) The desires of the mundane world.
    2) Discrimination of opposites arising from the thoughtless state.
    3) Idle thoughts leading to more of the same.
    4) Shameful thoughts upon realization that one's previous thoughts have been idle.
    5) Quietude where one is free from the thoughts of desire, of discrimination, of idleness, and of shame.

54. The Six Procedures for Achieving *Samatha*:
    1) Determining wherein lies your mistake:
       In discriminating between good and evil.

Metaphysical and Logical Approaches in Early Ch'an Teachings

   In the mind's attachment to its own innocence.
2) Remedies for these mistakes:
   Quietude is a remedy for discrimination.
   Consciousness is a remedy for innocence.
3) Application of these remedies to their corresponding mistakes.
4) From excessive quietude, innocence arises.
5) Quietude without consciousness leads to innocence.
   Consciousness without quietude leads to discrimination.
6) Consciousness supplemented by quietude leads to illumination, in which the mind is free from both discrimination and attachment.

55. The Three Vehicles include: (1) Śrāvakayāna, in which one understands the truth through the teachings of Buddha; (2) Pratyekabuddhayāna, in which one understands the truth through self-awakening; and (3) Bodhisattvayāna, in which one understands the highest level of *bodhi*, or wisdom.

56. The "dharma-eye" is the vision of the Bodhisattva, which perceives the sufferings of the sentient beings. This vision penetrates to the truth of actuality, through discrimination.

57. The "wisdom-eye" is the vision of the Śrāvaka and the Pratyekabuddha, which perceives the inner reality of the self, that is, the formless void, or *śūnyatā*.

58. The "Buddha-eye" is the vision of Buddha, which sees both the differentiations of the external world and the undifferentiated void of the inner self. This vision is omniscient because it embraces all kinds of vision including the two above.

59. The three truths are the awareness of *śūnyatā*, the proper discrimination of Bodhisattva, and the perfect wisdom of Buddha.

60. The symbol *yi*, which is neither vertical nor horizontal.

61. The three virtues are *dharmakāya*, *prajñā*, and *mokṣa* (emancipation).

62. That is, material things such as countries, clothes, foods, etc., upon which the personal existence depends.

63. Hsiang-t'ai, the hall where Buddha lived.

64. Originally, *nirvāna* meant tranquil extinction. In this case, it means liberation from existence, or death. Also, we have: "Nirvāna in its ultimate signification was an affirmation—an affirmation beyond opposites of all kinds" (Suzuki, *Essays in Zen Buddhism*, I, p. 56).

65. T'ai-tsung's reign was 976–997.

Part II

Introduction
Interfusion of Universality and Particularity

TUNG-SHAN LIANG-CHIEH (807–869)
"He Is the Same as Me, Yet I Am Not He!"

TS'AO-SHAN PÊN-CHI (840–901)
"Purity Is in the Impure"

Interfusion of Universality and Particularity

Among the five schools of Ch'an Buddhism established in China early in the ninth century, two are still active in present-day Japan, though in China all five have virtually lost their original identity. These two schools are the Ts'ao-tung Tsung and the Lin-chi Tsung (Sōtō School and Rinzai School in Japan). The former was founded by Tung-shan Liang-chieh and his disciple Ts'ao-shan Pên-chi, the latter by Lin-chi I-hsüan. When we study the basic teachings developed by these two schools we cannot neglect the metaphysical speculations of great Buddhist minds such as Fa-tsang (643–720) and Ch'êng-kuan (738–839), who expounded the Hua-yen philosophy. For example, the teachings of *wu wei*[1] *p'ien cheng,* or the Five Relations Between Particularity and Universality, maintained by Tung-shan Liang-chieh, and of *ssu liao chien,* or the Four Processes of Liberation from Subjectivity and Objectivity, by Lin-chi I-hsüan, are closely related to the doctrines of the Identification of Reality and Appearance, by Fa-tsang, and the Fourfold Dharmadhātu, by Ch'êng-kuan. Perhaps these adaptations of Hua-yen metaphysics to the teachings of Ch'an may serve as evidence of "the further leap after climbing to the top of a pole one hundred feet long" so often urged by Ch'an masters.

Interfusion of Universality and Particularity

In 798, the fourteenth year of the Chên-yüan period of the T'ang Dynasty, only ten years prior to the birth of Tung-shan Liang-chieh, the famous translation into Chinese of the *Avataṁsaka Sūtra* (*Hua-yen Ching*) celebrated its completion by Prajñā at the Chung-fu Monastery in the ancient capital of China. This translation was begun in 420; it then comprised only sixty fascicles, and is generally known as the Chin script. In 699 a second version of the translation, consisting of eighty fascicles, was completed by Śikṣānanda with the assistance of Fa-tsang under the direction of the Royal Court; it is called the T'ang script. The third script, *Gandavyūha*, which was the final chapter of the foregoing scripts, was transcribed by the King of Uda in India and sent to the Emperor of T'ang in 796. It was translated into forty fascicles and bears the title *Entering the Dharmadhātu*. Thus by 798 the *Avataṁsaka Sūtra*, "the King of Mahāyāna Sūtra," had been completely rendered into Chinese.

From Buddhist literary sources we learn that Buddha was in *samādhi*, known as *sāgaramūdra*, when he delivered the *Avataṁsaka Sūtra*. The fundamental idea of the sūtra is the unimpeded mutual solution of all particularities. Each particularity, besides being itself, penetrates all other particularities and is in turn penetrated by them. This harmonious interplay between particularities and also between each particularity and universality creates a luminous universe. This world of luminosity, absolutely free from spatial and temporal limitations and yet no less the world of daily affairs, is called *dharmadhātu*. In *dharmadhātu* the boundaries of each particularity melt away, and the reality of each becomes infinitely interfused with every other being. The metaphysical speculation of the Avataṁsaka was further expounded and systematized by Chinese Buddhists and the philosophy of Dharmadhātu was classified into the fourfold world:

1. A world of *shih*, or event, or appearance, or particularity
2. A world of *li*, or reality, or universality
3. A world of *li* and *shih*, completely interfused and identified
4. A world of perfect unimpeded mutual solution between *shih* and *shih*, or between particularity and particularity

Interfusion of Universality and Particularity

To understand the philosophy of Hua-yen we must be familiar with the basic ideas of *li* and *shih*. In Chinese script *li* literally means the veins in a polished gem; figuratively, it refers to basic principles. Thus the word *li* means reason, or Heavenly Reason, often used by Confucianists in contrast to human desire. The word *shih* literally means events or happenings.

When Chinese Hua-yen Buddhists adopted the terms *li* and *shih*, they identified them with the Sanskrit *śūnyatā* and *rūpa*. *Śūnyatā* has been translated in Chinese as *k'ung*, which is often used to indicate unoccupied space—that is, something was there before and now is not. But the real meaning of *śūnyatā*, or *k'ung*, is ontological. It is the absolute reality, free from the dichotomy of being and non-being, form and formlessness. Because the Chinese *k'ung* easily leads to its relative sense, the absence of things, Hua-yen scholars chose to use the term *li*, which denotes the absolute reality, to coexist with *shih*. Where there is no *shih*, there is no *li*. Thus *li*, or reality, exists only within *shih*, or appearance.

Fa-tsang was born 150 years before Tung-shan Liang-chieh, and his *Treatise on the Golden Lion* was a noted contribution to the Buddhist literature. When Fa-tsang expounded the philosophy of Hua-yen to the Royal Court, he used the golden lion in the palace to illustrate the unimpeded mutual solution between *li* and *shih*. The lion symbolizes *shih*, or appearance, which has no reality without the gold. On the other hand, gold lacks meaningful expression without the form of the lion as its appearance. The existence of each is dependent upon the other. Yet the gold and the lion distinctly exist by themselves. When by mutual solution gold is lion and lion is gold, the dichotomy between reality and appearance disappears.

This approach to enlightenment is through metaphysical reasoning, and few can really reach this level of intellection. This is the intellectual process that Ch'an Buddhists call "the pole one hundred feet long." Even if the devotee reaches the top of the pole, he still needs "a further leap." This is why zealous learners of Ch'an would rather concentrate on mind-awakening than on the pursuit of intellectual profundity. However, the leading masters of Ch'an

Interfusion of Universality and Particularity

Buddhism, such as Tung-shan Liang-chieh and Lin-chi I-hsüan, thoroughly mastered the metaphysical structure of Hua-yen and developed it up to "the further leap." In the following sermons we find Tung-shan's application of the basic principle of unimpeded mutual solution between *li* and *shih*—reality and appearance. His approach differs from Hua-yen in that he concentrates on the concrete experience rather than on the abstract principle.

> Once a monk asked Master Tung-shan, "Winter comes and summer comes. How do we avoid them?" The Master answered. "Why should you not go where there is neither summer nor winter?" The monk persisted: "How could it be that there is neither a summer nor a winter?" The Master said, "You feel hot in summer and cold in winter."

What Tung-shan meant is that there is no separation between feeling hot and the summer, and between feeling cold and the winter. When "hot" is identified with summer and "cold" with winter, reality interfuses appearance. As soon as one actually realizes this, one has Ch'an. In Hua-yen, however, it is the world of *li* and *shih*, completely interfused and identified, that one enters.

Ts'ao-shan Pên-chi, the great disciple of Tung-shan, also applied the doctrine of the identification of *li* and *shih* in his teachings. This may be seen in his interpretation of the answers made by Hsiang-yen Chih-hsien to a disciple's question, "What is Tao?" Hsiang-yen's first reply was, "In the dry woods a dragon is singing." When the disciple failed to understand this, the Master then said, "The eye is in the skull." Another Ch'an master, Shih-shuang Hsing-k'ung, when asked for an interpretation, said that the first statement meant, "There is still joy there," and the second, "There is still consciousness there." When Ts'ao-shan heard of this, he composed the following poem:

> He who says that a dragon is singing in the dry woods
> Is he who truly sees Tao.
> The skull has no consciousness,
> But wisdom's eye begins to shine in it.
> If joy and consciousness should be eliminated,

> Then fluctuation and communication would cease.
> Those who deny this do not understand
> That purity is in the impure.

Ts'ao-shan did not accept Shih-shuang's saying that the dragon's singing signifies joy, nor that the eye in the skull means consciousness. Shih-shuang's teaching was known as K'u-mu Ch'an, or "Ch'an in the dry woods." His students often did not sleep on beds, but sat in meditation day and night. But the essence of Ch'an is not merely non-action, but also action which reveals non-action. Thus non-action and action are interfused and identified. So, in the dry woods the dragon is singing, in the skull the eye is shining: it is the same as to say that *li* is identified with *shih*. Therefore Ts'ao-shan maintained that purity is revealed through impurity. In other words, the dragon's singing is the manifestation of the dry woods. Without its singing, there would be no expression of the dry woods. The two are mutually identified: the dragon's singing is the dry woods and the dry woods is the dragon's singing. In the language of Hua-yen, *li* is *shih* and *shih* is *li*.

In Tung-shan's own work *Inscription on Ch'an*, we read:

> In action there is no labor,
> In non-action there is illumination,
> Thus *li* and *shih* are clearly understood,
> And substance and action are unimpededly interfused.
> This is the essence of Ch'an!

From this statement we can see how Tung-shan applied the basic principle of the perfect unimpeded mutual solution between reality and appearance, which had been illustrated by Fa-tsang with the parable of the golden lion.

In Hua-yen philosophy we find an even more complex structure of the interrelation between one and many, or universality and particularity. It was also Fa-tsang's ingenious invention to use the mutual reflections of ten mirrors for illustration. He put ten mirrors above and below and around, all facing one another. In the center stood an illuminated figure of Buddha. The reflection of the image was cast into each mirror. Each mirror reflected the image of every other mirror, each multiplying the others' images

Interfusion of Universality and Particularity

endlessly. The one mirror takes in the nine other mirrors; all nine others at the same time take in the one. In other words, one is in all and all is in one. In Tsung-mi's *Commentary on Contemplation of Dharmadhātu* we have the formula:

> When one is absorbed by all, one penetrates into all.
> When all is absorbed by one, all penetrates into one.
> When one is absorbed by one, one penetrates into one.
> When all is absorbed by all, all penetrates into all.

This idea of interfusion is called *shih shih yuan yung wu ai*, or unimpeded perfect mutual solution between particularity and particularity. It is an infinite interplay of all forces and all units, as drawn in the formula above. Intellectually, this is a distinguished contribution to human thought. But it is hardly possible to achieve enlightenment through this systematization of speculation. Therefore the Ch'an master Tung-shan Liang-chieh made a step further and developed what is called *wu wei p'ien cheng*, or the Five Relations Between Particularity and Universality. The formula given by Tung-shan is this:

1. *cheng chung p'ien*, or particularity in universality
2. *p'ien chung cheng*, or universality in particularity
3. *cheng chung lai*, or enlightenment emerging from universality
4. *p'ien chung chih*, or enlightenment arriving from particularity[2]
5. *chien chung tao*, or enlightenment achieved between universality and particularity

When a monk asked Ts'ao-shan the meaning of *wu wei p'ien cheng*, Ts'ao-shan explained:

> *Cheng* means the world of the Void, in which there is nothing from the beginning. *P'ien* means the world of appearance, which consists of ten thousand forms and images. *Cheng chung p'ien* indicates particularity in universality. *P'ien chung cheng* refers to universality in particularity. *Chien* is that which responds silently to all conditions, yet is attached to none of them. It is free from impurity and purity,

particularity and universality. Thus it is the great Way of Ch'an, the real teaching of non-attachment.

As *cheng*, or universality, refers to the Void and *p'ien*, or particularity, to events, the first *wei* relation, *cheng chung p'ien*, means that objective events are in the Void, which is free from subjective distortion. As Ts'ao-shan expresses it, it is the revealing of the entirely objective being, emancipated from any subjective stain. In the *Pao-ching San-mei*, or *Samādhi as Reflection from the Precious Mirror*, which was handed down from generation to generation in the Ts'ao-tung Tsung, we read:

> As snow is contained in a silver bowl, and as a white heron hides in the bright moonlight, when you classify them they are different from each other, but when you unify them they are the same in the Source.

The images "snow" and "white heron" are symbols of particularity, the objective events. The symbols "silver bowl" and "bright moonlight" refer to the Void, or universality. It is in this world of universality that the particularities join together and enter the Source. Hung-chih Cheng-chio (1083–1159) gave the same idea in a *gāthā*:[3]

> The white bird disappears in vapor;
> The autumn stream unites with heaven.

When the objective event is not distorted by a subjective stain, it unites with the world of the Void. The white bird and the autumn stream both symbolize the unstained objective events, and heaven, the Source, or universality. When we read the literature of Ts'ao-tung masters we know that they are following the first *wei*, *cheng chung p'ien*, or particularity in universality.

The second *wei* is *p'ien chung cheng*, or universality in particularity, which can be illustrated by a verse of William Blake:

> To see a world in a grain of sand
> And a heaven in a wild flower.
> Hold infinity in the palm of your hand
> And eternity in an hour.

Interfusion of Universality and Particularity

The idea of universality penetrating into particularity has been carried even further by Ch'an Buddhists, who often describe the power of reality or universality in illogical and symbolic expressions. In the *Pao-ching San-mei* we also have:

> While the wooden man is singing,
> The stone maiden starts to dance.
> This cannot be reached by our consciousness.
> How can you give any thought to this?

Through the power of universality even the wooden man can sing and the stone maiden dance. As a matter of fact, when we are deprived of the sustenance of our universe, we are as dead as the wooden man and the stone maiden. This is the function of *p'ien chung cheng*, or universality in particularity.

The third *wei* is *cheng chung lai*, or enlightenment emerging from universality. Ts'ao-shan's explanation is: "The meaning of a word exists in no words." A monk once asked Master Chao-chou Ts'ung-shen whether a dog has the Buddha-nature. Chao-chou's answer was "*Wu.*" The original meaning of *wu* is "to have not," or "nothing," or "non-being." But according to Ch'an Buddhists' understanding, none of these meanings convey what Chao-chou had in mind. It was just absolute *wu*, a meaningless syllable. Nonsensical as it appears, this meaningless sound *wu* is full of meaning. When Ta-hui Tsung-kao (1089–1163) wrote to his lay disciple Liu Yen-chung, he advised him to meditate on "*wu*" as given by Chao-chou in his *kung-an*, because from the absolute *wu*, or *cheng*, or universality, enlightenment will emerge.

In the *Recorded Dialogues of Ch'an Master Ta-hui* we read:

> When habitual anxiety arises, do not purposely get rid of it by pressure; but at the very moment when it arises, meditate on the *kung-an:* Has a dog the Buddha-nature, or not?

The answer *wu* indicates the absolute moment, similar to that moment when a snowflake falls on the burning stove. No one can save the snow no matter how he tries. So the moment one begins to meditate on *wu*, one dissolves one's self in the absolute realm of *wu*, or Void; and enlightenment emerges from that instant.

Interfusion of Universality and Particularity

When Hung-chih Cheng-chio was asked, "How is it that substance is lacking in the reality of purity and Void?" he replied: "It is the instant of origin where refinement has not yet made any marks, and the moment when a message has not yet been conveyed." When one collects one's thoughts at the instant of *wu*, one will be led to sudden enlightenment. This is called *cheng chung lai*, or enlightenment emerging from universality.

The fourth *wei* is *p'ien chung chih*, or enlightenment arriving from particularity. In Tung-shan's fascicle we are told that when Master Tung-shan was crossing the water and saw his image reflected, he was awakened. In a *gāthā* which he wrote about this experience, he said:

> I meet him wherever I go.
> He is the same as me,
> Yet I am not he!
> Only if you understand this
> Will you identify with what you are.

An image is a concrete objective form. When one grasps the reality through objectivity, one is enlightened. So it was with Master Tung-shan: when he saw his image reflected in the water, his mind was suddenly opened up and he achieved enlightenment. Chü-shih often lifted one finger when a devotee sought Ch'an from him. He meant that when he lifted a finger, the whole universe came along with it. When Yün-mên Wên-yen took his staff and drew with it on the ground, he said to the assembly, "All Buddhas, numberless as grains of sand, are here engaged in endless dispute." When Chao-chou was asked about the meaning of Bodhidharma coming from the West, his answer was, "The cypress tree in the courtyard." Tung-shan Shou-ch'u's answer to this same question was, "Three *chin*[4] of flax." These answers are either an ordinary object or an event which requires no intellectual analysis or logical reasoning. However, this objectivity, meaningless as it is, may suddenly break the wall of one's consciousness and penetrate into the deeper recesses of one's mind. It all serves as a key to open the mind of the Ch'an learner. This key is what Tung-shan called *p'ien chung chih*, enlightenment arriving from particularity.

Interfusion of Universality and Particularity

The fifth *wei* is *chien chung tao*, or enlightenment achieved between universality and particularity. Ts'ao-shan's interpretation is, "It is neither words nor no-words." Primarily it is free from both, yet it directly hits the point. His illustration of this *wei* is the answer given by Yüeh-shan to Yün-yen, recorded in a sermon by his master:

> When Yüeh-shan roamed about the mountain with Yün-yen, the sword worn by Yüeh-shan made a rattling sound. Yün-yen asked him, "Where does this sound come from?" Yüeh-shan immediately drew the sword and lifted it as if he were going to split something. Master Tung-shan quoted this story and said to the assembly, "Look here! Yüeh-shan reveals Ch'an through his action. Learners in present days should understand Ultimate Reality and try to experience it through self-realization."

This is indeed, as Ts'ao-shan pointed out, the direct approach to Ch'an, which is free from both verbal expression and silence.

Here is an example of Tung-shan's own application of *chien chung tao*, the fifth *wei* approach to Ch'an. Once a monk asked the Master, "When a snake swallows a frog, should you save the frog's life or should you not?" The Master answered, "If you save it, it means that 'both of your eyes are blind.' If you do not save it, it means that 'both your body and your shadow are not visible.' " It is through this unusual profundity of expression that Tung-shan's inner experience is revealed. He was free from both saving the life of the frog and not saving it. His answer followed the approach of *chien chung tao*.

In 1961, when I was having dinner with Rōshi Yamada Mumon in his Myōshinji Temple, some fragments of cracker dropped on the floor, and ants immediately went to work carrying off the food. Rōshi Yamada gently pushed the ants away, but they kept on working. So I asked him, "Our ants are in such a hurry to gather their supply. Do they crave or not?" Rōshi smiled and replied, "Ask the ants!" He was free from both assertion and negation of the question. Thus his answer was in accordance with the fifth *wei* of Tung-shan.

In addition to the *wu wei p'ien cheng*, or the Five Relations

INTERFUSION OF UNIVERSALITY AND PARTICULARITY

Between Particularity and Universality, Tung-shan Liang-chieh further developed *wu wei kung hsün,* or the Five Levels of Achievement, which are closely related to the former set of formulas. So it is another application of the Fourfold Dharmadhātu maintained by the Hua-yen School.

1. *hsiang,* or subjectivity
2. *feng,* or objectivity
3. *kung,* or non-action (from which action emerges)
4. *kong kung,* or the interfusion between action and non-action
5. *kung kung,* or the absolute freedom from both action and non-action

The first two levels both belong to the Hua-yen world of *shih;* and the Ch'an Buddhists' commentaries identified these two levels as universality in particularity and particularity in universality. The third level, *kung,* is explained by Tung-shan himself as "that which is symbolized by dropping one's hoe." He says further: "One stops work in order to sit quietly, and one has one's leisure in the depth of white clouds." This apparently indicates non-action. The fourth level, *kong kung,* was interpreted by Ta-hui Tsung-kao: "Non-action identifies with action; and action identifies with non-action." It is the same as the world of interfusion between *li* and *shih.* The fifth level, *kung kung,* indicates perfect freedom from subjectivity and objectivity, as Master Chia-shan once said: "In myself there is no Chia-shan [subjectivity]; in front of me there is no monk [objectivity]." This is the world of perfect mutual solution between *shih* and *shih* according to Ta-hui Tsung-kao and others.

In the foregoing we have discussed the Fourfold Dharmadhātu maintained by the Hua-yen masters, and also the Five Relations Between Universality and Particularity as well as the Five Levels of Achievement taught by Ts'ao-tung masters. We have seen each of these formulas illustrated and have noted the progress brought about by Tung-shan. Perhaps the chart on page 53 below may help us to grasp more clearly the essential relations between Ts'ao-

Interfusion of Universality and Particularity

tung and Hua-yen and between Tung-shan's two sets of formulas and the Fourfold Dharmadhātu of Hua-yen, and thereby facilitate a better understanding of Ch'an.

According to the Ts'ao-tung School, *cheng chung lai* refers to "the meaning of the word exists in no words." This means that the awakened mind emerges from nothingness. Since non-action is the same as nothingness, it follows, as the Five Levels of Achievement given in the chart on page 53 indicate, that from non-action action emerges.

This theory of mind-awakening was often criticized by the Lin-chi School, which opposed the idea of mere meditation. As is shown in the chart below, for example, Wan-ju T'ung-chê maintained that he who stays at the top of the solitary peak should still be given thirty blows. But the Ts'ao-tung masters, such as Hung-chih Cheng-chio, the leading master of this school in twelfth-century China, maintained that meditation is the fundamental approach to enlightenment, and it was Hung-chih who established the School of Silent Illumination. At the same time, his opponent, Ta-hui Tsung-kao, favored the discipline of *kung-an* training and opposed the approach of silent illumination, though he nevertheless advised his disciples to meditate on the absolute *wu* as a means toward enlightenment, as we have mentioned previously.

Let us first take a brief glance at the teachings of silent illumination. Here we have Hung-chih Cheng-chio's own words, translated from the *Hung-chih Ch'an-shih K'uang-lu*, or the *Extensive Records of Ch'an Master Hung-chih*, Section 6:

> In learning to be a Buddha, and in seeking the essence in the teaching of our school, man should purify his mind and allow his spirit to penetrate the depths. Thus he will be able to wander silently within himself during contemplation, and he will clearly see the origin of all things, obscured by nothing, not even by a mustard seed or a thread of hair. His mind is boundless and formless, just as the pure water contains the essence of autumn. It is glistening white and lustrously bright in the same way that moonlight envelops the entire night. During that absolute moment there is illumination without darkness; there is transparency free from stain. It is what it

FOURFOLD DHARMADHĀTU OF HUA-YEN (CH'ENG-KUAN)	FIVE RELATIONS BETWEEN UNIVERSALITY AND PARTICULARITY, BY TUNG-SHAN	FIVE LEVELS OF ACHIEVEMENT, BY TUNG-SHAN	ILLUSTRATION GIVEN BY WAN-JU T'UNG-CHÊ
The world of *shih* (events)	Particularity in universality	Subjectivity	When one stays in the center of the market and is ready to engage in all kinds of work at any time, he is entitled to receive thirty blows, because he neglects the cultivation of *li*, or reality, or non-action.
	Universality in particularity	Objectivity	
The world of *li* (reality)	Enlightenment emerging from universality	Non-action (from which action emerges)	When one stays on top of the solitary peak and gazes at the sky, he may swallow all the Buddhas, past, present and future, in one gulp, but he will neglect the all-sentient beings. He should also be given thirty blows because he neglects *shih*, or action.
The world of *li* and *shih* perfectly interfused	Enlightenment emerging from particularity	Interfusion of action and non-action	One stays on top of the solitary peak gazing at the sky, yet he is in the center of the market engaged in all kinds of work. One is in the center of the market engaged in all kinds of work, and yet he stays on top of the solitary peak, gazing at the sky. If these two men come to me, I will have nothing to offer them.
The world of perfect mutual solution between *shih* and *shih*	Enlightenment achieved between universality and particularity	Absolute freedom from both action and non-action	Do you understand where I shall be? Holding a staff and sitting in front of the door. When a lion or an elephant or a fox or a wolf comes, every one of them will receive my blows in like manner.

Interfusion of Universality and Particularity

is, absolutely tranquil and absolutely illuminating. When it is tranquil, this is not annihilation of cause and effect; when it is illuminating, this is not the objective reflection. It is simply pure light and perfect quiescence which continues through endless time. Being motionless but free from obscurity; being silent but self-aware. When one steadily enters the depth, the crystal vase [mind] freely revolves and turns over. Through one shift of the direction of the moving force he engages himself in all world affairs.

All the world situations and their manifold appearances are simply established by one's self. As I and the four elements of all things are from the same source, there will be no obstruction to our interfusion, and as soon as we all freely interpenetrate, man and things are non-differentiated. Self and others are not understood to be separate as their names are. In the midst of the visible and audible world we are engaging in each event one after another, but we transcend them airily and gracefully. Therefore we say that there is no mountain barrier and no river separation; the bright light penetrates every corner of the world. This is what we should be aware of and grasp.

In this passage Hung-chih maintains that the enlightened man deals with world affairs and every single happening of the day. However, in the midst of world affairs he is free from attachment and transcends them. Thus the affairs of the world are no longer a barrier or an obstacle to him. To reach such mental integrity man begins with the training of silent illumination. In other words, through meditation he attains enlightenment. This is the essential point in the Ts'ao-tung School's teaching. What Hung-chih said in his sermon is the essence of this teaching. To understand his sermon, one must first understand his teachings on meditation. The following translations of "Admonition on Sitting in Meditation" and "Inscription on the Chamber of Bliss in Purity" may open the way to the understanding of silent illumination.

ADMONITION ON SITTING IN MEDITATION

This is the essence of all Buddha's teaching,
And the essence of all that the Patriarchs taught:
Understanding should be gained free from objectivity;
Illumination should be achieved without causation.

Interfusion of Universality and Particularity

That which is understood, free from objectivity, is invisible.
That illumined, without causation, becomes a wonder.
When the understanding is invisible, it is the consciousness of non-differentiation.
When illumination becomes wonder, it is instantaneous enlightenment.
The consciousness of non-differentiation is awareness of the Absolute One beyond duality.
The instantaneous enlightenment is the light which is self-illuminating.
Pure is the water and transparent, where fish move slowly, slowly in it.
Boundless is the sky where flying birds disappear, disappear into the unseen.

Master Hung-chih here gives a brief description of what silent illumination is and how to achieve it. In only a dozen lines he summarizes his philosophy on inner awareness free from objectivity, and illumination free from causation, which serve as the foundation of instantaneous enlightenment. "Fish" indicates the circulation of light, and "birds" symbolizes the idle thoughts which are eliminated eventually. The foregoing passage gives us only a philosophical comprehension of enlightenment through meditation, but the following passage tells us briefly how to experience it.

INSCRIPTION ON THE CHAMBER OF BLISS IN PURITY

To search with eye or ear,
This is indeed a wrong path to undertake.
The profound source of inner joy
Is the absolute bliss from one's purity.
When purity is absolute,
Therein I have bliss.
Purity and bliss sustain one another
As the fuel maintains the flame.
The bliss of one's Self is limitless,
And absolute purity is infinite.
They are transparency beyond form,
And consciousness illuminating the empty chamber.
The empty chamber is Void,
Neither a being nor a non-being;
Yet it silently moves the spiritual potentiality

Interfusion of Universality and Particularity

And subtly revolves on the mystic axis.
When the mystic axis is turned round,
The original light is auspiciously revealed.
As there is nothing germinating in the mind,
How can it be determined by verbal expression?
Who is he who is aware of this?
Distinctly and clearly it is self-awareness,
Perfectly and extensively it is one's own consciousness,
Which is different from intellectual thinking
Since it has no concern with intellection.
It is just like snow shining upon white blossoms of reeds.
Thus it becomes a real illumination,
Boundless and void, lustrous and transparent.
[The rest is omitted.]

When we understand the process of silent illumination, we can understand Master Hung-chih's sermon:

Let a screen be hung unto the yellow chamber;
And who will carry messages in and out?
Let the curtains of purple silk be joined together,
And all the shining pearls will be dispersed in the darkness.
The very moment cannot be reached either by seeing or hearing;
Nor can it be expressed in words.
How can any news be sent there?
When darkness gradually turns to the light of dawn,
Your breeze will emerge from the glittering spring.
This I want to point out to you with a smile.

And another sermon, also a symbolic presentation, reads in part:

When by the side of the ancient ferry
The breeze and moonlight are cool and pure,
The dark vessel turns into a glowing world.

Both of these selections can be understood when we realize that they are descriptions of meditation turning darkness into illumination. The "screen" is down and the "curtains" are pulled together, which means darkness; the dispersion of the "shining pearls" symbolizes illumination. So it is true that the "dark vessel turns into a glowing world." This glowing world is just as Master Lin-chi expressed it in his last *gāthā*:

INTERFUSION OF UNIVERSALITY AND PARTICULARITY

Being carried by the endless stream you ask why,
The real infinite illumination is the answer.

Both of these leading masters of Ch'an Buddhism, in the Ts'ao-tung (Sōtō[5]) School and the Lin-chi (Rinzai) School, reached the highest achievement, although through different processes. While I was engaged in translating the biography of Master Hung-chih, I asked Rinzai Zen Asahina Sogen, the great master of Engakuji in Kamakura, whether he thought that the silent illumination maintained by the School of Sōtō was the highest achievement of enlightenment. His answer was, "Yes, it is!" But he stressed that the illumination must be genuine. Thus the aim of the Ts'ao-tung School is the same as that of the Lin-chi School. The only difference is in their approaches.

TUNG-SHAN LIANG-CHIEH
(807–869)

"He Is the Same as Me, Yet I Am Not He!"

(*From* The Transmission of the Lamp, *Chüan 15*)

CH'AN Master Tung-shan Liang-chieh of Yün-chou[6] was a native of Kuai-chi.[7] His original surname was Yü. In his childhood, while studying the *Prajñāpāramitā-hridaya Sūtra* with his teacher, he asked him about the meaning of the "rootless *guna.*"[8] Greatly amazed, the teacher said, "I am not the right teacher for you." He advised him to go to Mount Wu-hsieh to study under the Ch'an master Ling-mo. He went there and had his head shaved. At the early age of twenty-one, Liang-chieh was ordained at Mount Sung, after which he journeyed on foot all over the country. The first master he visited was Nan-ch'üan, and it happened to be at the time when the Master was conducting the annual memorial service for Ma-tsu.[9] Nan-ch'üan remarked, "When we serve food for Master Ma-tsu tomorrow, I do wonder whether he will come for it." None of the monks made a reply, but Liang-chieh came forth out of the crowd and said, "As soon as he has companions he will come." Hearing this, Nan-ch'üan praised him: "Although this man is young, he is worthy of being trained." Liang-chieh said to him, "Master, you should not make a slave out of an honorable person."

[After visiting Nan-ch'üan] Liang-chieh went to see Master

Kuei-shan and said to him, "I have just heard that Dharma[10] may also be taught by non-sentient things and that this is being practiced by the National Teacher Nan-yang Hui-chung. I have not yet understood its real meaning." Kuei-shan replied, "I teach it here too. However, I have not yet found the man to whom I can teach it." Liang-chieh then urged Kuei-shan to tell him about it. Kuei-shan remarked, "My mouth, which I inherited from my parents, never dares to utter a word." But Liang-chieh persisted: "Is there anyone else besides you who has also devoted himself to this teaching?" Kuei-shan answered, "When you leave here and come to a place where there are stone chambers[11] connected with each other, you will find Master Yün-yen there. If you don't mind the hardship of climbing up there to visit him, he will be the man whom you will respect."

When Liang-chieh came to Yün-yen, he asked him, "What kind of man is able to hear the teaching of Dharma through non-sentient things?" Yün-yen replied, "The Dharma taught by non-sentient things will be heard by non-sentient things." Liang-chieh asked, "Can you hear it?" Master Yün-yen said, "If I hear it, you will not, now I am teaching the Dharma." Liang-chieh replied, "If this is so, it means that I do not hear you teaching the Dharma." Master Yün-yen challenged him: "When I taught the Dharma, even you did not hear it. How can you expect to be taught by non-sentient things?" Thereupon Liang-chieh composed a *gāthā*, and presented it to Yün-yen.

> It is strange indeed!
> It is strange indeed!
> Dharma taught by non-sentient things is unthinkable.
> Listening through your ear you cannot understand;
> But you will be aware of it by listening with your eyes.

After presenting the *gāthā*, Liang-chieh took his leave of Master Yün-yen, who said to him:

"Where are you going?"

"Although I am leaving you, I have no idea where my next stop will be," replied Liang-chieh.

"Are you not going south of the Lake?" asked Yün-yen.

Interfusion of Universality and Particularity

"No!" said Liang-chieh.

"Then are you returning to your native town?" asked Yün-yen.

The answer from Liang-chieh was again no. Then Yün-yen continued, "Come back here soon."

"When you become the head of a monastery,[12] I will come back to you," replied Liang-chieh.

"After you leave here, it will be very hard for us to see each other again," said Master Yün-yen.

"It will be very hard for us not to see each other again," answered Liang-chieh. "After you have passed away, how can I answer someone if he wants me to describe what you were like?"

"You just say to him, 'This is!'" Yün-yen replied. Liang-chieh kept silent for a while. Then Yün-yen said to him, "You must be very careful, as you are carrying this great thing."

Liang-chieh was still puzzled. Later when he was crossing the water and saw his image reflected, he suddenly understood the teaching of Yün-yen. Thus he made the following *gāthā*:

> You should not search through others,
> Lest the Truth recede farther from you.
> When alone I proceed through myself,
> I meet him wherever I go.
> He is the same as me,
> Yet I am not he!
> Only if you understand this
> Will you identify with *tathatā*.[13]

Another day, on the occasion of offering food before the portrait of Master Yün-yen, a monk asked Master Liang-chieh:

"Is this [portrait] not what our late Master meant when he said that 'This is'?"

"Yes, it is!" Master Liang-chieh answered.

"What did 'This is' mean when Master Yün-yen said it?"

"I almost misunderstood him when he said it," replied the Master.

"I wonder whether the late Master knew the Truth," continued the monk.

"If he did not know 'This,' how could he know to say 'This'? If he did know 'This,' how could he say 'This'?" said Master Liang-chieh.

In Lê-t'an, Master Liang-chieh attended the reverend monk Ch'u's sermon. "It is wonderful indeed!" Ch'u said to the assembly. "It is wonderful indeed! How immeasurable are Buddhism and Taoism!" Master Liang-chieh made his reply: "As for Buddhism and Taoism, let us leave them for a moment. Could you tell me what kind of man is he who is speaking of Buddhism and Taoism? Please just give me a simple statement." For a while Ch'u was silent without answering. Master Liang-chieh pressed him: "Why don't you say something immediately?" Ch'u replied, "If you want to dispute with me you will get nowhere." To this Master Liang-chieh said, "You have not yet uttered a word. What do you mean nothing will be gained by dispute?" Ch'u made no answer. Master Liang-chieh continued, "The difference between Buddhism and Taoism lies simply in their names. Should we not bring out their teachings?" Ch'u replied, "What teachings do you want to discuss?" Master Liang-chieh gave his illustration by a quotation: "When ideas are obtained, words are forgotten." Ch'u challenged him, saying, "You are letting the teachings stain your mind." The Master then said, "How much more you are staining your mind by talking about Buddhism and Taoism!" It is said that the reverend monk Ch'u died because of this challenge.

By the end of the period of Ta-chung [847–859], Master Liang-chieh received disciples and taught them at the Hsin-feng Mountain. After that his teachings were widespread at Tung-shan [Mount Tung] in Kao-an of Yü-chang.[14] One day, when the Master was conducting the annual memorial service for Master Yün-yen, a monk asked him:

"What instruction did you receive from the late Master Yün-yen?"

"Although I was there with him, he gave me no instruction," answered the Master.

"Then why should you conduct the memorial service for him, if he did not instruct you?" persisted the monk.

Interfusion of Universality and Particularity

"Although this was the case, how could I disobey him?" explained the Master.

"You became known after you visited Nan-ch'üan. Why should you conduct the memorial service for Yün-yen?" pressed the monk.

"It is neither for his moral character nor for his teaching of Dharma that I respect him. What I consider important is that he never told me anything openly," stated the Master.

Again the memorial service for Yün-yen caused a monk to raise a question:

"Master! you conduct a memorial service for the late Master Yün-yen. Do you agree with what he has said to you?"

"Half agree and half not!" replied the Master.

"Why don't you entirely agree with him?" continued the monk.

"If I entirely agreed with him, I would be ungrateful to him," replied the Master.

A monk asked, "How can I see your original master?"

"If two people are the same age, then there is no barrier between them," answered the Master.

The monk tried asking about what still puzzled him. The Master said to him, "Do not trace the previous steps, but raise another question." The monk made no answer. Yün-chü [another disciple] replied for him: "According to what you say, I cannot see your original master." The Master then continued: "Is there anyone who does not show his gratitude to the 'Four Graces'[15] and the 'Three Existences'?"[16] If he does not understand the meaning of these, how can he be free from the suffering of the beginning and end of existence? Every thought he has in his mind should be free from attachment to things, and also every step he takes should be free from attachment to his dwelling place. When he keeps on in such a way without interruption, he will be close to the answer."

When the Master asked a monk where he came from the answer was:

"I came after wandering from mountain to mountain."

"Have you reached the top?" asked the Master.

"Yes, I have reached it," answered the monk.

"Is there anyone there?" said the Master.

"No, no one is there," replied the monk.

"If so, it means that you have not yet reached the top," said the Master.

"If I have not yet reached the top, how can I know there is no one there?" argued the monk.

"Then why don't you stay there?" said the Master.

"I wouldn't mind staying there, but there is someone in the Western Heaven[17] who will not permit me," answered the monk.

The Master said to the abbot T'ai, "There is something which upwardly supports the heaven and downwardly sustains the earth. It is constantly in action and is as dark as tar. Is there any mistake in this?"

"The mistake is in its action," answered the abbot.

"Go away!" cried out the Master.

Someone asked the Master what the meaning was of Bodhidharma coming from the West. The Master answered:

"It is as big as a rhinoceros, whose horn often frightens chickens."

The Master asked Hsüeh-fêng where he came from. Hsüeh-fêng answered, "I came from T'ien-t'ai."

"Have you seen Master Chih-i?"[18] continued the Master.

"I-ts'un [Hsüeh-fêng] deserves to be beaten with an iron stick," answered Hsüeh-fêng.

A monk asked the Master, "When a snake swallows a frog, should you save its life or not?"

The Master answered, "If you save it, it means that 'both of your eyes are blind.' If you do not save it, it means that 'both your body and your shadow are not visible.'"

A monk came forward to ask a question, and then retreated into the crowd. Because there was no lamp lit that night, the Master asked the attendant to light a lamp and then called the inquiring monk forward. The monk stepped up in front of him. The Master said, "Give this man three ounces of flour." The monk shook his sleeves and left. From that time on he was awakened. Consequently he sold his belongings and offered food for sacrifice in the monastery. Three years afterward the monk bid good-bye to

Interfusion of Universality and Particularity

the Master, who told him, "Be careful of what you are doing!" During the interview Hsüeh-fêng stood by the side of the Master and said, "This monk is leaving you. When will he come back again?" The Master replied, "He knows how to go away, but he does not know how to come back." In the meantime the monk had gone back to the hall, and there, sitting beside his robe and bowl, he died. Thereupon Hsüeh-fêng reported the incident of the earnest monk to the Master, who said:

"Although he has shown us such devotion, it is still far less than the course of 'three lives'[19] that I followed in achieving Buddhahood."

Once Hsüeh-fêng went to greet the Master. The latter said to him:

"If you want to enter the door, you have to say something. You cannot take it for granted that you already have entered the door."

"I-ts'un has no mouth," answered Hsüeh-fêng.

"Forget your mouth; give me back my eyes," remarked the Master. To this Hsüeh-fêng made no answer.

The Master asked a monk where he came from. The monk answered that he came from the Pagoda of the Third Patriarch. The Master said:

"You have come from the Patriarch. What do you want to see me for?"

"As for the Patriarch, he lives differently from us; but you and I live in the same world," answered the monk.

"Is it possible for me to see your original master?" asked the Master.

"It will be possible only when your Self is revealed," replied the monk.

"Just a short time ago I was not within myself for a moment," stated the Master.

Yün-chü asked what the meaning was of Bodhidharma coming to China from the West. The Master replied:

"Sometime later you will have a bundle of thatch[20] covering your head. Then if someone asks you the same question, what will you tell him?"

A government officer wanted to know whether there was anyone approaching Ch'an through cultivation. The Master answered:

"When you become a laborer, then there will be someone to do cultivation."

A monk asked, "What is that moment as described in the ancient sayings: 'One meets the other without showing what he has, and through his suggestions the other is able to know what it is'?"

The Master then put his palms together and bowed.

The Master asked the attendant of Master Tê-shan, "Where do you come from?"

"From Tê-shan," was the answer.

"What do you come here for?" continued the Master.

"To show filial piety to you," said the attendant.

"What is that which is most filial in the world?" demanded the Master.

The visitor gave no answer.

Once the Master said:

"When one has experienced the Ultimate of Buddhahood, then one will be qualified to speak about it."

"What is this speaking?" a monk asked immediately.

"When these words are delivered, you cannot hear them," the Master replied.

"Will you be able to hear it?" demanded the monk.

"As soon as I do not speak, I hear it," answered the Master.

A monk asked, "What is the correct question and answer?"

"It is that which one does not speak from the mouth," replied the Master.

"Then if there is someone who asks you about it, do you answer him?" the monk asked further.

"I have not yet been asked," answered the Master.

A question was addressed to the Master:

"What is that which is not precious when it enters through the entrance?"

"Stop! Stop!" answered the Master.

The Master questioned the monk who lectured on the *Vimalakīrti-nirdeśa Sūtra*:[21]

Interfusion of Universality and Particularity

"What are the words which one cannot apprehend by intelligence or understand by consciousness?"

"The expressions that praise *dharmakāya*,"[22] answered the monk.

"*Dharmakāya* itself is a praise. Why then should it be praised once more?" replied the Master.

Once the Master said to the assembly:

"Even when you say plainly that from the very beginning nothing exists, you will still not be qualified to receive the bowl-bag."[23]

"Then who is entitled to have it?" asked a monk.

"The one who does not enter the door," answered the Master.

"As for this man who does not enter the door, will he really be able to receive the bowl-bag?" pressed the monk.

"Although he is outside the door, one cannot help but give it to him," replied the Master.

The Master repeated, "Even when you say plainly that from the beginning nothing exists, you will not be able to receive the bowl-bag. In this connection you have to make one statement which leads to a further leap. What is this one statement?"

There was an elder monk[24] who tried ninety-six times to make this statement, but he failed each time. Finally, in his ninety-seventh trial, the Master agreed that his answer was correct, and cried out:

"Sir! Why didn't you say this sooner?"

There was another monk who heard the story and wanted to find out the final answer. For three years he attended the elder monk in order to get the secret from him, but unfortunately the elder monk told him nothing. Later on the elder monk fell ill. The earnest learner came to him, saying:

"I have been with you three years hoping you would tell me the answer you gave the Master, but you have never been kind enough to do so. Now, since I have failed to get it from you honestly I will get it in the worst way."

Thereupon he drew a sword, and brandishing it at the elder monk, threatened him: "If you don't give me the answer this time, I will kill you."

Taken aback, the elder monk said, "Wait! I will tell you." Then he continued, "Even if I were to give it to you, you would have no place to put it."

The repentant monk made a deep bow.

Failing to understand the meaning of "the birds' track," a monk asked why the Master oftentimes told his disciples to walk in the birds' track. The Master answered:

"It is the path where you meet no one else."

"How do you walk in it?" the monk asked further.

"You have to walk without a thread tied to your feet," answered the Master.

"If one walks in the birds' track in this way, is it the same as seeing one's original face?" asked the monk.

"Why should you put things upside down?" exclaimed the Master.

"Where have I put things upside down?" asked the monk.

"If you have not put things upside down, why should you take a servant for the master?" replied the Master.

"Then, what is the original face?" persisted the monk.

"It is that which does not walk in the birds' track," said the Master.

The Master told the assembly, "When you are aware of reaching the Ultimate of Buddhahood, then you are qualified to say something about it."

"What is the man who reaches the Ultimate of Buddhahood?" a monk immediately asked.

"Not usual," answered the Master.

Once the Master asked a monk where he came from. The monk replied:

"From where I made my shoes."

"Did you understand by yourself, or depend on others?"

"I depended on others."

"Did they teach you?"

"To consent means not to disobey."

A monk came from Master Chu-yü and reported that he had asked him, "What are the actions of a Buddhist monk?" Master

Interfusion of Universality and Particularity

Chu-yü had answered, "To act means no more non-action; to be conscious of one's own actions is wrong."

The Master sent the same monk back to Chu-yü, saying, "I do not understand what these actions are."

"Buddha's action! Buddha's action!" answered Chu-yü. The inquiring monk returned to the Master and reported this answer to him. Thereupon the Master remarked:

"As for Yu-chou it is all right; but as for Korea, what a pity!" But the monk insisted that the Master answer his question about what a monk's actions are. The Master replied, "The head is three feet long, the neck two inches."

When the Master saw the elder monk Yu coming, he immediately stood behind his bed. Monk Yu said to him:

"Why did you hide yourself from me?"

"I thought you would not see me,"[25] answered the Master.

There was a question asked: "What is the further mystery in the mystery?"

The Master answered, "It is like the tongue of a dead man."

While he was washing his bowl, the Master watched two crows fighting over a frog. A monk came up and asked him:

"Why should they reach such a state?"

"It is simply because of you," answered the Master.

A monk asked, "What are the teacher of *vairocana*[26] and the master of *dharmakāya*?"

"A stem of rice plant and a stack of millet," answered the Master.

"Of the Threefold Body [of the Buddha], which one does not suffer a worldly fate?" asked the monk.

"I often think about it," replied the Master.

Once, when the Master visited the rice field, he saw the elder monk Lang leading a cow. The Master said to him:

"Watch this cow carefully, lest she eat the rice plants."

"If she is a good cow, she will not eat the rice plants," Lang said.

The Master asked a monk what in this world is most painful. The monk answered, "Hell is most painful." The Master said to him, "No!" The monk pressed him to say what he thought. The Master's answer was:

"Wearing the monk's robe and yet being ignorant of enlightenment is the most painful."

Once the Master asked a monk what his name was. The monk answered that his name was so-and-so. The Master then asked:

"Which one is your real self?"

"The one who is just facing you."

"What a pity! What a pity! The men of the present day are all like this. They take what is in the front of an ass or at the back of a horse and call it themselves. This illustrates the downfall of Buddhism. If you cannot recognize your real self objectively, how can you see your real self subjectively?"

"How do you see your real self subjectively?" the monk immediately asked.

"You have to tell me that yourself."

"If I were to tell you myself, it would be seeing myself objectively. What is the self that is known subjectively?"

"To talk about it in such a way is easy to do, but to continue our talking makes it impossible to reach the truth."

The Master announced his departure for *nirvāna* and sent a monk to inform Yün-chü. He told the monk that if Yün-chü should ask for his words, he should tell him this: "The path to Yün-yen is going to be cut off." The Master also warned his messenger that while speaking to Yün-chü he should stand far away from him, so that Yün-chü would not strike him. However, when the monk took the message to Yün-chü, he was struck even before finishing his words. The monk fell silent.

When he was going to die, the Master told the assembly, "I have made a useless name in this world. Who will remove it for me?" None of his disciples made an answer, but a novice stepped forward and said, "Please tell us your Dharma title." The Master answered, "My title has already faded away."

A monk said to the Master, "You are sick, Master, but is there anyone who is not sick?"

"Yes, there is one."

"Will the one who is not sick visit you?"

"I am entitled to see him."

"How can you see him?"

"When I see him, I do not see the one who is sick." The Master then said, "After I leave this shell, where will you go to see me?" All the disciples were silent.

One day, in the third month of the tenth year of the Hsien-t'ung period [860–873], Master Tung-shan Liang-chieh, having had his head shaved and having put on his robe, ordered the gong struck. He was going to pass away by sitting solemnly. In the meantime all his disciples, deeply moved, were crying. After a while the Master suddenly opened his eyes and stood up, and spoke to the assembly:

"Those who are Buddhists should not attach themselves to externalities. This is the real self-cultivation. In living they work hard; in death they are at rest. Why should there be any grief?"

Thereupon the Master ordered the head monk in the temple to prepare "offerings of food to ignorance" for everyone in the monastery. Thus a lesson was given to those who clung to passion. However, all his disciples were still yearning for him. Seven days passed, and on the last day when dinner was served, the Master shared it with his disciples. After they had finished their dinner, the Master said to them:

"When a Buddhist acts, he should not be heedless. What a noise and disturbance you made, when I started my departure!"

On the eighth day, when he had finished bathing, he sat still and passed away. His age was sixty-three. This was forty-two years after he was ordained. His posthumous name bestowed by the Court was Great Master Wu-pên, or Original Consciousness, and his pagoda was entitled Hui-chüeh, Wisdom and Enlightenment.

TS'AO-SHAN PÊN-CHI
(840–901)

"Purity Is in the Impure"

(*From* The Transmission of the Lamp, *Chüan* 17)

CH'AN Master Ts'ao-shan Pên-chi was a native of P'u-t'ien of Ch'üan-chou.[27] His original surname was Huang. When he was young he became interested in Confucianism. At the age of nineteen he left his home to become a Buddhist monk, entering the monastery of the Ling-shih Mountain in Fu-t'ang of Fu-chou.[28] At the age of twenty-five he was ordained. In the beginning of the Hsien-t'ung period [860–873] Ch'an Buddhism was flourishing. At this time Ch'an Master Tung-shan Liang-chieh was the head of the Ch'an monastery[29] and Ts'ao-shan went there frequently to learn from him. Once Tung-shan asked him:

"What is your name?"

"My name is Pên-chi."

"Say something toward Ultimate Reality."

"I will not say anything."

"Why don't you speak of it?"

"It is not called Pên-chi."

Hence Tung-shan regarded him as a man with a great capacity for Buddhism. After that Ts'ao-shan became the disciple of Tung-shan and had the privilege of receiving private instruction and ap-

Interfusion of Universality and Particularity

proval from the Master. After he had studied several years under Tung-shan, Ts'ao-shan came to bid him good-bye, and Tung-shan asked him:

"Where are you going?"

"I go where it is changeless."

"How can you go where it is changeless?"

"My going is no change."

Thereupon Ts'ao-shan left Tung-shan. He wandered all over and expounded Ch'an whenever the opportunity arose.

At first the Master was invited to stay in Ts'ao Mountain of Fu-chou. Later he stayed in Ho-yü Mountain. In both places disciples came to him in great crowds.

A monk asked him, "Who is he that is not accompanied by ten thousand things?"

The Master replied, "There are many people in the city of Hung-chou.[30] Can you tell me where they disappear?"

Monk: "Do eyes and eyebrows know each other?"

Master: "They do not know each other."

Monk: "Why do they not know each other?"

Master: "Because they are located in the same place."

Monk: "In such a way, then, there is no differentiation between eyes and eyebrows?"

Master: "Not so. Eyebrows certainly cannot be eyes."

Monk: "What is an eye?"

Master: "Straight ahead."

Monk: "What is an eyebrow?"

Master: "Ts'ao-shan is still in doubt about it."

Monk: "Why should you, Master, be in doubt?"

Master: "If I were not in doubt, it would be straight ahead."

Monk: "Where is the reality in appearance?"

Master: "Wherever there is appearance, there is reality."

Monk: "How does it manifest itself?"

The Master lifted his saucer.

Monk: "Where is the reality in illusion?"

Master: "Illusion was originally real."

Monk: "How can reality manifest itself in illusion?"

Master: "Whenever there is illusion there is the manifestation of reality."
Monk: "In such a way, then, reality can never be separated from illusion."
Master: "Where can you possibly find the appearance of illusion?"
Monk: "Who is he who is always present?"
Master: "It is the time when Ts'ao-shan happens to be out."
Monk: "Who is he who is never present?"
Master: "Impossible to achieve."
Monk Ch'ing-jui came to the Master and said, "I am very poor and fatherless. Please, my Master, help me!"
Master: "Ch'ing-jui, come over here." When Ch'ing-jui went over to the Master, the Master said, "You had three cups of wine from the Pai House of Ch'üan-chou and yet you claim not to have had even one sip."
Monk: "Is not imitation the same as identification?"
Master: "As matter of fact non-imitation is the same as identification."
Monk: "What is the difference between them?"
Master: "Do not ignore the sensation of pain and itching."
Ching-ch'ing asked, "How is it that the pure void is formless?"
Master: "It is this way with reality, but what is appearance?"
Ching-ch'ing: "Since reality is this way, so appearance is like this also."
Master: "You can easily deceive Ts'ao-shan alone. But how can you escape the judgment of all wise men?"
Ching-ch'ing: "If there are no wise men, who can tell that it is not this way?"
Master: "Publicly one is not allowed to miss even a needle, but secretly a carriage and horse can pass unnoticed."
Yün-mên asked, "If a man who cannot be converted comes to see you, do you receive him?"
Master: "I have no time to waste on such a man."
Monk: "As the ancient one says, we all have [Buddha-nature]. But I am in confusion: do I still have it, or not?"

Interfusion of Universality and Particularity

Master: "Give me your hands." Then he pointed at his fingers and said: "One, two, three, four, five, enough."

Monk: "When Master Lu-tsu saw a monk coming to him, he immediately turned and faced the wall.[31] What did he intend to reveal?"

The Master covered his ears with his hands.

Monk: "Ever since the early days there has been a saying: 'No one who falls can get up without the support of the ground.' What is a fall?"

The Master: "To assert is to fall."

Monk: "What is getting up?"

The Master: "You are getting up now."

Monk: "In the ancient teaching there is a saying: 'A corpse cannot remain in the great sea.' What is the sea?"

The Master: "It is that which embraces all things."

Monk: "Why should the corpse not be able to remain in it?"

The Master: "It is not the place where the lifeless would be able to stay."

Monk: "As it embraces all things, why should the lifeless be unable to stay?"

The Master: "To embrace all things is not its merit; to exclude the lifeless is its virtue."

Monk: "Is there any activity whereby one may approach the Ultimate Reality?"

The Master: "You can talk about doing and not doing as you wish. What can you do to the dragon-king[32] who raises his sword against you?"

Monk: "What kind of understanding should one have when one stands in front of people and skillfully answers their questions?"

The Master: "Do not say a word."

Monk: "Then what can you discuss?"

The Master: "Neither a sword nor an ax will penetrate it."

Monk: "If we are able to discuss things in such a way, is there still someone who does not agree with us?"

The Master: "Yes, there is."

Monk: "Who is he?"

The Master: "It is Ts'ao-shan [the Master himself]."
Monk: "What can you reveal, if you are speechless?"
The Master: "I do not reveal anything in that way."
Monk: "Where do you reveal it?"
The Master: "In the middle of last night I lost three pennies in my bed."
Monk: "What is there before the rising of the sun?"
The Master: "Ts'ao-shan also comes that way."
Monk: "What is there after the sun has risen?"
The Master: "In comparison with Ts'ao-shan, it is still behind him by a half-month's journey."
The Master asked a monk what he was doing. The monk replied, "Sweeping the floor."
The Master said, "Do you sweep in front of Buddha or at the back of Buddha?"
The monk replied, "I sweep both places at once."
The Master: "Bring my slippers here."
The Master asked the elder monk Ch'iang-tê, "In what sūtra do we have the saying: 'When Bodhisattva was in *samādhi*, he heard that the fragrant elephant was crossing a river'?"
Ch'iang-tê answered, "It is in the *Nirvāna Sūtra*."
The Master: "Did Bodhisattva hear it before his *samādhi* or after it?"
Ch'iang-tê: "Master! You are flowing in the river."
The Master: "In talking about it, even though you try your best, you can only achieve half the truth."
Ch'iang-tê: "What is your answer, Master?"
The Master: "Receive it at the shore."
A monk asked, "How can I maintain what I have achieved in my meditation during the twelve periods of a day?"[33]
The Master: "It is just as when one passes through an infected country. One should not touch even one drop of water."
Monk: "Who is the master of the essence of all things?"
The Master: "They say that there is no great man in the Kingdom of Ch'in."
Monk: "Is this not Suchness?"

Interfusion of Universality and Particularity

The Master: "Cut off!"

Monk: "With what man of Tao should one associate, so that one will hear constantly what one has never heard?"

The Master: "That which is under the same coverlet with you."

Monk: "This is still what you, Master, can hear yourself. What is it that one will hear constantly which one has never heard?"

The Master: "It is not the same as wood and stone."

Monk: "What is the first and what is the last?"

The Master: "Have you not heard what one hears constantly which one has never heard?"

Monk: "Who is he in our country that holds a sword in his hand?"

The Master: "It is Ts'ao-shan."

Monk: "Whom do you want to kill?"

The Master: "All those who are alive will die."

Monk: "When you happen to meet your parents, what should you do?"

The Master: "Why should you have any choice?"

Monk: "How about yourself?"

The Master: "Who can do anything to me?"

Monk: "Why should you not kill yourself, too?"

The Master: "There is no place on which I can lay my hands."

Monk: "What does this mean: 'When one cow drinks water, five horses do not neigh'?"

The Master: "Ts'ao-shan is free to eat everything." Later the Master answered again: "Ts'ao-shan is free from wearing mourning."

Monk: "Who is he who is often tossed upon the sea of life and death?"

The Master: "The shadow of the moon."[34]

Monk: "Does he want to come out of the sea?"

The Master: "Yes, he does, but there is no way out."

Monk: "If he wants to come out of the sea, who can help him?"

The Master: "The man who carries an iron casque."

A monk asked the meaning of the following dialogue between Yüeh-shan and a monk:

Yüeh-shan: "How old are you?"
The monk: "Seventy-two."
Yüeh-shan: "Is your age seventy-two?"
The monk: "Yes, it is."
Yüeh-shan struck him immediately.

The Master said, "The first arrow is all right, but the second arrow penetrates deeply."

The monk asked, "How can a blow be avoided?"

The Master answered, "When an emperor's mandate is made known, all the princes will avoid it."

Monk: "What is the general idea of Buddhism?"

The Master: "To fill a ditch and a ravine."

Monk: "What is a lion?"

The Master: "It is the one that no other animal can come near."

Monk: "What is a lion's son?"

The Master: "It is the one that devours its parents."

Monk: "Since the lion is one that no other animal can come near, how can it be devoured by its son?"

The Master: "If the lion's son should roar, its parents would be completely devoured."[35]

Questioner: "As for grandparents, does the lion's son also devour them?"

The Master: "Yes, it does."

Questioner: "What will happen to it after all the others are devoured?"

The Master: "Its body will completely dissolve into its father."

Monk: "Why should you say that the lion's son also devours its grandparents?"

The Master: "Haven't you seen that a prince can successfully manage the affairs of the whole country, and from dry wood the buds of blossoms can be gathered?"

Monk: "Why is it that as soon as there is affirmation and negation, the mind is lost in confusion?"

The Master: "Cut off! Cut off!"

A monk said that there was someone who asked Master Hsiang-

Interfusion of Universality and Particularity

yen, "What is Tao?" Master Hsiang-yen answered, "In the dry woods a dragon is singing." The monk said that he did not understand. Hsiang-yen then said, "The eye is in the skull." Some time later the monk asked Master Shih-shuang what he thought of the statement: "In the dry woods a dragon is singing." Master Shih-shuang answered, "There is still joy there." The monk again asked, "What is the meaning of 'The eye is in the skull'?" Shih-shuang replied, "There is still consciousness there." Master Ts'ao-shan, hearing of this, composed a poem which reads:

> He who says that a dragon is singing in the dry woods
> Is he who truly sees Tao.
> The skull has no consciousness,
> But wisdom's eye begins to shine in it.
> If joy and consciousness should be eliminated,
> Then fluctuation and communication would cease.
> Those who deny this do not understand
> That purity is in the impure.

After hearing this the monk asked the Master, "What does it mean: 'In the dry woods a dragon is singing'?"

The Master said, "Consanguinity never ceases."

The monk asked, "What about the eye that is in the skull?"

The Master replied, "It can never be dried up completely."

The monk went on, "I wonder whether there is anyone who can hear this?"

The master said, "There is no one in the entire world who does not hear this."

The monk continued, "I do not know what kind of composition the dragon's song is."

The Master answered, "I also do not know what kind of composition the dragon's song is. But all those who hear it lose themselves."

Thus without using rigid methods the Master enlightened his devotees with great capacity. When he received the great teachings such as the *wu wei** from Tung-shan, he became an exemplary Bud-

---

* The Five Relations Between Particularity and Universality, as explained on pages 50–51 above.

dhist. Several times the leader Chung in Hung-chou invited him to go there, but the Master repeatedly declined the invitations. He simply copied a Shan-chü hymn written by Master Ta-mei and sent it to Chung. One night in the late summer in the first year [Hsin-yü] of the T'ien-fu period [901–903], the Master asked the monk manager in the temple, "What day is it today?" The monk answered, "It is the fifteenth day of the sixth month." The Master said, "In my lifetime, when I travel by foot, wherever I go I spend a period of just ninety days." The next morning during the Cheng period [7–9 A.M.] the Master entered *nirvāna*. His age was sixty-two. It was thirty-seven years after he was ordained. His disciples built a pagoda and enshrined his bones in it. The Royal Court bestowed on him a posthumous name, Yüan-cheng, and named the pagoda Fu-yüan.

NOTES

1. The word *wei* in Chinese originally meant position or rank. Here, however, *wei* means the situation between universality and particularity, therefore, the relationship between the two.

2. This cannot be rendered as *chien chung chih* (Japanese *ken chu shi*), as this would not be different from *chien chung tao*. The distortion is all due to the later interpolation of the Chinese word *chien* instead of *p'ien*. When Ts'ao-shan interprets his master Tung-shan's philosophy of the Five Relations the word is *p'ien*, not *chien*. There is a good deal of literature concerning the pros and cons of this issue. The commentary given in the *Lin Chien Lu* by Hung Chueh-fan is especially sound, supporting *p'ien chung chih* as referring to the interfusion between particularity and universality.

3. A *gāthā* is a metrical hymn or chant, usually four lines long.

4. The *chin* is a Chinese unit of measure corresponding to the pound in the West. Usually it equals sixteen ounces.

5. In 1224, Dōgen came from Japan to the Ching-tê Monastery in the T'ien-tung Mountain to study Ch'an under Ju-ching, the disciple of Hung-chih Cheng-chio. After his return to Japan in 1228, he founded the Sōtō School of Zen there. His contributions to the philosophy of Zen are somewhat different from the teachings of Tung-shan and Hung-chih.

6. Now the town of Kao-an in northern Kiangsi Province.

7. The original script usually reads *hui*, meaning "to meet," or a society;

Interfusion of Universality and Particularity

but it reads *kuai* when it refers to the ancient town of Kuai-chi, now Shaohing in northeastern Chekiang Province.

8. In Sanskrit *guna* means "a secondary element"; in Chinese, it means "dust defiling a pure mind."

9. It is a Chinese custom to conduct a memorial service every year on the anniversary of a person's death.

10. *Dharma* is used variously to mean truth, doctrine, object, substance, existence, etc.

11. According to *Records of Pointing at the Moon*, these stone chambers were in Yuhsien of Liling in Hunan Province.

12. *Chu*, in Ch'an literature, means to be an abbot of the monastery.

13. *Tathatā* means things as they are in absolute reality. It is often used to mean "suchness" or "thusness."

14. A town in northern Kiangsi Province.

15. The "Four Graces": (1) grace of parents; (2) grace of all beings; (3) grace of the Ruler; (4) grace of Triratna (Buddha, Dharma, Saṅgha).

16. The "Three Existences": (1) present body and mind; (2) the future state; (3) the intermediate state between death and reincarnation.

17. This indicates the Buddha in India.

18. Chih-i (531–597) was the founder of the T'ien-t'ai School in China. As Hsüeh-fêng was born more than two hundred years after Chih-i, he could not possibly have met Chih-i when he visited T'ien-t'ai.

19. The course of "three lives" means the achievement of Buddhahood through the three stages of life, past, present, and future.

20. Meaning, the thatched roof of a monastery. This indicates that he will become the abbot of that monastery.

21. The *Vimalakīrti-nirdeśa Sūtra* is an account of conversations between Śākyamuni and some residents of Vaiśālī, translated into Chinese by Kumārajīva as *Wei-ma Chi Ching*.

22. *Dharmakāya* means the absolute nature of the Buddha-mind.

23. The bowl-bag is a symbol for the transmission of Ch'an. Traditionally, this was the bag in which the monk carried his eating bowl.

24. The original Chinese word for elder is *shang tso*, or higher seat, which refers to a monk who has practiced meditation for twenty to forty-nine years.

25. Other versions say "would look for me."

26. *Vairocana* is the essential body of Buddha-truth, pervading everything.

27. Now Chin-chiang (Tsingkiang), in southeastern Fukien Province, on the Formosa Strait.

28. Foochow, now the capital of Fukien Province.

29. Master Tung-shan Liang-chieh was then the leading Ch'an master on Mount Tung in Kao-an in Kiangsi Province.

30. Now Nan-ch'ang, the capital of Kiangsi Province.

31. The story of "Lu-tsu facing the wall" is recorded in the fascicle of Ch'an Master Pai-yun of Mount Lu-tsu in Ch'ih-chou. See *The Lamp*, Chüan 7.

32. According to Chinese legend, the dragon-king is the one who kills the devils. To talk about doing or not doing is a devil, which may be killed by the dragon-king's sword.

NOTES

33. The day of the ancient Chinese was divided into twelve two-hour periods.

34. Buddhists call this "the second moon." When one's eyes are covered with cataracts one cannot see the real moon, but only its shadow.

35. The original text reads "grandparents" as well as "parents," but this is a printer's error.

Part III

Introduction
Liberation from Subjectivity and Objectivity

HUANG-PO HSI-YÜN (?–849)
To Roar Like a Tiger

MU-CHOU TAO-TSUNG
"Before a Donkey and After a Horse"

LIN-CHI I-HSÜAN (?–866) *
"Here I Will Bury You Alive"

---

* The seventh year of the Hsien-t'ung period, when Lin-chi entered into *nirvāna*, is 866, according to Tung Tso-pin, *Chronological Tables of Chinese History*, Vol. II, p. 109.

Liberation from Subjectivity and Objectivity

This introduction will deal chiefly with the teachings of Lin-chi I-hsüan, founder of the school which bears his name. Two other masters, however, played important roles in the life of Lin-chi, and we must consider them briefly first. These were Huang-po Hsi-yün, the master under whom he first studied, and Mu-chou Tao-tsung, head monk in the monastery where Lin-chi attained enlightenment, and a decisive influence on his life and work.

In addition to such records as we have of Huang-po in *The Lamp*, we have his work entitled *Essentials of the Transmission of the Mind*. And just what is this "transmission of the mind"? Let us consider the following dialogue. Once Huang-po was asked, "If you say that mind can be transmitted, then how can you say it is nothing?" He answered, "To achieve nothing is to have the mind transmitted to you." The questioner pressed, "If there is nothing and no mind, then how can it be transmitted?" Huang-po answered, "You have heard the expression 'transmission of the mind' and so you think there must be something transmitted. You are wrong. Thus Bodhidharma said that when the nature of the mind is realized, it is not possible to express it verbally. Clearly, then, nothing

Liberation from Subjectivity and Objectivity

is obtained in the transmission of the mind, or if anything is obtained, it is certainly not knowledge."

When Lin-chi approached his master Huang-po three times in order to ask him the meaning of Buddhism, he hoped he might be able to learn some knowledge of truth. On each occasion Huang-po, instead of explaining doctrine to him, administered sharp blows, this characteristic non-verbal gesture being meant to transmit the mind of the master to his disciple. We may say that what Huang-po tried to transmit to Lin-chi was the "mind of no-mind." Later, when Lin-chi attained enlightenment, he realized that Huang-po was being not harsh but kind, indeed almost motherly, in his ministrations, and that what he was teaching was extremely simple and direct—so uncomplicated, in fact, that very little could be said of it.

Lin-chi came to be considered the dharma-heir of Huang-po. From *The Lamp* we learn that Lin-chi was enlightened by such non-verbal simplicity. This is a good example of what the Ch'an Buddhists call the transmission of the mind. Kuei-fêng Tsung-mi (780–841) says in his *Preface to the Complete Explanation of the Source of Ch'an:*

> When Bodhidharma came to China, he saw that most Chinese learners did not grasp the truth of Buddhism. They merely sought it through interpretation of textual terminology, and thought of the changing phenomena all around them as real action. Bodhidharma wished to make these eager learners see that the finger pointing at the moon is not the moon itself. The real truth is nothing else but one's own mind. Thus, he maintained that the real teaching must be transmitted directly from one mind to another, without the use of words.

This transmission of the mind in a direct and non-verbal manner became the tradition of Ch'an. Hui-nêng, the Sixth Patriarch, in his *Platform Sūtra*, says: "In the early days, when the great Master Bodhidharma first came to this country, he transmitted the true wisdom, using his robe as a symbol. But as for the real teaching, no symbol was necessary. It was transferred spontaneously from mind to mind."

Liberation from Subjectivity and Objectivity

Thus it is that the mind of the master, the transmitter, and the mind of the disciple, the receiver, ultimately identify with one another. Through such mind transmission, Ch'an was carried on from generation to generation. According to Kuei-fêng Tsung-mi, in the early days of Ch'an, in order to avoid error, the transmission of the mind was made only to one's successor of the following generation. In later dynasties, however, when the practice of Ch'an was well established, a master could transmit to as many disciples as were capable of being illuminated. To understand Ch'an, therefore, one must have an understanding of the nature of this "mind" that was transmitted.

In Chinese, the word for mind is *hsin*. This means, more literally, kernel or essence. For the Confucianists, *hsin* meant moral consciousness. For the Buddhists it was the depths of the unconscious, or the abyss of absolute nothingness. Mind, when considered in a state of quiescence, may be identified with the Christian concept of innocence, the primal mind of man before the fruit of the tree of knowledge was eaten. The Buddhists sometimes refer to it as the "original face of man before he is born." In dynamic terms, mind produces the "ten thousand things" of the world. It is seen as creativity itself, simultaneously encompassing and penetrating the entire universe. But it must be realized that mind considered either in quiescence or in action cannot be related to the customary standards of time or space. In *Essentials of the Transmission of the Mind*, Huang-po says: "People in the world cannot identify their own mind. They believe that what they see, or hear, or feel, or know, is mind. They are blocked by the visual, the auditory, the tactile, and the mental, so they cannot see the brilliant spirit of their original mind."

He further says: "This mind is illuminated, and pure as the Void, without form. Any thought deviates from the true source." The "pure and illuminated" mind that Huang-po refers to cannot be understood in any relative sense. He means absolute purity, beyond light or darkness. As he puts it, the sun rises and shines all over the world but it does not light the Void; when the sun sets, darkness comes to the world but the Void is not darkened. Light

Liberation from Subjectivity and Objectivity

and darkness are conditional phenomena, alternating and contrasting with each other. The Void is free from any such alternatives. If one should take Buddha as the image of purity and liberation, and all other sentient beings as vessels of defilement and ignorance, one would never reach enlightenment, because the mind of Buddha and the mind of ordinary beings are one and the same; in Buddha there is no more, in ordinary men there is no less. This aspect of mind is often discussed in the work of Huang-po.

Another aspect of mind, according to Huang-po, is that all things—mountains, rivers, sun, earth, stars, all things and everything—are the products of mind. Outside mind, nothing exists. Put another way, mind embraces all things and reflects all things. He says: "Words and silence, action and non-action, all these things are Buddha's things. And where can you find Buddha? You are the Buddha!" Huang-po uses the example of mercury as a symbol illustrating the relationship of the one to all and all to the one. Mercury, when divided, becomes small pearl-like droplets, each separate and whole in and of itself. But when the mercury is allowed to run together, it forms one totality in which the separate parts are indistinguishable from the whole. In Huang-po's words, when things are separate, a mountain, for example, is a mountain, a monk a monk, an ordinary fellow an ordinary fellow, but the totality of the mind encompasses them all. This view of the one and the all is also expounded by the Hua-yen and T'ien-t'ai schools, but Huang-po applied this teaching to Ch'an.

What we have discussed so far might be called the theoretical framework of the teachings of Huang-po. Recorded in *The Lamp*, however, are some practical examples of his theories. Huang-po used the *kung-an* as a vehicle for the transmission of his mind to his disciples. His approach was close to that of Ma-tsu, his grandfather-in-dharma. Once he was asked by Pei Hsiu, "We see the portrait of a monk, but where is the real monk?" Huang-po cried out, "Pei Hsiu!" Pei Hsiu immediately answered, "Yes, Master?" And Huang-po said, "Where is he now?" Pei Hsiu was suddenly awakened.

This abrupt calling out of a disciple's name, and the follow-up

LIBERATION FROM SUBJECTIVITY AND OBJECTIVITY

question, such as Where is it? or What is it? was a technique initiated by Ma-tsu. As we record elsewhere, a monk known as Liang of Szechwan came to visit Ma-tsu. When the monk was taking leave of Ma-tsu the latter suddenly called out his name. The monk turned and Ma-tsu cried out, "What is it?" Liang was suddenly enlightened. He later told his own disciples that as of that moment all his doubts melted away as ice melts in the heat of the sun. This technique of awakening a disciple is what the Ch'an masters often refer to in the context of confronting the "initial consciousness," or *yeh-shih*. This term is often used by Nan-ch'üan and Yang-shan, as discussed in their respective sections. Here we see how Huang-po applied it in his teaching.

Another common technique of enlightenment, that of hitting or striking, a method also originated by Ma-tsu, was frequently used to great effect by Huang-po. Once Huang-po traveled to Hangchow to visit Yen-kuan Ch'i-an. In the monastery he met a young novice. Unknown to Huang-po, this young man was none other than the Royal Prince, who was then living in exile in the monastery because of treachery at the Royal Court, but who would eventually return to become the Emperor. One day Huang-po was bowing before the image of Buddha when the novice, who had been observing him, asked, "Since we are taught to seek nothing from Buddha, nothing from Dharma, and nothing from Sangha, why do you bow in such a fashion before Buddha's image? What can you hope to gain?" Huang-po answered, "I seek nothing from Buddha, Dharma, or Sangha. I bow to Buddha's image as a customary gesture of respect." The novice asked, "But what is the purpose of the gesture? Why should you follow this custom?" Huang-po immediately slapped the novice's face. The novice said, "What rude behavior is this!" Huang-po answered, "Do you know where you are? How can you talk of rudeness and refinement here?" And he promptly slapped the young man's face once more.

This incident is not the only one recorded of Huang-po's application of the "strike." In a story which appears in the following fascicle we find that Huang-po once slapped the face of Po-chang Huai-hai (720–814), who was his master. He did this in an expression of his own free spirit, and Po-chang was not at all offended. He was, in fact, delighted that his student had achieved such freedom. Subsequently, when Lin-chi was enlightened and returned to Huang-po for a visit, he in turn, in the course of a dialogue, slapped Huang-po's face. Huang-po, needless to say, accepted the gesture. On a relative plane and in the course of everyday affairs, certain gestures are considered polite and others insulting. But for the Ch'annist who has achieved absolute freedom, each of his actions is a direct expression of his liberated spirit; he does not abide by customary standards and he cannot be judged by them.

In the first fascicle which follows, there is an anecdote wherein Huang-po was asked by Master Po-chang whether or not he had seen a tiger while he was out that day picking mushrooms at the foot of the mountain. Huang-po's answer was free from the trap of logical assertion or negation: instead, he immediately roared like a tiger. In this way he revealed the total and perfect integrity of his being. This response is comparable to Yüeh-shan's drawing his sword when he was asked about the rattling sound it made as he walked: both illustrate freedom from the alternatives of words or silence. As I have indicated elsewhere, Tung-shan Liang-chieh considered this mode of expression one of the highest achievements of Ch'an.

As we know, Huang-po criticized Niu-t'ou Fa-yung for talking excessively about Ch'an but never knowing the secret that led to the real experience of Ch'an. The various techniques he used—striking, calling out the disciple's name, his tiger's roar, his silences—all were intended to enable his disciples to take that final leap into the limitless realm of Ch'an awakening. But while Huang-po criticized Niu-t'ou Fa-yung's lectures, he himself delivered lectures on the transmission of the mind, as recorded by Pei Hsiu. Some question might arise as to whether or not this lecturing was against his own principles. To answer this question we may refer to the episode of Pei Hsiu bringing his own written interpretation of Ch'an to Huang-po for his perusal. Huang-po put it aside without reading it, and was silent for some time. Finally he leaned toward Pei Hsiu and asked, "Do you understand?" If we grasp the mean-

LIBERATION FROM SUBJECTIVITY AND OBJECTIVITY

ing of his silence in this instance, we may be on the road to making that further leap into Ch'an enlightenment.

Carrying on the teachings of Huang-po, besides Lin-chi, we have Mu-chou Tao-tsung, who is often referred to as Chên Tsun-su, or the Reverend Old Master Chên. In the literature of Ch'an we find that he has left no recorded lectures or theoretical analyses such as we have from Huang-po and later Lin-chi. Mu-chou's teachings, however, were so powerful and direct that he was responsible for the enlightenment of two of the most famous figures in Ch'an annals, Lin-chi I-hsüan and Yün-mên Wên-yen, thereby paving the way for the development of two famous schools of Ch'an Buddhism in China. For this alone Mu-chou is accorded a significant position in the development of Ch'an.

Before we discuss what we know of Mu-chou's teachings it might be worthwhile to tell a little about his character and personality. Mu-chou was a very poor man who supported himself and his aged mother by making straw sandals, which he often left in the streets for the poor who could not afford to buy them. At first no one knew who the anonymous benefactor was, but the sandals were finally traced to Mu-chou. He was greatly admired by the people of his village for his generosity and sympathy, and became widely respected for his wisdom, earning the affectionate name of Sandal Chên. One day it was rumored that the village was about to be attacked by bandits. On hearing the news, Mu-chou constructed a huge sandal and hung it from the village gate. When the bandits arrived they saw the sandal and turned away, sparing the village out of respect for the old sandal maker. Mu-chou's reputation is said to have spread throughout the country before he died at the advanced age of ninety-eight.

In both the T'ien-t'ai and the Hua-yen schools an interfusion of appearance and reality is strongly maintained. But this interfusion and identification are present in the abstract, in terms of philosophical principles. Ch'an maintains, however, that these principles are never fully grasped by the intellect alone but must be personally experienced through one's own efforts. The merely intellectual search for truth splits our being into two separate and warring camps; one is the transcendental, the other the concrete. In seeking transcendence, one abandons the concrete; remaining with the concrete, one is unable to transcend it. But for the Ch'an Buddhist nothing is transcendental apart from the concrete. In other words, the man of Ch'an engages in ordinary daily activities and simultaneously transcends them, so that the concrete and the transcendental in his life are one and the same. He lives, as do all men, in time and space, but he is not limited by either. For him the finite dwells within the infinite, the infinite within the finite. They are totally and inseparably identified as one.

Mu-chou Tao-tsung is considered one of the great masters who actually experienced this identification and was able to transmit the experience to his disciples. In fact, the reason for his not lecturing or engaging in the formulation of abstract principles was that he adhered strictly to the traditional Ch'an teachings handed down from Ma-tsu. These teachings are distinguishable from other schools of Buddhism as well as from their Indian predecessors.

Once Mu-chou was asked how one could be free from the tiresome tasks of dressing and eating each day. He replied that one should put on one's clothes and eat each day. When the questioner said that he did not understand this reply, Mu-chou remarked, "If you don't understand, just dress and eat each day anyway." According to Mu-chou salvation must be found in concrete activity. Enlightenment is not something which exists above or beyond the ordinary ground of human affairs. Rather it is immediate, immanent. Once when Mu-chou was asked for a statement surpassing the wisdom of all the Buddhas and Patriarchs, he held up his staff and said, "I call this a staff. What do you call it?" When the monk made no answer, Mu-chou flourished his staff and said, "A statement surpassing all the Buddhas and Patriarchs, is that not what you asked for, O monk?" The simple concrete gesture of flourishing the staff surpassed any statement of formulated wisdom that could possibly be made. Mu-chou made his disciples see that only within this sphere of immanence can the true nature of enlightenment be found.

However, if in the common gesture the revelation of the highest wisdom is not implicit, then the gesture may be mere imitation. Once Mu-chou asked a monk where he had come from. The monk cried out, "Ho!" Mu-chou said, "So now you give me 'Ho!'" Again the monk said, "Ho!" "Well," Mu-chou said, "after the third or fourth 'Ho!' what will you do?" When the monk was unable to reply, Mu-chou struck him, saying, "You are a shallow faker!"

It is traditionally said by Ch'annists that before one is enlightened one sees a mountain as a mountain and a river as a river; in the process of attaining enlightenment, mountains are no longer mountains, rivers no longer rivers; but when one has finally achieved enlightenment, mountains are once more mountains, rivers once more rivers. So it was with Mu-chou's teaching. Only after supreme enlightenment did he reach this state of wisdom.

Lin-chi I-hsüan, as we have said, was the disciple of Huang-po and the grandson-in-dharma of Po-chang. He is considered the most powerful master in the entire history of Ch'an. The school which he founded became the most influential of the five major Ch'an sects. Lin-chi died in the middle of the ninth century, but up until the middle of the twelfth century his direct followers from generation to generation were the leading masters of Ch'an. It was in the twelfth century that his teaching was brought to Japan, where it flourishes to this day.

Lin-chi's methods include certain features which represent a typical orthodoxy as descended from Ma-tsu. He used the "Ho!" and the striking approaches to awaken his disciples, and, like Ma-tsu, was in fact notorious for the rough treatment he meted out. (We may recall the story of Ma-tsu slapping Po-chang so hard that the latter was deaf for three days.) Lin-chi's method of applying the "strike" was similar to that of Tê-shan Hsüan-chien: he emphasized directness, spontaneity, absolute freedom. He once said:

> Many students come to see me from all directions. Many of them are not free from the entanglement of objective things. I treat them right on the spot. If their trouble is due to grasping hands, I strike there. If their trouble comes from their mouths, I strike them there. If their trouble is hidden in their

Liberation from Subjectivity and Objectivity

eyes, it is there I strike. So far I have not found anyone who can be set free by himself. This is because they have all been entangled in the useless mechanics of their old masters. As for me, I do not have a single method to give to everyone, but what I can do is relieve the troubled and set men free.

However, it is necessary to be free oneself before one can free others. Lin-chi once said that when people came to him asking about Buddha, his answers emerged from the realm of purity; when they asked him about Bodhisattva, his answers derived from the realm of wonders; and when they asked about *nirvāna*, he responded from the realm of quiescence. When he entered all these different realms, he said, he was not entangled in any of these situations; none of them could enslave him. When a man came to him asking for help he was in a position to observe him, free from entanglements.

Lin-chi discovered that because he was absolutely free of entanglements, his disciples often had difficulty recognizing him. Therefore, he would put on various garments to enable them to do so. Sometimes when he took off his coat and entered into the realm of purity, his disciples would know him and be pleased to see him. But when he stripped away even his garment of purity, they would be at a loss and run away, complaining that he was no longer the same man. Yet as soon as he told them he was a real man who wore clothes, they would suddenly recall him. Thus Lin-chi warns the learners of Ch'an that they should not attempt to recognize the man by what he wears, for what he wears is a mere attachment, a fixation. There are many kinds of fixations, such as purity, *bodhi*, *nirvāna*, patriarch, and even Buddha. So whenever we encounter a famous name or a refined expression, we must recognize them as simple attachments. To be a great Ch'an master one must be free from all these attachments, and to be a good disciple one must be able to see the master's freedom. When the sun is not covered with clouds, the illumination of the sky shines all over the world. This should be true of the master himself as well as of his disciples. To set one free from attachments, Lin-chi developed his distinctively abrupt and unconventional approach to enlightenment, as we shall see in his fascicle.

Liberation from Subjectivity and Objectivity

On the first reading of the *Recorded Dialogues of Ch'an Master Lin-chi*, we may expect to be completely lost. However, as we go over Lin-chi's teachings, we find they are not so incomprehensible as they seem at first glance. He has formulated a number of basic principles intended to lead us to enlightenment. These include *ssu pin chu*, or the Fourfold Relationship Between Questioner and Answerer; and *ssu liao chien*, or the Four Processes of Liberation from Subjectivity and Objectivity. Both of these approaches lead to the transformation of the limited ego-form self to the unlimited universal Self—briefly, we may say the transformation of the ego into the Self.

A. *Ssu pin chu*, the Fourfold Relationship Between Questioner and Answerer.

1. *Pin chien chu*, or guest sees host. *Pin*, or guest, means the ego-form self, and *chu*, or host, means the universal Self. Thus "guest sees host" means that the questioner is in the form of ego when he meets the answerer, who is in the form of Self.

2. *Chu chien pin*, or host sees guest. This means that the questioner is in the form of Self, when he meets the answerer, who is in the form of ego.

3. *Chu chien chu*, or host sees host. This means the questioner is in the form of Self, when he meets the answerer, who is also in the form of Self.

4. *Pin chien pin*, or guest sees guest. This means that the questioner and the answerer are both in the form of ego.

By way of illustrating the first point, "guest sees host" (or the questioner with his limited ego-form self interviewing the answerer with his unlimited universal Self), we may look at the first story in Lin-chi's fascicle. After three years of study Lin-chi was confused in his search for Ultimate Truth and went to his master Huang-po three times. At that time Lin-chi was apparently nothing other than the representative of a limited ego-form self, full of anxiety and exhausted by intellectual inquiry. On the other hand Huang-po, the "answerer" interviewed by the "questioner" Lin-chi, was master of himself. Inwardly there was no thought stirring him; outwardly he did not seek serenity. The blows that he gave Lin-chi were a direct reflection from his center of being, the reservoir of

Liberation from Subjectivity and Objectivity

all potentialities. Therefore, his striking was similar to the swift movement of the sacred sword Vajra, or the "flash of lightning." In Hua-yen philosophy we learn that a single hair of a lion contains the potentialities of all the hairs. This is a metaphysical approach through which we can only expect to gain an intellectual understanding. When Huang-po struck he manifested the integrity of his own mind, far beyond any verbal expression or intellectual analysis. Thus Master Ta-yü called Huang-po's blows "motherly kindness." They came from a mind full of potentialities and yet without intellectual discrimination or conceptual distinctions. So it was the universal Self, or host, unlimited and unbiased, that interviewed the ego-form self of Lin-chi before his enlightenment. Thus we have the illustration of "guest sees host."

The relationship in the case of "host sees guest," or the unlimited Self interviewing the limited ego, can be illustrated by the dialogue between Master Lin-chi and the director of the Bear's Ear Pagoda. When Lin-chi said that he would not visit and bow to the images of Buddha and the Patriarchs, he meant that his mind was the absolute Void, which is not only free from the worldly trap of opposites but also from attachment to images of the divine. As he points out in his *Dialogues*: "When you meet a Buddha, kill the Buddha, when you meet a Patriarch, kill the Patriarch. . . . Only then will you obtain absolute emancipation from any attachment. Thus you are liberated and reveal your real self at ease." Lin-chi's answer to the director of the pagoda was a manifestation of his real self, the unlimited universal form of Lin-chi, the "host" in our schemata. The director of the pagoda did not understand the meaning of Lin-chi's remarks and, shocked, declared that he had insulted the holy images. Buddha and the Patriarchs, he said, had not done any injustice to Lin-chi! Obviously his mind was conditioned to a relative level; he had not been freed from his limitations to a comprehension of the absolute Void. His grumbling represented the ego-form self, the "guest," which interviews the Self, i.e. Lin-chi, the "host."

The third relationship, "host sees host," is the most desirable one. Both questioner and answerer reach the state of enlighten-

LIBERATION FROM SUBJECTIVITY AND OBJECTIVITY

ment and become entirely different personages. This can be illustrated in the story of Lin-chi when he went to seek enlightenment from Master Ta-yü. On this occasion Ta-yü approved the instruction given by Huang-po, Lin-chi's original master, and praised Huang-po's rough treatment as "motherly" teaching. His mind was harmonious with that of Huang-po. Here Ta-yü is the "host" who possesses the universal Self. As soon as Lin-chi's mind was opened by Ta-yü's penetrating remarks, he suddenly attained enlightenment. Ta-yü's comment on Huang-po's teaching is the spontaneous reflection of his universal Self, which has been set free from previous confusion and the entanglements of anxiety. Lin-chi is now no longer limited by his ego-form self, but is liberated as "host" to interview the "host" of Ta-yü. The story of this interview concludes with Ta-yü testing the authenticity of Lin-chi's self-realization by asking him, "What have you seen, after all?" Lin-chi responded by striking his chest three times and saying nothing. This "knocking" indicated that the message was sent from the center of his being, the universal Self of Lin-chi, the "host." This interview with Ta-yü is an example of "host sees host," the goal of Ch'an Buddhism.

The fourth relationship, "guest sees guest," is a case where the questioner and answerer both are entangled in their ego-form selves and are unable to free themselves of their obstructions. Furthermore, each imposes on the other the burden of his own entanglements. The situation is not an uncommon one, as Master Lin-chi himself observes in his *Dialogues:*

> There are some students who carry the cangue and wear a lock [such as were worn by prisoners] and appear thus before the Ch'an master. The master puts on another cangue and lock to add to his burden. The students, however, are very well pleased since both the master and the pupil fail to realize what has happened. This is called "guest interviews guest."

B. *Ssu liao chien,* the Four Processes of Liberation from Subjectivity and Objectivity.

The purpose of the "Ho!" or the *kung-an* method is, of course, to liberate the learner from his unseen entanglements.

97

Liberation from Subjectivity and Objectivity

However, the procedure for reaching this goal varies with circumstances and the individual involved. According to Lin-chi, the master must determine what kind of person the disciple is and then apply the appropriate technique for opening his mind. This procedure involves four steps.

1. *Tuo jen pu tuo ching.* A literal translation of this first process would be "to take away the man but not his objective situation." There are many poetic and symbolic paraphrases by various Buddhist scholars, including some by Lin-chi himself, for example: "Silently I meditate in the temple, the white clouds rise from the tops of the mountains." This is suggestive, but does not tell us the exact meaning of this process of liberation. After studying many such symbolic and poetic paraphrases of this idea, and reviewing the actual cases of enlightenment through *kung-an*, "Ho!," or striking, I have come to the conclusion that the meaning is, to free from the attachments of subjectivity but to let objectivity remain. This procedure is suggested in the following lines by Master Fên-yang (947–1024) of the Lin-chi School:

> Under the moonlight are the towers and chambers of a
>   thousand houses;
> Lying in the autumn air are lakes and rivers of myriad *li.*
> Blossoms blow in the reeds, differing not in their colors.
> A white bird descends the white sandbank of a stream.

In this poem there is no mention of subjectivity; what we have is the actual situation, sheer objectivity. Similarly the subjectivity of man is liberated, freed from its attachments; only objectivity remains. Hence, "to take away the man but not his objective situation."

2. *Tuo ching pu tuo jen.* This means to take away the objective situation but not the man. Less literally, it translates "to be free from the attachments of objectivity, but let subjectivity remain." This may be illustrated by one of Lin-chi's sermons:

> There are some Buddhist learners who have already made the mistake of seeking for Mañjuśrī at Mount Wu-t'ai. There is no Mañjuśrī at Wu-t'ai. Do you want to know Mañjuśrī? It is

Liberation from Subjectivity and Objectivity

something at this moment working within you, something which remains unshakable and allows no room for doubt. This is called the living Mañjuśrī.

Lin-chi's remarks on Mañjuśrī stress the fact that man must desist from seeking outside himself, even from famous masters. This approach of non-attachment to objectivity liberates one's self from bondage to the outside and thus leads to enlightenment. This is Lin-chi's second principle, "to take away the objective situation but not the man."

3. *Jen ching chu tuo*. This is to take away both the man and his objective situation. In other words, it is the liberation from both the subjective and the objective bondage. We may say that it is to free from the attachments of subjectivity and objectivity. Lin-chi's famous "Ho!" and Yüeh-shan's staff often served this purpose. Let us look at the following story in Lin-chi's *Dialogues:*

> The monk Ting came to the Master [Lin-chi] and asked, "What is the essence of Buddhism?" The Master came down from his straw chair, slapped his face, and pushed him away. Ting, the questioner, stood there unmoved. A monk standing by said to him, "Ting! Why don't you bow to the Master?" As the monk Ting started to make a bow he suddenly attained enlightenment.

Such slapping and pushing would be insulting in ordinary circumstances, but when applied in the teaching of Ch'an they become a means of opening the mind, beyond any intellection and free from the bondage of both subjectivity and objectivity. The question was put to the Master about the essence of Buddhism. The Master, instead of attempting to explain intellectually, simply administered a slap. There is nothing of intellection in Ting's response. He could not respond with subjective reasoning, nor could he find any help in traditional teachings to add to his understanding. He was lost in a world where he could lean on neither subjectivity nor objectivity. He stood frozen. But when he started to move, it shook the dam of the reservoir of his vitality and broke it. His awakening was like the rushing of water through the shattered dam. This technique of breaking the "mental

Liberation from Subjectivity and Objectivity

dam," is what Lin-chi referred to as *jen ching chu tuo*, or freeing from the attachments of both subjectivity and objectivity.

In Lin-chi's biography we have a story concerning the Master's treatment of an earnest but humble man who frequently came in and out. When he finally approached the Master to ask a question, Lin-chi came down from his seat, took hold of the man, and demanded that he speak out. As he was about to speak Lin-chi pushed him away. This rough treatment was applied for the same purpose as in the case of the monk Ting.

4. *Jen ching chu pu tuo*. This means to take away neither the man nor the situation. Or, to let both subjectivity and objectivity be what they are and be perfectly identified with one another. The following quotation from Lin-chi may throw some light on this concept:

> Fellow learners! To achieve Buddhahood there is no need for cultivation. Just carry on an ordinary task without any attachment. Release your bowels and water, wear your clothes, eat your meals. When you are tired, lie down. The fool will laugh at you, but the wise man will understand.

This is the gist of the teaching of Ch'an. The ultimate reality lies right at the heart of daily existence, if one but knows how to grasp the absolute moment. Thus it is that we say, "Carrying water and chopping wood—therein is the wonder of Tao." Let us see how Lin-chi applied this in his famous teaching of *jen ching chu pu tuo*:

> When Chao-chou sought his enlightenment by foot travel, and came to visit Master Lin-chi, it happened that the latter was bathing his feet. Chao-chou asked, "What is the meaning of Bodhidharma coming from the West?" Master Lin-chi answered, "You ask at a time when I am bathing my feet!" Chao-chou moved nearer and made a gesture of listening. Master Lin-chi said, "Do you want a second ladle of dirty water poured on you?" Chao-chou thereupon went away.

Lin-chi's remarks were a perfectly straightforward statement of the real situation. He was bathing his feet, and he said so to his visitor. The subjectivity, the doer, is exactly identified with ob-

Liberation from Subjectivity and Objectivity

jective activity, the thing being done. This is the same as is reflected in the statement, "Bodhidharma came from the West." It is through this inner experience of perfect identity that Lin-chi answered Chao-chou's question. All that he could convey was shown by his own activity, perfectly representing himself. This is nothing that one can say in words. Therefore, when Chao-chou came nearer and tried to hear something more from the Master, the lesson was, did he want a second ladle of dirty water? This self-identification with objectivity cannot be achieved by outward search. As Lin-chi maintains in his *Dialogues*: "When you search outwardly you are a fool. What you should do is be master of yourself under any circumstances. The objective situation which you are in is sure to be a real one. Then when anything untoward happens, you are not turned about."

When one is inwardly master of oneself and outwardly in the situation true to oneself, then we may say that subjectivity and objectivity are perfectly identified, or, in Lin-chi's words, *jen ching chu pu tuo*. This is the basic principle that Lin-chi used in his *kung-an* as we find them compiled in *The Lamp*.

When we understand the foregoing principles, we may begin to see that the "Ho!" and the striking and the other typical gestures, and the irrelevant questions and answers of Ch'an literature, are no more and no less than a means of attaining the inner experience of enlightenment, or awakening. Ch'an itself remains inexpressible; it cannot be contained in any rigid formula. Intellectual comprehension may be an obstacle rather than an aid to opening the mind. However, these "objective" observations on the teachings of Ch'an may be of some help to us before we plunge into the strange world of apparently meaningless questions and answers. These fundamentals, as set forth by Lin-chi himself, may help us to grasp the meaning of his teachings as they flash forth from a context so different from the comfortable and conventional one that we all know.

HUANG-PO HSI-YÜN
(?–849)

To Roar Like a Tiger

(*From* The Transmission of the Lamp, *Chüan 9*)

CH'AN master Huang-po Hsi-yün of Hung-chou[1] was a native of Min.[2] When still very young he left his home and became a Buddhist monk in the Huang-po Mountain[3] of his native district. In the middle of his forehead there was a swelling resembling a pearl. His voice was articulate and melodious, and his character was plain and pure. Once when he visited the T'ien-t'ai Mountain[4] he met a monk who chatted with him as if he were an old friend. When Huang-po looked at him, the monk's eyes were very bright and penetrating, so Huang-po decided to travel with him. It happened that a mountain stream overflowed the valley. The monk took off his straw hat, put down his staff, and halted their journey. However, the monk wanted Huang-po to cross the water with him. Huang-po said to him, "If you want to walk across the water, please do so by yourself." The monk lifted the hem of his garment and walked on the current as if he were walking on the ground. He turned his head and called to Huang-po, "Cross over! Cross over!" Huang-po said, "Oh! This fellow wants only to save himself. Had I known earlier what he was like, I would have chopped off his feet." The monk sighed deeply and said, "You have really been endowed with a capacity for being a Mahāyāna Buddhist, which I have not." After he said this he disappeared.[5]

Later Huang-po traveled to the capital. He was advised to visit Po-chang Huai-hai,[6] so he went to him and asked, "How did the early Ch'an masters guide their followers?" Po-chang remained silent. Huang-po said, "You cannot let the original Ch'an teachings be lost in the hands of later followers." Po-chang answered, "I say that you shall be the man [who loses Ch'an]." After having said this Po-chang went to his room. But Huang-po followed him and entered the room, saying, "I came here especially [to learn from you]." Po-chang said, "If so, you had better not disappoint me in the future."

One day Po-chang asked Huang-po, "Where have you been?" The answer was that he had been at the foot of the Ta-hsiung Mountain picking mushrooms. Po-chang continued, "Have you seen any tigers?" Huang-po immediately roared like a tiger. Po-chang picked up an ax as if to chop the tiger. Huang-po suddenly slapped Po-chang's face. Po-chang laughed heartily, and then returned to his temple and said to the assembly, "At the foot of the Ta-hsiung Mountain there is a tiger. You people should watch out. I have already been bitten today."

Some time later Huang-po was with Nan-ch'üan.* All the monks in Nan-ch'üan's monastery were going out to harvest cabbage. Nan-ch'üan asked Huang-po, "Where are you going?" Huang-po answered, "I am going to pick cabbage." Nan-ch'üan went on, "What do you use to pick cabbage?" Huang-po lifted his sickle. Nan-ch'üan remarked, "You take the objective position as a guest, but you do not know how to preside as a host in the subjective position." Huang-po thereupon knocked on the ground three times with his sickle.

One day Nan-ch'üan said to Huang-po, "I have a song for herding cows. Could you make a sequel to it?" Huang-po said, "I have my own teacher here."

When Huang-po bid good-bye to Nan-ch'üan, who saw him off at the door, Nan-ch'üan held out Huang-po's straw hat and said,

* Nan-ch'üan P'u-yüan (738–824), whose dialogues appear in Part IV.

Liberation from Subjectivity and Objectivity

"Your body is unusually big. Isn't your straw hat too small?" Huang-po said, "Although my hat is small, the entire universe is in it." Nan-ch'üan said, "How about me, Teacher Wang?"* Huang-po just put on his straw hat and left.

Huang-po later stayed in the Ta-an Temple of Hung-chou, where many devotees gathered around him. When the Prime Minister Pei Hsiu[7] was stationed at Wan-ling,[8] he built a great Ch'an monastery and invited Master Huang-po to lecture there. Because the Master was fond of the old mountain where he had lived before, the new monastery was named after it. The Prime Minister invited the Master to the city and presented his own written interpretation of Ch'an to him. The Master took it and put it on the table. He did not read it. After a short silence, he asked the Prime Minister, "Do you understand?" The minister answered, "I do not understand." The Master said, "It would be better if you could understand immediately through inner experience. If it is expressed in words, it won't be our teaching." Thereupon the Prime Minister wrote a poem and presented it to him:

You, great Bodhisattva, are seven feet tall with a pearl on your forehead.
After you received the mind-seal you expounded Ch'an in the district of Shu-shui[9] for about ten years.
Today your devotees cross the River Chang[10] to come to you.
Thousands of earnest monks esteem and follow you.
Incense and flowers are brought in from far distances for the great cause.
They all wish to serve you as disciples
But no one knows to whom the Dharma will be transmitted.

After reading the poem the Master did not feel pleased. However, from that time on the spirit of the teaching of Huang-po's school became widespread south of the Yangtze River.

One day the Master came to the assembly, where all his disciples were gathered. The Master said, "All of you! What are you seeking?" Thereupon he took a staff and scattered them, and then said:

"You are all idiots. Seeking the Truth through traveling as

* Nan-ch'üan often called himself this; Wang was his family name.

you do now will only make others ridicule you. You join the crowd whenever there are several hundred or a thousand people. You should not do this just for fun. When I was traveling by foot, if I happened to meet someone who at first glance I realized understood the hardships[11] of Ch'an, I would offer him my own rice. Should I have taken things as lightly as you do now, there would be no teaching here today. Since you are learning Ch'an through your travels, you should put all your effort into it. Do you know that in the great kingdom of T'ang there is really no master of Ch'an?" Just then a monk stepped forward and asked, "All over the country we have many old masters who gather their disciples and teach them Ch'an. Why should you say that there are no Ch'an masters?" The Master answered, "I did not mean that there is no Ch'an; what I do mean is that there is no teacher. Do you know that eighty-four disciples of the great Ma-tsu taught Ch'an, but only two or three of them had really received his genuine wisdom? The great Master Kuei-tsung[12] was one of them.

"Every Buddhist should possess inner awareness of the Ultimate Reality. For example the great master Niu-t'ou Fa-yung,* a disciple of the Fourth Patriarch, expounded Ch'an in every way, but he did not know the secret of making the further leap to the Ultimate. With such vision one is able to judge which Ch'an sect has the correct teaching. Furthermore, if one does not actually realize the truth of Ch'an from one's own experience, but simply learns it verbally and collects words, and claims to understand Ch'an, how can one solve the riddle of life and death? Those who neglect their old masters' teachings will soon be led far astray. As for them, I recognize them immediately, as soon as they step through my door. Do you understand what I mean? You must study hard, and not take things lightly. If you just keep yourself going, and waste your lifetime for nothing, wise men will laugh at you. And finally you will fade away as a common ignorant man. Be sure to understand that this serious task is yours alone. If you understand, you will immediately see it. If you do not, please leave."

A monk asked, "What is the meaning of Bodhidharma coming from the West?" The Master immediately struck him. The teach-

---

* The teachings of Niu-t'ou Fa-yung appear in Part I.

Liberation from Subjectivity and Objectivity

ings of the Master embodied the highest vision, so those who were mediocre failed to understand him.

In the [third] year of the Ta-chung period [847–859] of the T'ang Dynasty, the Master passed away, on his mountain.[13] The Royal Court bestowed upon him the posthumous name of Ch'an Master Tuan-chi, or Liberator from Limitations, and named his pagoda Kuang-yeh, or Grand Deeds.

MU-CHOU TAO-TSUNG

"Before a Donkey and After a Horse"

(*From* The Transmission of the Lamp, *Chüan 12*)

THE Old Reverend Master Chên lived at the Lung-hsin Monastery in Mu-chou.[14] He concealed his fame among the learners of Ch'an and in no way made himself known to the outside world. He used to make sandals and secretly put them by the road. After many years, people found out that it was he who did this. Thus he was called "Sandal Chên." Scholars often came to ask him questions, to which he would respond instantaneously. His words were sharp and cutting, indicating that his teachings were beyond the conventional way of thinking. Therefore, the shallow and the superficial often laughed at him. But those Ch'an learners who were highly endowed with talents greatly respected him. Hence devotees came to him from all directions and called him Chên Tsun-su, or Old Reverend Master Chên.

One evening the Master said to his assembly:

"All of you! Those who do not yet have insight into Ch'an must seek it; those who do have it should not be ungrateful to me afterward." Just then a monk stepped out from the crowd, bowed, and said, "I will never be ungrateful to you, sir!" The Master rebuked him, "You have already been ungrateful to me." The

Liberation from Subjectivity and Objectivity

Master then said, "Ever since I came to preside here, I have not seen one man free from attachment. Why don't you come forward?" A monk then came up to him. The Master said, "My supervisor is not here, so you had better go outside the gate and give yourself twenty blows." The monk protested: "Where is my mistake?" The Master said, "You have added a lock to your cangue."[15]

Often when the Master noticed a Ch'an monk coming to see him, he would immediately shut his door. Sometimes when he was visited by a lecturing monk, the Master would call him, "Sir." When the monk answered the call, the Master would say to him, "What a lumber carrier!"[16] Or sometimes he said, "Here is a bucket; please fetch me some water."

One day when the Master was standing on the stone steps of the corridor, a monk came upon him and asked, "Where is the chamber in which Old Reverend Master Chên lives?" The Master took off his sandal and beat the monk on the head with it. When the monk was about to leave, the Master called to him, "Sir!" The monk turned his head and looked back. The Master pointed to him and said, "Please leave that way!"

A monk knocked on the door. The Master asked, "Who is it?" The monk answered, "It is so-and-so." The Master said, "A drill used for making wheels in the Ts'in Dynasty [252–207 B.C]."

One day an envoy sent by the Royal Court asked the Master, "All three doors are open: through which one should I enter?" The Master addressed him, "Your Highness!" The officer responded, "Yes, Master!" The Master said, "You must enter through the door of faith." The officer saw the mural painting on the wall and asked, "What are these two *aryas*[17] talking about?" The Master knocked on the pillar and said, "Each of the Triple Bodies[18] of a Buddha preaches Buddhism."

The Master asked a lecturing monk, "Are you not lecturing on 'Mere Ideation'?" The answer was "Yes!" The Master said, "You are not following the first five of the ten commandments."[19]

The Master asked an abbot, "When one understands, a drop of water on the tip of a hair contains the great sea, and the great earth is contained in a speck of dust. What do you have to say about this?" The abbot answered, "Whom are you asking?" The Master said, "I am asking you." The abbot said, "Why don't you listen to me?" The Master said, "Is it you or I who does not listen to the other's words?"

The Master saw a monk coming toward him and said, "According to the well-known *kung-an* you will be given thirty blows." The monk answered, "I am what I am." The Master said, "Why should the image of the *vajra*[20] at the monastery gate raise his fist?" The monk replied, "The *vajra* is what he is." The Master struck him.

A question was asked: "What is the upward passage?"[21] The Master said, "It is not hard to tell, if I wish to do so." The monk said, "Please tell me." The Master said, "The third day, the eleventh, the ninth, and the seventeenth."

Question: "I am not going to ask you how to negate one level through another level. But how do you not negate one level, if not through another?"

Answer: "Yesterday I planted the eggplant, today the winter melon."

Question: "What is the real meaning of the teaching of the Six Patriarchs?"

Answer: "I am fond of anger, but not joy!" The questioner went on: "Why should you like this?"

Answer: "When you meet a swordsman on the road, you should show him your sword; when you meet a man who is not a poet, you should not talk about poetry."

A monk came to visit the Master, who asked him, "Where do you come from?" The monk answered, "Liu-yang." The Master asked, "What did the Ch'an master in Liu-yang[22] say about the meaning of Ch'an?" The monk answered, "You can go anywhere, but you cannot find the road." The Master asked, "Is that what the old master there really said?" The monk answered, "Yes, it is." The Master picked up his staff and gave the monk a blow, saying, "This fellow remembers only words."

The Master asked an abbot, "If a brother monk comes to ask you something, what would you answer?" The abbot said, "I'll

Liberation from Subjectivity and Objectivity

tell him when he comes." The Master: "Why don't you say it now?" The abbot said, "What do you lack, Master?" The Master said to him, "Please do not bother me with your creepers."[23]

A monk came to visit the Master, who asked him, "Are you not one of those monks who travel on foot?" The monk answered, "Yes." The Master then asked him, "Have you bowed to the image of Buddha?" The monk answered, "Why should I bow to that lump of clay?" The Master exclaimed, "Go away and give yourself blows!"

A monk asked, "I give lectures, as well as travel on foot. How is it that I do not understand the teaching of Buddhism?" The Master said, "If your words are true, you should repent." The monk asked, "Please tell me how to do it." The Master said, "If you do not understand, I will shut my mouth without a word." The monk insisted, "Please tell me." The Master said, "If you are not ungrateful, you will not appear ashamed."

Question: "What is that which can be expressed in one word?"
Answer: "The meaning is lost."
The questioner went on: "Where is the lost meaning?"
Answer: "Who deserves thirty blows?"
Question: "Are the teachings of Buddha and the teachings of the Patriarch [Bodhidharma] the same?"
Answer: "A green mountain is a green mountain, and white clouds are white clouds."
The monk continued: "What is a green mountain?"
The Master: "Return a drop of rain to me."
The monk: "I cannot say it. Please say it yourself."
The Master: "The 'troops' that stay in the front of the Peak of the Dharma-Flower will be recalled after the word of *nirvāna* is announced."

The Master asked a monk, "Where were you this summer?"
The monk answered, "I will tell you when you have a place to stay."
The Master: "The fox is not the same as the lion, and lamplight cannot be compared to the brightness of the sun and moon."

The Master asked a newly arrived monk where he came from. The monk stared at him. The Master said, "You are a fellow running before a donkey and after a horse." The monk said, "Please look at me." The Master said, "You, fellow, running before the donkey and after the horse, say something to me." The monk gave no answer.

When the Master was reading the sūtras, the Minister Chen Tsao[24] asked him, "Master! What sūtra are you reading?" The Master said, "The *Diamond Sūtra!*"[25] The Minister said, "The *Diamond Sūtra* was translated in the Sixth Dynasty;[26] which edition are you using?" The Master lifted up the book and said, "All things produced by causation are simply an illusive dream and the shadow of a bubble."

When the Master was reading the *Nirvāna Sūtra*,[27] a monk asked him what sūtra he was reading. The Master picked up the book and said, "This is the last one for cremation."

The Master asked a newly arrived monk, "Where did you go for this summer session?"

The monk: "To Ching-shan."[28]

The Master: "How many disciples were there?"

The monk: "Four hundred."

The Master: "This fellow eats dinner at night."[29]

The monk: "In your honorable assembly, how can you even mention a fellow who eats dinner at night?"

The Master raised his staff and chased the monk off.

Master Mu-chou heard of an old Ch'an master who was practically unapproachable. He went to visit him. When the old Ch'an master saw Mu-chou entering his chamber, he immediately uttered, "Ho!" Mu-chou slapped him with his hand, and said, "What an imitation this is." The old master said, "Where is my fault?" Mu-chou scolded him, "You! You wild fox spirit!" After saying this, Master Mu-chou returned home immediately.

The Master asked a monk where he had been recently.

The monk: "Kiangsi."[30]

The Master: "How many sandals have you worn out?"

The monk made no answer.

The Master shared his tea with a lecturer monk, and said, "I cannot save you."

The monk: "I do not understand. Please explain, Master." The

Liberation from Subjectivity and Objectivity

Master picked up a cream cake and showed it to him, asking, "What is this?"

The monk said, "A material object."

The Master said, "You are the kind of fellow who boils in hot water."

A high-ranking monk, who had been given a purple robe by the court, came to the Master and bowed to him. The Master took hold of the ribbon of the monk's hat and showed it to him, saying, "What is this called?"

The monk: "A court hat."

The Master: "If that's so, then I will not take it off."

The Master asked him what he was studying.

The monk answered, "The Teaching of Mere Ideation."[31]

The Master: "What is this?"

The monk: "The Triple World is nothing else but mind, and all things are but consciousness."

The Master pointed at the door and asked, "What is this?"

The monk: "This is a material object."

The Master: "In the court, the purple robe was bestowed on you; to the Emperor you have spoken the sūtra. Why do you not keep the five commandments?"[32]

The monk made no answer.

A monk asked, "I just came to the assembly. Please give me guidance!"

The Master: "You don't know how to ask a question."

The monk: "How would you ask it?"

The Master: "I will release you from thirty blows. Give them to yourself and get out of here."

A monk asked, "Please explain the basic principles of the teaching of the Buddha."

The Master said, "You may ask me and I will tell you."

The monk: "Please, Master, say it."

The Master: "Burning incense in the Buddha Hall and joining your hands outside the gate of the monastery."[33]

A question was asked: "What word illustrates?"

The Master: "To evaluate a man's talent, give him an appropriate position."

The monk went on: "How can one be free from the trap of verbal illustration?"

The Master said, "May I beg you to accept this offer?"[34]

The Master called Chaio-shan to him, and also called a boy to bring in an ax. The boy brought him an ax and said, "There is nothing to measure with, so you will only be able to cut roughly."

The Master shouted, "Ho!" and called the boy back, saying, "What is your ax?"

The boy held the ax as if he were chopping with it.

The Master: "You should not cut off the head of your old master."

A question was asked: "What is the direct way to the Truth?"

The Master said, "To evaluate a man's talent and give him an appropriate position."

The question was rephrased: "What is not the direct way to the Truth?"

The Master: "May I beg you to accept this offer?"

A newly arrived monk visited the Master, who asked him, "Are you newly arrived?" The answer was, "Yes, Master!"

The Master said, "Cast off your creepers.[35] Can you understand this?"

The monk said, "I do not understand."

The Master said, "Carry a cangue, present a statement of your crime, and get out of here by yourself." As the monk was leaving, the Master said to him, "Come back, come back. I really want to ask you where you come from." The monk answered that he was from Kiangsi. The Master said, "Master Pê-t'an[36] is at your back, and he is afraid that you might say something wrong. Have you seen him?" The monk made no answer.

Someone asked, "When the image of the guardian spirit [*vajra*] at the temple door wields the thunderbolt, he possesses all the power of heaven and earth. When he does not wield it, nothing happens. What does this mean?" The Master cried out, "Huṁ! Huṁ![37] I have never heard such a question before." Then he continued: "To leap forward three thousand times first, and then retreat backward eight hundred steps: what does this mean?" The monk said, "Yes!" The Master said, "First I will rebuke your crime

Liberation from Subjectivity and Objectivity

with a written statement, and then I will grant you blows." The monk was about to leave, but the Master called him back: "Come here! I'll share your creepers. When we wield the thunderbolt we possess all the power of heaven and earth. Can you tell me how deep the water is in Lake Tung-ting?"[38] The monk said, "I have not measured it." The Master said, "Then what is Lake Tung-ting?" The monk answered, "It exists just for this moment." The Master said, "Even this simple creeper you cannot understand." He gave the monk a blow.

A question was asked: "What word is entirely free from attachment?"

The Master said, "I would not say it this way."

The monk pressed, "Then how would you say it?"

The Master answered, "An arrow is shot through India for about a hundred thousand miles, but you wait for it in the great kingdom of T'ang."

A monk knocked on the Master's door. The Master asked, "What is it?" The monk answered, "I do not yet understand my own affairs of life and death. Please, Master, guide me." The Master replied, "What I have for you here is a stick." Then he opened the door. The monk was going to challenge him. The Master immediately slapped his mouth.

A question was asked: "What character neither completes *i* nor resembles *pa*?"[39] The Master snapped his fingers once and asked, "Do you understand this?" The monk answered that he did not understand it. The Master said, "To ascend to heaven and present a memorial to the throne for the infinite surpassing cause, a frog jumps into the Brahman Heaven and an earthworm passes through the East Sea."

The Abbot Hsi-feng came to visit the Master. The Master offered him a seat and refreshments, saying, "Where were you teaching Ch'an this summer?" The Abbot answered, "Lan-ch'i." The Master went on: "How many people were there?" The Abbot: "About seventy." "What did you teach your disciples then?" The Abbot picked up an orange and presented it to him, saying, "It's done." The Master rebuked him: "Why should you be in such a hurry?"

A newly arrived monk came to visit the Master. As he was bowing, the Master cried out, "Why should you steal the ever abiding fruit[40] to eat?" The monk said, "I just arrived here. Why should you, Master, steal the fruit?" The Master said, "The stolen goods are here."

The Master asked the monk, "Where have you just come from?" The monk said, "From Mount Yang." The Master went on: "Why don't you follow the five commandments?" The monk replied, "In what way did I lie to you?" The Master said, "This place does not defile a novice."

[The Master entered *nirvāna* in his ninety-eighth year. See the *Amalgamation of the Sources of the Five Lamps*, Chüan 4.]

LIN-CHI I-HSÜAN
(?–866)

"Here I Will Bury You Alive"

(*From* The Transmission of the Lamp, *Chüan 11*)

CH'AN Master Lin-chi I-hsüan of Chen-chou[41] was a native of Nan-hua in Ts'ao-chou.[42] His original surname was Hsing. In his early boyhood he made up his mind to become a Buddhist. As soon as he had had his head shaved and was ordained, he devoted himself to Ch'an. In the beginning he studied with Master Huang-po Hsi-yün, by following the group of monks who visited the Master and attended his sermons. One day the head monk[43] suggested that he should go to see Master Huang-po and question him. So Lin-chi went to Huang-po and asked him, "What is the real meaning of Bodhidharma coming from the West?" Losing no time, Huang-po struck him at once. Lin-chi persisted and visited his master three times, and each time he received blows. Thereupon he went to the head monk and asked to leave the monastery: "You previously encouraged me to question the Master, but all that was granted me were blows. Since to my regret I have such a dull mind, I had better set out on foot and seek everywhere for enlightenment." The head monk reported to Huang-po that Lin-chi, in spite of his youth, was a man of unusual qualities and asked the Master to help him again when he came to bid him farewell. The following day, when Lin-chi took leave of Huang-po, the latter advised him to go to Master Ta-yü.[44] So Lin-chi went to see Master Ta-yü, who asked him:

"Where do you come from?"

"From Huang-po."

"What instruction did Huang-po give you?"

"When I asked him for the real meaning of Buddhism, he immediately struck me. Three times I put this question to him, and three times I received blows. I don't know where I was at fault."

Thereupon Master Ta-yü exclaimed, "Your master treated you entirely with motherly kindness, and yet you say you do not know your fault."

Hearing this, Lin-chi was suddenly awakened and said, "After all, there isn't much in Huang-po's Buddhism!"

Master Ta-yü took hold of him and exclaimed, "You young devil! A moment ago you complained that you did not understand your master's teaching, and now you say that there is not much in Huang-po's Buddhism. What have you seen after all? Speak out! Speak out!"

Three times Lin-chi poked Ta-yü in the ribs with his fist. Ta-yü pushed him away and said, "Your teacher is Huang-po. There is nothing here that is of any concern to me."

After that Lin-chi left Ta-yü and returned to Huang-po, who asked him, "Have you not come back too soon?"

"It is simply because you have been as kind as a mother to me." Then he bowed to Master Huang-po and stood beside him. Huang-po inquired about the instruction that Master Ta-yü had given him. Lin-chi told him all about it. Master Huang-po remarked:

"When next I see this old fellow Ta-yü, I should like to give him hard blows."

"Why should you talk about waiting? Here, I give them to you now." Saying this, Lin-chi slapped his master Huang-po, who cried out:

"What a crazy fellow! He is coming to pluck the tiger's beard!" Lin-chi immediately cried out, "Ho!"

Huang-po called the attendant: "Let this madman go to the assembly hall!"

One day Master Lin-chi went with Huang-po to do some work in which all the monks participated. Lin-chi followed his master

Liberation from Subjectivity and Objectivity

who, turning his head, noticed that Lin-chi was carrying nothing in his hand.

"Where is your hoe?"

"Somebody took it away."

"Come here: let us discuss something," commanded Huang-po, and as Lin-chi drew nearer, he thrust his hoe into the ground and continued, "There is no one in the world who can pick up my hoe."

However, Lin-chi seized the tool, lifted it up, and exclaimed, "How then could it be in my hands?"

"Today we have another hand with us; it is not necessary for me to join in."

And Huang-po returned to the temple.

One day Huang-po ordered all the monks of the temple to work in the tea garden. He himself was the last to arrive. Lin-chi greeted him, but stood there with his hands resting on the hoe.

"Are you tired?" asked Huang-po.

"I just started working; how can you say that I am tired!"

Huang-po immediately lifted his stick and struck Lin-chi, who then seized the stick, and with a push, made his master fall to the ground. Huang-po called the supervisor to help him up. After doing so, the supervisor asked, "Master, how can you let such a madman insult you like that?" Huang-po picked up the stick and struck the supervisor. Lin-chi, digging the ground by himself, made this remark: "Let all other places use cremation; here I will bury you alive."

One day Lin-chi was sleeping in the monks' living quarters. Huang-po came in and tapped on the side of his bed three times. Lin-chi lifted his head and saw that it was his master, but went back to sleep. At that, Huang-po tapped on his mat three times and then left for the upper room, where he saw the head monk sitting in meditation. Master Huang-po said to him, "In the outer room a young man is sitting in meditation, so what are you thinking about so idly?" The head monk answered, "This old fellow must have gone crazy." Thereupon Huang-po struck the board and left.

Lin-chi was planting fir trees with Huang-po, when the latter questioned him:

"Why should we plant so many trees in these mountains?"

Lin-chi answered, "In the first place, for later generations; they may be used as a record of the old days; in the second place, these trees improve the scenery of the monastery."

Having said this, he took the hoe and struck the ground with it three times. Huang-po remarked:

"Although you now answer this way, previously you deserved my blows." Thereupon Lin-chi struck the ground three times with his hoe again, and puffed, "Hsu! Hsu!" Huang-po then said:

"When the teachings of our school are transmitted to you, the prophecy of our prosperity will be fulfilled."

One day after half the summer session had already passed, Lin-chi went up the mountain to visit his master Huang-po, whom he found reading a sūtra. Lin-chi said to him:

"I thought you were the perfect man, but here you are, apparently a dull old monk, swallowing black beans [Chinese characters]."

Lin-chi stayed only a few days and then bid farewell to Huang-po, who said:

"You came here after the summer session had started, and now you are leaving before the summer session is over."

"I came here simply to visit you, Master!"

Without ado, Huang-po struck him and chased him away. After having walked a few *li*, Lin-chi began to doubt his enlightenment in Ch'an, so he returned to Huang-po for the rest of the summer.

One day, when Lin-chi came to bid him farewell, Huang-po asked him where he was going. Lin-chi said:

"If it is not south of the river, it must be north of it."

Huang-po quickly picked up the stick and struck him. Lin-chi, grabbing the stick, said:

"This old fellow should not use the stick blindly. Later he may strike someone by mistake."

Huang-po called the attendant, asking him for a small table and leaning board. Lin-chi told him, "Bring some fire with you."

Huang-po cried out:

Liberation from Subjectivity and Objectivity

"No, don't! You may leave now. But in the future you will break the tongues of all the people under heaven."[45]

Thereupon Lin-chi left Master Huang-po and arrived at the Pagoda of the Bear's Ear.[46] The director of the pagoda asked him to whom he would first bow, the Patriarch or the Buddha?

"I will bow to neither," was Lin-chi's answer.

"What hostility is this that exists between Buddha and the Patriarch and you, O sir, that you do not want to bow to either of them?"

Waving his wide sleeves,[47] Lin-chi left the pagoda.

Later, Lin-chi returned to the North and was invited by the people of Chao-chou to stay at the Monastery of Lin-chi, where disciples and lay scholars gathered from all over the country.

One day, Master Lin-chi delivered a sermon to the assembly, saying:

"Within your body of red flesh there exists a true man without status who is frequently entering and going out through one's face. If any one of you has not seen him yet, look, look!"

To this a monk responded immediately, asking, "Who is the true man without status?" Master Lin-chi rushed down from his seat, took hold of him, and commanded:

"Speak! Speak!"

But when the monk was about to speak, the Master pushed him away, exclaiming: "What worthless stuff is this true man without status!" He then went back to his chamber.

Master Lin-chi asked Lo-p'u,[48] "From the early days on, some taught by means of the stick; others through 'Ho!' Which of the two means do you prefer?"

"I prefer neither."

"What is wrong with having a preference?" retorted the Master.

Lo-p'u immediately exclaimed "Ho!" and Master Lin-chi struck him.

Master Lin-chi asked Mu-kou,[49] "What is a white cow in the open field?"[50]

Mu-kou answered, "Moo!"

The Master responded, "Dumb!"
Mu-kou asked, "How about you?"
The Master said, "Beast!"

Ta-chio[51] came to visit Master Lin-chi. Lin-chi lifted his *fu-tzu*.[52] Ta-chio unfolded his sitting cloth.[53] Then Master Lin-chi threw down his *fu-tzu*, whereupon Ta-chio folded his sitting cloth and went to the assembly hall. The monks in the hall whispered that Ta-chio must be a close relative of the Master; therefore he did not need to bow, nor did he receive a blow. When the Master overheard this, he sent for the newly arrived monk Ta-chio, who came out from the crowd.

Master Lin-chi announced, "All the monks here are saying that you have not yet bowed to the abbot."

Ta-chio greeted him and went back into the crowd.

Ma-yü came to visit the Master. He unfolded his sitting cloth and asked:

"There are twelve faces of the Goddess of Mercy. Which is the one in front?"

Master Lin-chi came down from his seat, picked up the sitting cloth with one hand and took hold of Ma-yü with the other, and asked:

"Now where are those twelve faces of the Goddess?"

Ma-yü turned around and was about to seat himself in the Master's straw chair. Lin-chi picked up a stick and struck Ma-yü, who grabbed it. Thus, both holding the stick, they went to the Master's chamber.

Once the Master addressed the assembly:

"Listen, all of you! He who wants to learn Dharma must never worry about the loss of his own life. When I was with Master Huang-po I asked three times for the real meaning of Buddhism, and three times I was struck as if tall reeds whipped me in the wind. I want those blows again, but who can give them to me now?"

A monk came forth from the crowd, answering:

"I can give them to you!"

Master Lin-chi picked up a stick and handed it to him.

Liberation from Subjectivity and Objectivity

When the monk tried to grab it, the Master struck him instead.

A monk asked, "What is the first word?"

The Master answered, "Once the three essentials are asserted, they are as distinct as the red marks of a stamp. Thus, subjectivity and objectivity are already differentiated, even before you say anything."

"What is the second word?" the monk continued.

"How can subtle awareness be reached by Wu-chu's[54] intellectual inquiry? How can any means separate the ever flowing stream?"

The monk pressed him for the third word, and the Master answered:

"Take a look at the puppets on the stage! Their performance is directed entirely by the man behind."

Master Lin-chi remarked further, "Each word we say should possess the three mystic entrances, and each mystic entrance must possess the three essentials, manifested in temporary appearance and action. What do you understand by this?"

It was on the tenth day of the fourth month of the seventh year of the Hsien-t'ung period [860–873] of T'ang that Lin-chi announced his going to *nirvāna*. He then came to the assembly and said, "After my death, the treasure of my correct understanding of the Dharma should not disappear!" San-sheng[55] came forward and said, "How can we dare let your teaching of the Dharma disappear?" The Master asked, "Hereafter, if someone should ask you about it, what would you say?" San-sheng uttered a "Ho!" The Master then said, "Who could believe that the treasure of my teachings would be transmitted to this blind ass?" Thereupon he made a *gāthā*, as follows:

> Being carried away by the endlessly flowing stream, you ask what to do.
> Achieve real infinite illumination, is my answer.
> However, to be free from forms and names is not innate in man.
> Even the sharpest sword[56] must be constantly resharpened.

After chanting this *gāthā*, he passed away. The Royal Court bestowed upon the Master the posthumous name of Hui-chao, or

Wise Illumination; and his pagoda is called Ch'eng-ling, or Pure Spirit.

NOTES

1. Now Nan-ch'ang, the capital of Kiangsi Province.
2. Now Fukien Province.
3. West of the Fu-ch'ing district in Fukien Province.
4. North of the T'ien-t'ai district in Chekiang Province. It was on this mountain that the T'ien-t'ai School was founded.
5. In *The Wan-ling Records* the story is a slightly different one. The scripts of Wan-ling have been translated by John Blofeld in *The Zen Teaching of Huang-po* (see p. 94). This story in *The Lamp* implies that the other monk followed the Hīnayāna tradition of saving himself alone, whereas Huang-po considered that self-salvation alone was not the correct answer to the truth, which is why he said, "I would have chopped off his feet."
6. According to the *Records of Pointing at the Moon*, Chüan 10, Huang-po was advised to go to Nan-ch'ang to visit Ma-tsu, but when he arrived there Ma-tsu had passed away. So he visited Ma-tsu's pagoda. Po-chang had built a hut by the side of Ma-tsu's tomb; thus Huang-po first met him there and studied under him. According to *The Lamp*, Huang-po was the disciple of Po-chang. But according to Pei Hsiu's introduction to *Essentials of the Transmission of the Mind*, Huang-po was the nephew-in-dharma of Po-chang Huai-hai and Hsi-t'ang Chih-tsang.
7. According to Pei Hsiu's introduction to *Essentials of the Transmission of the Mind*, he first invited Huang-po to lecture at Lung-hsing Temple in Chung-ling in 842. Six years later, when Pei Hsiu was in Wan-ling, he again invited Huang-po to the Temple of K'ai-yan.
8. Now the town of Hsüan-ch'eng in southern Anhwei Province.
9. The River Shu (also called Ho-shu Shui), flows through northern Sui-ch'uan district in Kiangsi Province.
10. The River Chang, or Chang Chiang, flows through southern Fukien Province, south of the Huang-po Mountain, where the Master was originally ordained.
11. In the original text the literal meaning is "to know pain and itching." This means having experienced the hardship of the task—in this case, Ch'an.
12. Kuei-tsung refers to Ch'an Master Chih-chang of Kuei-tsung Monastery in Lu-shan, or Mount Lu. He was one of the best disciples of Ma-tsu.
13. According to *Records of Buddhas and Patriarchs in Various Dynasties*, Chüan 16, Huang-po died in the third year of the Ta-chung period, or 849. According to *General Records of Buddhas and Patriarchs*, Chüan 42, however, he died in the ninth year of the Ta-chung period, or 855.
14. Now Chien-te (Kienteh), located west of Shun-an in Chekiang Province.
15. The cangue is a wooden frame that confines the neck, formerly used as a punishment in China.
16. This is a T'ang colloquial expression which indicates one-sidedness: a coolie can carry lumber on one shoulder only.

17. An *arya* is an honorable person, such as an *arhat*.
18. The Triple Bodies (Trikāya) of the Buddha are *dharmakāya*, or the Body of Essence; *sambhogakāya*, or the Body of Bliss; and *nirmanakāya*, or the Body of Magical Transformation.
19. The first five commandments are against killing, stealing, adultery, lying, and intoxicating liquors.
20. The *vajra* is the guardian spirit of the Buddhist order, who holds a large thunderbolt in his hand.
21. The Ch'an master Pan-san once said: "As for the upward passage, a thousand saints could not give it to you. The learners toiled in search of it. The result was the same as when the monkey was trying to catch the moon." In other words, "the upward passage" is the Ch'an expression for the way leading to ultimate enlightenment.
22. A town east of Ch'ang-sha in Hunan Province.
23. This is the expression used by Ch'an Buddhists to indicate that our intellectual arguments lead to others, like a vine that never ends.
24. Chen Tsao was governor of Mu-chou at that time. He was a statesman and a Buddhist scholar, as was Pei Hsiu. See *The Lamp*, Chüan 12.
25. The *Diamond Sūtra* sets forth the doctrines of *śūnyatā*, emptiness, and *prajñā*, wisdom.
26. The Six Dynasties were the Wu, Eastern Chin, Sung, Ch'i, Liang, and Ch'ên. These dynasties had Chien-kang, now Nanking, as their capital.
27. The *Mahāparinirvāna Sūtra*, first translated into Chinese by Dharmaraksa in 423, advocated the doctrine that the *dharmakāya* is everlasting and that all human beings possess the Buddha-nature.
28. Ching-shan Hung-yen became the chief abbot in Ching Mountain in 865. Ching Mountain was located in Hangchow.
29. According to Ch'an monastery rules, the monks only eat two meals a day, breakfast and lunch. They have no third meal, but in the afternoon they eat some biscuits. Those who eat dinner at night are considered immoral.
30. In the T'ang Dynasty, Kiangsi was one of the centers for the study of Ch'an, where great masters such as Ma-tsu presided.
31. The doctrine of Vijñāptimātra, or Mere Ideation (Wei-shih in Chinese), originated in India as the Yogācāra School.
32. See above, note 19. Among the five commandments is "Do not tell a lie."
33. A practice meant to express piety and devotion. It was also a gesture of salutation.
34. The original text, *fu wei shang hsiang*, is the usual expression used as the last sentence in every eulogy. Because this is such a common expression, it does not have any particular meaning as used by Mu-chou.
35. See above, note 23.
36. According to *The Lamp*, Chüan 6, Fa-huei and Wei-chien were both abbots of Pê-t'an in Hung-chou, and both disciples of Mu-chou. Therefore either Fa-huei or Wei-chien can be referred to as Master Pê-t'an. We do not know to whom Mu-chou makes reference in this context.
37. *Huṁ* is the last syllable of *Oṁ-mani-padme-huṁ*, which is the Jewel in the Lotus, a mantra of Tantric Buddhism. It is interpreted as the *bodhi* of all Buddhas, with magical power when spoken.

NOTES

38. One of the large lakes of the Yangtze River valley in central China, in northern Hunan Province.

39. The character for *i* has five strokes and that for *pa* two strokes. There is, however, a partial resemblance between the two characters.

40. This indicates the fruits of cultivating Buddhahood: in other words, enlightenment, variously referred to as *bodhi, tathatā, nirvāna,* etc.

41. Now Chên-hsien, southwest of Peking in Hopeh Province.

42. Now Tsou-hsien, southwest of Chi-ning in Shantung Province.

43. Mu-chou Tao-tsung, or Chên Tsun-su, who later became a great master himself and enlightened Yün-mên Wên-yen.

44. Kao-an Ta-yü, a disciple of Kuei-tsung Chih-chang of Mount Lu.

45. By this he meant that he would induce all people to be quiet and listen to him.

46. This is where Bodhidharma was buried.

47. A sign of disapproval.

48. Lo-p'u Yuan-an of Li-chou, a disciple of Chia-shan Shan-hui. See *The Lamp,* Chüan 16.

49. Mu-kou's name was Hsing-shan Chien-hung. See *The Lamp,* Chüan 15.

50. "Open field" indicates the mind of purity which is free from thought and confusion. "White cow" indicates the absolute reality, free from defilement, which is achieved through pure contemplation.

51. Wei-fu Ta-chio, a disciple of Master Lin-chi. See *The Lamp,* Chüan 12.

52. The *fu-tzu* (Japanese *hossu*) was the pointer used by the ancient masters as they gave sermons or led discussions. It was a short staff of wood, bamboo, or jade, with a brush of long hair at one end. It was first called *chu-kwei* after the large deer from whose tail came the hair for the brush; *fu-tzu* refers to the horsehair from which the brush was later made.

53. The Buddhist monk unfolds his sitting cloth as a gesture of reverence toward his master.

54. In the text, Wu-chu, the name of a Buddhist, is often used for two different persons and causes confusion. One is the Chinese transliteration of Asaṅga (310–390), the elder brother of Vasubandhu in India. The other is a Chinese Ch'an master, Wu-chu Wen-hsi (820–899), who was famous in the south of China during Lin-chi's time. Because Asaṅga was the founder of the Yogācāra School, his teaching centers upon *vijña,* or consciousness, which requires differentiation. Subtle understanding cannot be grasped by this differentiation according to Ch'an. Therefore, the name Wu-chu may refer to Asaṅga. However, there was a well-known story concerning Wu-chu Wen-hsi, the Chinese Ch'an master in the south. When he visited Mount Wu-t'ai, he asked many questions and was lost by subtle Ch'an answers. In this case, perhaps Lin-chi refers to this popular story.

55. The monastery of San-sheng in Chang-chou, where Ch'an Master Hui-jan stayed. When he became known, he was called San-sheng after the monastery. He was a disciple of Lin-chi.

56. According to the *Blue Cliff Records, ch'ui-mao* is a sharp sword which is capable of cutting a hair in half when it is blown against the blade.

Part IV

Introduction
Illogical and Unconventional Approaches to Ch'an

KIANGSI TAO-I (709–788)
"The Mind Is the Buddha"

NAN-CH'ÜAN P'U-YÜAN (748–834)
"To Be a Buffalo Down the Hill"

CHAO-CHOU TS'UNG-SHEN (778–897)
"You See the Logs, But Not the Chao-chou Bridge"

P'ANG YÜN (?–811)
Inner Harmony in Daily Activity

Illogical and Unconventional Approaches to Ch'an

The teachings of Ch'an as given to us by Hui-nêng (638–713), the Sixth Patriarch, are concerned with *chien-hsin*, which we may translate as "seeing one's true nature." This approach to the problem of self-knowledge could be called an intuitive one, and in that respect it differs basically from those of his predecessors. Hui-nêng once said to the monk Ming, "Show me your original face, as it was before you were born." This approach, as we shall see, was not an intellectual one; we do not reveal our "original face" through a process of cogitation and analysis, or indeed at all through intellectual concepts. It is revealed, rather, through a direct intuition, a process which takes place instantaneously and of its own power. We can say of it that it is "consciousness which is conscious of itself," and that in a single moment of realization. It is quite different from the process of intellection. Our self-nature is to be apprehended in the midst of our daily activities. Ch'an is not the cessation of action, but rather penetration directly into action: it is thus that we fulfill the process of self-realization. This instantaneous act of realization disperses all confusions in a moment; it enables us to return to our self-nature, to achieve Buddhahood. We find this seemingly illogical and certainly unconventional theory in the teachings of Hui-nêng, but it was not developed fully until the time of Kiangsi Tao-i, known as Ma-tsu, grandson-in-dharma of Hui-nêng.

Enlightenment, according to the teachings of the Middle Way theorists, comes either by "transcending the four alternatives,"[1] or by the method of the "hundredfold negation."[2] But this approach is one of incessant negation which is essentially logical in its method and which can scarcely lead us to true enlightenment. The Mere-Ideation School criticized the method of transcending the four alternatives thus: Asserting being is false addition; denying being is false reduction; asserting both being and non-being is false contradiction; and the last, denying both being and non-being, is a joke.

Logical negation could not lead to enlightenment, so the Mere-Ideation School held, but neither could criticism of the negation achieve it. The instantaneous awakening that was sought could only be achieved through the attainment of *p'ien ch'ang hsin*, or everyday-mindedness, which is free from any taint of assertion or denial, purity or impurity, birth or death. It is the mutual identification of reality and appearance, sometimes called *tathatā*, or "suchness," which can only be reached through non-cultivation. In his *Dialogues* Ma-tsu says:

> Cultivation is of no use for the attainment of Tao. The only thing that one can do is to be free of defilement. When one's mind is stained with thoughts of life and death, or deliberate action, that is defilement. The grasping of the Truth is the function of everyday-mindedness. Everyday-mindedness is free from intentional action, free from concepts of right and wrong, taking and giving, the finite or the infinite. . . . All our daily activities—walking, standing, sitting, lying down—all response to situations, our dealings with circumstances as they arise: all this is Tao.

In this passage Ma-tsu attempts to lead his disciples beyond intellectual understanding, beyond the limitations of concentration and contemplation.

Illogical and Unconventional Approaches to Ch'an

When Ma-tsu dwelt at Mount Heng he sat in meditation day after day. Master Huai-jang (677–744) came to see him, and asked him what it was he sought through meditation. Ma-tsu replied that he wished to achieve Buddhahood; whereupon Huai-jang took a piece of brick and began grinding it against a stone. When Ma-tsu asked why he ground the brick thus, Huai-jang answered that he was planning to make it into a mirror. Ma-tsu, surprised, demanded, "How can you ever make a brick into a mirror by polishing it?" Huai-jang in turn asked, "How can you ever achieve Buddhahood through meditation?"

What Huai-jang meant was that Tao cannot be achieved through cultivation. Artificial cultivation defiles the mind instead of cleansing it. Ma-tsu learned this from Huai-jang and exemplified it through his own experience, developing various methods other than meditation for the teaching of Ch'an.

The Ch'an masters, above all others in the history of Chinese philosophical teaching, are distinguished for their use of unconventional methods. One of these is referred to by the word "Ho!" a cry which is used to awaken the earnest devotee. Lin-chi I-hsüan was especially famous for developing the "Ho!" method into an effective and systematic tool, though we may well say that it was primarily an invention of Ma-tsu. For example, once when his disciple Po-chang Huai-hai approached him, Ma-tsu picked up the *fu-tzu* beside his seat and held it up. Po-chang asked, "At the very moment of this action, should you not be non-attached to it?" Ma-tsu put the *fu-tzu* back where it had been. Po-chang was silent for a moment. "You may open your mouth and go on talking," said Ma-tsu, "but what will make you an enlightened man?" Po-chang took the *fu-tzu* and held it up, and Ma-tsu asked him, "At the very moment of this action, should you not be non-attached to it?" As Po-chang put the *fu-tzu* back, Ma-tsu suddenly cried out "Ho!" so loudly that Po-chang was deaf for the next three days.

The thunderous exclamation achieves an effect opposite from that which is attained through intellectual disputation. This forceful approach is often used to awaken the mind of a devotee who

Illogical and Unconventional Approaches to Ch'an

is ready for enlightenment. After Ma-tsu, his followers Huang-po Hsi-yün, Mu-chou Tao-tsung, Lin-chi I-hsüan, and many others adopted "Ho!" for the purposes of mind-opening. Lin-chi ingeniously refined the "Ho" method into four types of application. Sometimes it was like a piercing sword. At other times it was like a lion crouching in front of you. Sometimes it was used as a sounding rod, testing the depth of a learner's understanding, and sometimes it was used without any specific purpose. "Ho!" is the manifestation of what is in one's mind. Whether it is sharp like a sword, forceful like a lion, or useful as a testing rod, it is in each case the expression of one's inner state. In the century following Lin-chi, Yün-mên Wên-yen replaced "Ho!" with "Kwan!" as the exclamatory utterance in Ch'an instruction.

In his teachings, Ma-tsu used any means at hand to open the minds of his disciples. One day when he was walking with Po-chang, a flock of wild geese flew overhead. Ma-tsu asked Po-chang, "What is there?" "Wild geese, Master." "Where are they now?" "They have flown away." Ma-tsu seized Po-chang's nose and gave it a violent twist, so that Po-chang cried out in pain. The Master said, "How could you say that the wild geese have flown away? They have been here from the very beginning." Hearing this, Po-chang was awakened to the Truth.

Po-chang's awakening took place after three years of devotion to Ch'an under Master Ma-tsu. His readiness for enlightenment was very well perceived by Ma-tsu. In ordinary conversation, when geese fly away and one says so, there is no mistake involved. But to the enlightened mind the fact that they have flown away is immaterial, since they have been there from the very first. To say that the geese have flown away is to work on the intellectual level, to apply simple logic. But this very use of intellectual logic is ignorance to the Buddhist; to rely upon this method of apprehension is to block one's inner light.

Intellectual and logical answers were conceived by Tung-shan Shou-ch'u as "dead words"; the irrelevant and illogical answers, on the other hand, were "living words." When Tung-shan first came to Master Yün-mên Wên-yen, the Master asked him where he had come from and his answer was, "From Ch'a-tu, sir!" Then the Master asked him where he had been during the summer, and he replied, "I have been in Pao-tzu Monastery in Hunan." The Master asked him when he had left there. He replied, "In the eighth month of last year." All these answers were straightforward and logical, but Master Yün-mên said to Tung-shan, "I absolve you from thirty blows." This was because the answers revealed no Ch'an; they were "dead words."

However, when Tung-shan became the abbot in Hsiang-chou and a monk asked him, "What is the duty of a Ch'an monk?" his answer was, "When the clouds envelop the top of Mount Ch'u, there must be a heavy rainstorm." This reply is quite different from the kind of answer Tung-shan had given to his master Yün-mên when he first arrived. The duty of Ch'an has nothing to do with the clouds enveloping Mount Ch'u, nor has it any relationship to the rainstorm. Yet these are "living words" in the teaching of Ch'an. The logical answers Po-chang gave to Master Ma-tsu proved that he was still immersed in the realm of "dead words." The Master twisted his nose to make him aware of his shortcomings.

Ma-tsu taught not only through the "Ho" method and by such devices as twisting the nose, but also originated the striking method, which Tê-shan Hsüan-chien and other masters often applied. When a monk asked Master Ma-tsu, "What is the meaning of Bodhidharma coming from the West?" the Master struck him, saying, "If I do not strike you, people all over the country will laugh at me." To teach Ch'an through the "strike" became a very popular practice among later masters. The most noted expert on strike teaching was Tê-shan Hsüan-chien. Once he came to the assembly hall and said, "If you say a word, you will get thirty blows. If you do not say a word, you will get the same thirty blows across the top of your head." This is similar to the mind-awakening of Lin-chi I-hsüan, who went three times to ask the meaning of Buddhism from his master Huang-po Hsi-yün, and on each occasion received blows for an answer. Finally, with the help of Ta-yü, he realized the meaning of these blows. To search outwardly for the meaning of Buddhism, to look for non-attachment from the outside, is entirely wrong. The Buddha-nature is found within. One only needs to realize that this is so. There is nothing more or less involved in the process of self-realization. Those who ask for the meaning of Buddhism all receive thirty blows.

Ma-tsu's teaching of Ch'an, besides the aspects stated above, took various other forms. When Shui-liao asked him the meaning of Bodhidharma coming to China, the Master kicked him in the chest, knocking him to the ground. This startling response suddenly awakened Shui-liao to the Truth. He rose from the ground laughing and clapping his hands, and shouted, "It is strange indeed! It is strange indeed! Numerous *samādhi* and all subtle truths are revealed in the tip of a single hair—it is thus that I have suddenly realized the Source!" He made a deep bow and departed. Later one of the monks made a poem about this incident:

> Receiving the transmission from Ma-tsu, Shui-liao grasps his teaching thoroughly.
> Just one kick from the Master leads him to the Source.
> The mere emptiness that once was an idle land is shattered.
> The iron boat sails directly into the Ocean of the Infinite.

What Shui-liao had grasped was the capacity to penetrate deeply into his innermost being. His awakened insight led him into the Truth, as though an "iron boat" were sailing into the World of the Infinite. Thus Ma-tsu's kick was an expression of the great action.

We find another innovation in the teachings of Ma-tsu which was frequently applied by the later masters. A lecturing monk named Liang of Szechwan came to visit Ma-tsu. During their interview Ma-tsu told him that his lectures on the sūtras could not lead to enlightenment. At this, the visitor left Ma-tsu and walked down the steps. Ma-tsu called his name, and the monk turned his head. Ma-tsu asked, "What is it?" Thereupon Liang was suddenly enlightened. When he went back to his own temple he had this to say: "I thought that my lectures on the sūtras were a supreme achievement, one that no one could match, but with Ma-tsu's question all that I had achieved in my lifetime melted away like ice."

Calling someone by name at the moment of his leaving may

awaken the initial consciousness that is called *yeh-shih*. It is from this initial consciousness that one is opened up to enlightenment. Nan-ch'üan P'u-yüan, Chao-chou Ts'ung-shen, Kuei-shan Ling-yu, Yün-mên Wên-yen, and many others often used this method for opening the minds of earnest seekers. Ma-tsu, however, is the earliest master in Ch'an literature to have used this unconventional means of awakening men. He also made extensive use of the technique of irrelevant responses to questions. All of his methods were further developed by his followers.

Of the more than 130 disciples who spread the teaching of Ch'an all over China, Nan-ch'üan P'u-yüan (748–834) was one of the finest and most famous. Once Nan-ch'üan, Hsi-t'ang (Chih-tsang), and Po-chang (Huai-hai) accompanied Master Ma-tsu on a stroll in the moonlight. Suddenly the Master said, "At this moment, what do you think you should do?" Chih-tsang gave the first answer, saying, "At this moment, one should take this opportunity to study the sūtras." Huai-hai said, "I should like to say that it would be the best time for meditation." Hearing these answers, Nan-ch'üan turned and left the group. Then the Master said, "As for the sūtras, I leave them to Chih-tsang. As for meditation, Huai-hai could do it well. But P'u-yüan transcends all these externals." Nan-ch'üan's later teaching of Ch'an was indeed of the finest.

Under the guidance of Nan-ch'üan P'u-yüan, Chao-chou Ts'ung-shen and Ch'ang-sha Ching-ch'en became noted masters in the history of Ch'an. Nan-ch'üan also taught Lu Hsüan, a lay disciple who was the Governor of Hsüan-chou. Once Lu Hsüan felt that he did not understand what Sêng-chao (394–414) meant when he said that all things share the same root and that consequently right and wrong are one and the same. Nan-ch'üan pointed to the peony blossoms in the courtyard and said, "Governor, when people of the present day see these blossoms, it is as if they see them in a dream." A comment in the *Blue Cliff Records* says that this vivid kind of teaching is like pushing a man off a ten-thousand-foot cliff—he loses his life immediately. But "to lose one's life" here means to drop one's burden of ignorance and enter into the new world of understanding that is Ch'an. This *kung-an* was dis-

Illogical and Unconventional Approaches to Ch'an

cussed in the *Blue Cliff Records*, but it was not fully understood by later Ch'an students. Once when Fa-ch'ang I-yü and his head monk were repairing a flower stand in the garden, they conversed in this fashion:

Master Fa-ch'ang: "How do you interpret Nan-ch'üan's saying that the people of the present day see the peony blossoms as if in a dream?"

Head monk: "Nan-ch'üan simply spoke of the non-existence of flowers."

Fa-ch'ang: "Your answer shows that you are still a captive of Nan-ch'üan."

Head monk: "Then what did Nan-ch'üan really mean?"

Fa-ch'ang: "Pass me a brick."

The head monk did pass a brick to the Master, but he still did not understand that this was the Master's answer and put his question again.

Fa-ch'ang sighed: "The ancient Buddha [Nan-ch'üan] passed away long ago."

What Master Fa-ch'ang meant here was that the answer should be sought by the head monk in his own inner experience and that it was something which could not possibly be expressed in words. In fact, Fa-ch'ang's answer, like that of Nan-ch'üan, was intended to push his listener off the "ten-thousand-foot cliff."

There is another *kung-an* through which Lu Hsüan was finally awakened by Nan-ch'üan. One day Lu Hsüan said to Master Nan-ch'üan, "A man raised a goose in a bottle. As the goose grew bigger, the man realized that he could not get it out of the bottle without killing it. He did not want to break the bottle or kill the goose. What would you do, Master?" Nan-ch'üan immediately cried out, "Oh! Governor!" "Yes, Master?" Then Nan-ch'üan said, "It is out!" At this the Governor was awakened. Ch'an cannot be achieved by the calculating mind. When a man is trapped in calculating intellection, it is not the goose that needs to get out of the bottle but the man himself. When Lu Hsüan realized that the dilemma originated in his own mind, it vanished and he was out of the bottle of confusion.

Another *kung-an* concerning Nan-ch'üan may help us to understand better his teaching of Ch'an and the importance of freedom from intellectual reasoning. When Tao-wu visited Nan-ch'üan, the Master asked him, "What is your name?" Tao-wu replied, "My name is Tsung-chih." (*Tsung* means devotion and *chih* means wisdom. *Tsung-chih* therefore means devotion to wisdom.) Nan-ch'üan continued, "When wisdom does not reach it, what do you do?" Tao-wu said, "We should not talk about it." Nan-ch'üan remarked, "Apparently, you are doing the talking, and horns will grow on your head." Three days later, when Tao-wu and Yün-yen were mending their clothes, Nan-ch'üan came upon them and asked, "The other day I said that that which cannot be reached by wisdom should not be talked about. What, then, would you do?" As soon as Tao-wu heard this he left the group and went to the hall. When Nan-ch'üan left, Yün-yen went to Tao-wu and asked, "Why did you not answer the Master a moment ago?" Tao-wu replied, "What a clever man you are!" Yün-yen did not understand this either and went to Nan-ch'üan and asked him, "Why should a brother monk not answer you?" Nan-ch'üan said, "It is because that is the way to walk in the path of other [non-human] beings." Yün-yen asked, "What is this path of other beings?" Nan-ch'üan answered, "Do you realize that that which cannot be reached by wisdom should not be talked about? If one speaks of it, horns will grow on one's head. What one really should do is walk immediately in the path of other beings." Hearing this, Yün-yen was lost and did not grasp what the Master meant.

Tao-wu, seeing that Yün-yen had such difficulty understanding him, advised Yün-yen to go back to see his own master, Yüeh-shan. As soon as he reached Yüeh-shan, Yün-yen asked him, "What is it to walk in the path of other beings?" Master Yüeh-shan replied, "I am tired today. Come see me some other time." To this Yün-yen said, "But I have come all the way from Nan-ch'üan to see you, Master!" However, Yüeh-shan sent him away. Tao-wu, who was waiting outside, asked Yün-yen, "How did the Master answer you?" Yün-yen answered, "He did not want to tell me."

Later, when both monks had returned to Master Yüeh-shan, the

Master repeated the words of Nan-ch'üan: "That which cannot be reached by wisdom should not be talked about. If one speaks of it, horns will grow on one's head." When Tao-wu heard this, he made a bow and left the Master. Yün-yen asked the Master, "Why should brother Tao-wu not reply to you, sir?" Yüeh-shan said, "My back pains me today. Tao-wu understood me. Go and ask him." But when Yün-yen returned to Tao-wu, Tao-wu said, "I have a headache today. You had better go back to the Master."

Yün-yen himself later became one of the leading masters of Ch'an. But before he was enlightened he beat quite a path between the Master and his brother monk in search of the Truth. Each wanted to help him, but neither could tell him the answer in the way that he sought it. In fact, not telling him was a way of helping him. Of this, Hsiang-yen Chih-hsien, a disciple of Kuei-shan, said at a memorial service for his master, "I praise him not for his moral conduct but because he did not tell me anything." Ch'an can be revealed only through one's inner experience. Even one's master or one's best friend cannot help.

The approach of tossing a seeker of Ch'an between the master and other enlightened brothers was first applied by Ma-tsu. The purpose of this, too, is to help the seeker to be awakened through self-realization. What Yün-yen experienced had its roots in the teachings of Ma-tsu. The following *kung-an* is a familiar one. One day a monk asked Master Ma-tsu what the real meaning was of Bodhidharma coming from the West. The Master told him he was tired and sent the man to see his brother monk Chih-tsang and ask him. When the monk came to Chih-tsang, he was told to go and see another brother, Huai-hai, because Chih-tsang had a headache. But Huai-hai advised him to return to seek the answer from the Master. The Master finally said to him, "Chih-tsang's hair is white and Huai-hai's is black." The color of one's brother monks' hair has nothing to do with one's enlightenment. What is important is the realization that enlightenment comes from within one's own mind, and that it is thus that one's mind is opened. There is nothing that one can seek from the outside.

One of the methods used by Nan-ch'üan but not found in the records of Ma-tsu's teaching is that of leaving the questioner alone without saying anything. This occurred, for example, when Nan-ch'üan was attending Master Ma-tsu along with Huai-hai and Chih-tsang in the incident related above. After Huai-hai and Chih-tsang had each given his opinion, Nan-ch'üan left the group without saying a word.

On another occasion, Chao-chou asked Nan-ch'üan, "Please tell me what it is that goes beyond the four alternatives and the hundredfold negations." Nan-ch'üan made no answer but went to his room. This method of "answering without words" was also applied by Chao-chou himself, who once answered a statement of Nan-ch'üan's by bowing and leaving his master, showing by this action that he understood Nan-ch'üan's idea. Subjectively, Chao-chou's mind was full of the Truth, and objectively, it was communing with another mind which had had this same experience.

Chao-chou Ts'ung-shen, one of the best disciples of Nan-ch'üan, came to be known as one of the great masters of Ch'an. He lived to a great old age, in fact, to the age of 120 years. He did not establish a distinctive school, but his teachings were unique, as was his personal style. He did not use a stick to give his questioners thirty blows, nor did he awaken their minds by the use of the exclamatory "Ho!" His words were always plain and ordinary, words used by common people in their everyday activities. In his dialogues we rarely find the sharp exchanges that occur in the dialogues of Yün-mên Wên-yen, nor the extremely forceful rebukes such as were uttered by Lin-chi I-hsüan. It was through very simple talk, effortless and unornamented, that he revealed his spiritual understanding and transmitted it to his devotees. Many of his sayings became classics and were used by later teachers of Ch'an.

Chao-chou's methods were greatly influenced by Ma-tsu and by Nan-ch'üan P'u-yüan. Once when Chao-chou was still a disciple of Nan-ch'üan, he asked his master for the real meaning of Ch'an. The Master pointed out to him that everyday-mindedness is Ch'an. Chao-chou then asked if it were possible to approach it. Nan-ch'üan answered, "If you approach it, you will miss it, but when one has really attained it without intention, one is as if in a great void, free from obstructions and limitations."

This non-intentional approach, free from assertion and negation, was applied later on by Chao-chou to his own disciples. Once a monk questioned Chao-chou about Ch'an, and Chao-chou awakened him in the following fashion. "Have you finished your rice gruel?" Chao-chou asked. "Yes, I have finished it," the monk replied. "Then go and wash your dishes," said Chao-chou.

This simple activity of the Ch'an monk, washing the dishes after eating gruel, is the most ordinary thing, the sort of activity that is completely spontaneous and requires no mental effort. While engaged in it, a man is free from assertion and negation. When one reaches this state of mind, one's inner power meets with no obstructions or limitations, and it was thus that the mind of Chao-chou's disciple was awakened.

Another time Chao-chou was asked, "Since all things return to One, where does this One return to?" His reply was, "When I was in Tsing-chou I had a robe made which weighed seven *chin*." This *kung-an* became famous and was used many times by later masters in their efforts to answer the question, "Where does the One return to?" Many students of this *kung-an* tried to reason out some answer in terms of the weight of the robe and in the relationship between Chao-chou and the town of Tsing-chou, but it was precisely this sort of intellectual interpretation that Chao-chou most wanted to avoid. To attain Ch'an one should be absolutely free from thought and merely respond to questions without deliberation. Chao-chou's answer simply reflected what was in his mind at that moment—indeed an effortless answer, without artificiality or intentional skill.

Once, when asked what the famous stone bridge of Chao-chou was, he replied, "Horses pass over it, donkeys pass over it." Again, when a disciple was going to see Hsüeh-fêng I-ts'un and asked him what he should say, Chao-chou told him, "When it is winter, speak cold; when it is summer, speak hot." Animals passing over a bridge, people talking about the weather—these are statements of everyday-mindedness. When a later master, Pao-tzu Wên-ch'i, commented on the teachings of everyday-mindedness as originated by Ma-tsu and handed down from Nan-ch'üan to Chao-chou, he sang:

ILLOGICAL AND UNCONVENTIONAL APPROACHES TO CH'AN

Drinking tea, eating rice,
I pass my time as it comes;
Looking down at the stream,
Looking up at the mountain,
How serene and relaxed I feel indeed!

Drinking tea, eating rice, looking at the stream and the mountain: all are as commonplace as Chao-chou's seven-*chin* robe, the stone bridge, the dishwashing, winter and summer, and many other such answers recorded in this fascicle. They are simple, free, and spontaneous.

Once Chao-chou asked his master, Nan-ch'üan, "Where should one rest after one has attained Tao [Ch'an]?" "One should become a buffalo down the hill," was Nan-ch'üan's answer. Chao-chou bowed deeply. Thereupon Nan-ch'üan remarked, "In the middle of last night the moonlight shone on the window." In the *Ch'an-lin Lei-chu*, or *Collection and Classification of Ch'an Materials*, we have this poem:

What our eyes see is "ordinary."
It does not frighten people,
But it always remains
Like the moonlight on the chilled window;
Even in the middle of the night it shines upon thatched
  cottages.

We must not be misled into thinking that references to the buffalo down the hill or moonlight on the windows limit us to what is plain and ordinary. Rather, it is through such directness and spontaneity that the "great function," so often stressed by the Ch'an Buddhists, takes place. When we look at the famous painting of six persimmons attributed to Mu-ch'i, now preserved in the Daitokuji Temple in Kyoto, we are enchanted by the clarity of vision of this great Chinese painter of the thirteenth century. These six contours, naive and unelaborated, reveal the wisdom of the artist. What is true of Mu-ch'i's brushwork is likewise true of Chao-chou's answers. The "seven-*chin* robe," "the cypress tree in the courtyard," "the clay statues in the hall"—all of these manifest the

Illogical and Unconventional Approaches to Ch'an

great potentiality of Chao-chou. If we feel joy when we look at the brushwork of a master of Chinese art, we can certainly derive a similar joy from concentrating on a *kung-an* of Chao-chou. Perhaps his own statement concerning his application of simple words in *kung-an* can give us a clearer understanding:

> It is as if a transparent crystal were held in one's hand. When a foreigner approaches it, it reflects him as such; when a native Chinese approaches it, it reflects him as such. I take a stalk of grass and let it act as a golden-bodied one, sixteen feet high, and I take a golden-bodied one, sixteen feet high, and let it act as a stalk of grass.

Thus the seven-*chin* robe, the cypress tree, and the others act, for Ch'an Buddhists, as does the stalk of grass identified with the Buddha's image sixteen feet high.

In the fascicle of Chao-chou we also see his progress to higher and higher levels of attainment through the study of Ch'an. When he was interviewed for the first time by Master Nan-ch'üan, the latter asked him, "Are you your own master or not?" Chao-chou answered, "In the middle of the winter the weather becomes bitterly cold. I wish all blessings on you, sir!" By his greeting Chao-chou indirectly revealed to Nan-ch'üan the greatness of his inner reality and his capacity as a student of Ch'an. Some years later, Kuei-shan Ling-yu put the same question to his newly arrived disciple Yang-shan Hui-chi, who made his answer by pacing from the west side of the hall to the east, and standing there mutely. His silent pacing, like Chao-chou's greeting, revealed his understanding of Ch'an.

These answers, however, merely illustrate an initial stage of understanding and training. Chao-chou's inward cultivation was not a static thing but a constant movement, gradually proceeding to higher and higher levels. Let us look now at a further stage in his progress. When Chao-chou went to visit Master Huang-po, the latter saw him coming and at once closed his door. Thereupon Chao-chou lit a torch in the hall and cried for help. Huang-po opened the door and grabbed him, saying, "Speak! Speak! What is it?" Chao-chou replied, "After the thief is gone, you draw your

Illogical and Unconventional Approaches to Ch'an

bow!" Huang-po closed the door to indicate to Chao-chou that the truth of Buddhism cannot be told. There was nothing that he could profitably discuss with his visitor. Chao-chou, however, understood this. He wanted to let Huang-po in turn know that one must not remain in the Void but must return from it, so he lit a fire to make Huang-po open his door. Huang-po understood this action, but wanted to make Chao-chou speak to find out if he understood correctly. However, Chao-chou's understanding went far beyond this —the demand for an explanation came much too late: "After the thief is gone, you draw your bow!" This interplay between Huang-po and Chao-chou is a good example of the working of immediate intuition; the same results could not have been generated by discursive thinking. Their responses to one another were "swift as thunder and lightning." This *kung-an* shows that through his inner experience Chao-chou had reached a higher level of understanding of Ch'an.

In the Nan-ch'üan fascicle in *The Lamp* we find this interesting illustration. Once Master Nan-ch'üan said, "Last night I gave Mañjuśrī and Samantabhadra twenty blows each and chased them out of my temple." Chao-chou asked him, "To whom have you given twenty blows?" Nan-ch'üan answered, "Could you tell me where I made a mistake?" Chao-chou bowed and left him. Nan-ch'üan had let his disciple know that in the search for the Truth one must not allow oneself to become attached even to Buddhism itself. This is exactly what the Ch'an masters often expressed in the following way: "When you meet the Buddha, kill the Buddha; when you meet the Patriarch, kill the Patriarch." When one enters the world of absolute truth, one must emerge again. Yet even in the thought of entering and coming out again, there is still the taint of attachment. One must be free from both, and it was thus that Chao-chou made a bow and left his master. In that moment, he reached a level far beyond the achievement of entering in or going out; he had reached that level which, until that moment, had been his master's concern.

Those who savor the flavor of fine wines often save them for many years. The longer some wines are preserved, the finer becomes

Illogical and Unconventional Approaches to Ch'an

their taste. It is at once milder and of greater quality. It is thus with the teachings of Chao-chou. Often his words seem very plain to us, certainly not strong in taste, but in reality they are of the highest quality. The more we drink of them, the greater is our joy.

In the history of Chinese Ch'an, there are a number of lay Buddhists who attained to great fame and whose words are worthy of perusal. Two figures of the early T'ang Dynasty especially deserve study: Wang Wei (699–759) and P'ang Yün (d. 811).

Wang Wei was a contemporary of Nan-yang Hui-chung, Shih-t'ou Hsi-ch'ien, and Ma-tsu Tao-i. From his full name we know that he was deeply devoted to Buddhism: to his formal name, Wei, he added the courtesy name Mu-chi; together these form the Chinese transliteration of the Sanskrit Vimalakīrti, the name of an Indian lay Buddhist and friend of Śākyamuni. However, Wang Wei's real achievement was in poetry and painting, and we find in his works a splendid reflection of his inner cultivation. Indeed, he is known for his beautiful lyric poetry rather than for his achievements in Ch'an, but his mastery of the latter was also remarkable. The beginning of his inscription for the Sixth Patriarch's biographical account indicates the depth of his understanding of Hui-nêng's Ch'an teaching:

> When there is nothing to give up
> One has indeed reached the Source.
> When there is no void to abide in
> One is indeed experiencing the Void.
> Transcending quiescence is no-action.
> Rather it is Creation, which constantly acts.

We also find applications of the *kung-an* theory in Wang Wei's poetry. There is an example in the last two lines of the verses entitled "Reply to the Court Valet Chang":

> You ask me to explain the reason for failure
>   or success.
> The fisherman's song goes deep into the river.

This, in fact, may well be the earliest example of the use of Ch'an *kung-an* techniques in Chinese poetry.

Illogical and Unconventional Approaches to Ch'an

P'ang Yün lived a few decades after Wang Wei. He studied under both Shih-t'ou Hsi-ch'ien and Ma-tsu, and was also a very close friend of Tan-hsia T'ien-jan. P'ang Yün maintained the doctrine of everyday-mindedness—*ping ch'ang hsin*—and was a follower of Ma-tsu's teachings. His assertion that "In the carrying of water and the chopping of wood—therein lies the Tao," is often referred to in Ch'an literature. The truth of Tao, or Ch'an, however, is ultimately inexpressible. Therefore when Shih-t'ou Hsi-ch'ien asked him, "What is the daily activity?" P'ang Yün answered him, "If you ask about my daily activity, I cannot even open my mouth." Daily activity is *ping ch'ang hsin*, which is inexpressible.

In the *Dialogue of P'ang Yün* and the *Records of Pointing at the Moon* we find that P'ang Yün and his wife had a son and daughter, and that the whole family were devoted to Ch'an. One day P'ang Yün, sitting quietly in his temple, made this remark:

"How difficult it is!
How difficult it is!
My studies are like drying the fibers of a thousand pounds
  of flax in the sun by hanging them on the trees!"

But his wife responded:

"My way is easy indeed!
I found the teachings of the Patriarchs right on the tops of
  the flowering plants!"

When their daughter overheard this exchange, she sang:

"My study is neither difficult nor easy.
When I am hungry I eat,
When I am tired I rest."

In the discussion above, one member of the family takes the position of affirmation, another the position of negation, and the third the position of the Middle Way. Although their approaches differ, all reflect upon no-birth, which is the same as *wu*, or the Void. This represents an application of the teachings of Mādhyamika, the Middle Way.

The dialogues between P'ang Yün and his daughter, Ling-chao,

Illogical and Unconventional Approaches to Ch'an are recorded in the *Records of Pointing at the Moon*. We find here one particular *kung-an* which characterizes the teachings of Ch'an:

P'ang Yün: "What do you say to the ancients' statement that the teachings of the Patriarchs are right on the tops of the flowering plants?"

Ling-chao: "A fine one you are, uttering such words!"

P'ang Yün: "What should I say?"

Ling-chao: "The teachings of the Patriarchs are right on the tops of the flowering plants."

When the father heard this, he was very well pleased. This type of *kung-an*, which repeats the questioner's words after first rejecting them, was adopted by the later Ch'an masters. As we see, such an exchange does not contain any intellectual reasoning, but simply reveals a sense of inner experience. Rejection of a statement does not imply that it is incorrect in any intellectual sense. Rather, when the purpose is to reveal one's inner experience, one should free oneself from the limitations of logic and discursive reasoning.

Once Tan-hsia T'ien-jan, P'ang Yün's good friend, went to visit him and found Ling-chao outside the house. Tan-hsia asked, "Is your father in?" Ling-chao laid down her basket and folded her hands together. Tan-hsia asked again, "Is your father in?" Lin-chao picked up the basket and immediately left him.

The real answer here is not in words but in Ling-chao's apparently irrelevant gestures. Those who share her inexpressible experience will understand this sort of implicit communication.

Once P'ang Yün came upon Chê-chuan picking tea leaves:

P'ang Yün: "Nobody can be contained in the world of Dharma. Do you still see me?"

Chê-chuan: "I am not your teacher. Why should I answer you?"

P'ang Yün asked his question several times, but Chê-chuan remained silent. Finally, as P'ang Yün grew insistent, Chê-chuan laid down his basket and went to his room.

We must understand that Chê-chuan was not being rude; he was simply revealing his inner experience. He gave a true answer to P'ang Yün's question in his actions. As we have seen, Nan-ch'üan and Chao-chou also often gave this sort of response to their questioners.

Once Shih-lin, lifting the *fu-tzu*, said, "Say a word, but do not fall into Tan-hsia's way!" P'ang Yün seized the *fu-tzu* from Shih-lin's hand.

Shih-lin: "This is Tan-hsia's way."

P'ang Yün: "Then say something that is not Tan-hsia's way."

Shih-lin: "Tan-hsia is dumb and P'ang Yün is deaf."

P'ang Yün: "Exactly so! Exactly so!"

Shih-lin was silent.

P'ang Yün: "What you have said happens to be correct."

Shih-lin still kept his silence.

When a Ch'an Buddhist abides in silence his inner nature is in harmony with the Ultimate Reality. His silence expresses the power of living nothingness. Silences in ordinary converse are silences in the relative sense; they are a dead stillness, which is quite the opposite of what silence is in Ch'an. Unless one's silence transcends both words and stillness, one's answer will not be correct at all. All of the leading Ch'an masters who answered questions with silence had in common this highest level of inner awareness. As absolute Emptiness, or *śūnyatā*, cannot be understood as dead nothingness, so the real meaning of silence is not truly silent at all. When we grasp the truth of this, we can understand the teachings of Ch'an as they are recorded in the following fascicles.

KIANGSI TAO-I
(709–788)

"The Mind Is the Buddha"

(*From* The Transmission of the Lamp, *Chüan* 6)

CH'AN Master Tao-i* of Kiangsi was a native of Shih-fang in the district of Han-chou.³ His original surname was Ma. In appearance and bearing he was most striking. He glared as a tiger does and ambled like a cow. He could touch his nose with his tongue, and on the soles of his feet were wheel-shaped marks.⁴ As a child he went to Tzu-chou and had his head shaved by Master T'ang. Subsequently he was ordained by the Vinaya master Yüan of Yü-chou.⁵

During the period of K'ai-yüan [713–741] he studied the *dhyāna* in the Monastery of Ch'uan-fa on Heng Mountain.⁶ It was there that he studied under Master Huai-jang, who then had nine disciples. Of these only Tao-i received the sacred mind-seal.⁷

Later he moved from Fu-chi-ling of Chien-yang⁸ to Lin-ch'uan,⁹ and then to the Kung-kung Mountain in Nan-k'ang.¹⁰ In the middle of the Ta-li period [766–779], while he was in the Monastery of K'ai-yüan, the Governor of Lu Szu-kung heard of him and admired

---

* Popularly known in both Eastern and Western literature as Ma-tsu, which means Patriarch Ma.

his spirit and teachings so deeply that he came to receive the Dharma personally from him. From that time on disciples traveled from all parts of the country to study under the Master.

One day the Master spoke to his assembly as follows: "All of you should realize that your own mind is Buddha, that is, this mind is Buddha's Mind. The great master Bodhidharma came from India to China to transmit the Mahāyāna Buddhist doctrine of the One Mind in order to enlighten us all. He used the texts of the *Laṅkāvatāra Sūtra* to prove the presence of the Mind in all beings. He thought that people might become confused and cease believing that within each of them this mind is innate. Therefore he quoted the *Laṅkāvatāra*: 'Buddha teaches that the Mind is the source of all existence, and that the method of Dharma is no-method.'"

The Master continued: "Those who seek for the Truth should realize that there is nothing to seek. There is no Buddha but Mind; there is no Mind but Buddha. Do not choose what is good, nor reject what is evil, but rather be free from purity and defilement. Then you will realize the emptiness of sin. Thoughts perpetually change and cannot be grasped because they possess no self-nature. The Triple World is nothing more than one's mind. The multitudinous universe is nothing but the testimony of one Dharma. What are seen as forms are the reflections of the mind. The mind does not exist by itself; its existence is manifested through forms. Whenever you speak about Mind you must realize that appearance and reality are perfectly interfused without impediment. This is what the achievement of *bodhi* is. That which is produced by Mind is called form. When you understand that forms are non-existent, then that which is birth is also no-birth. If you are aware of this mind, you will dress, eat, and act spontaneously in life as it transpires, and thereby cultivate your spiritual nature. There is nothing more that I can teach you. Please listen to my *gāthā*:

Anytime you wish to speak about Mind, speak!
In this way, *bodhi* is tranquil.
When appearance and reality are perfectly interfused without
    impediment,
Birth is simultaneously no-birth.

Illogical and Unconventional Approaches to Ch'an

A monk asked why the Master maintained, "The Mind is the Buddha." The Master answered, "Because I want to stop the crying of a baby." The monk persisted, "When the crying has stopped, what is it then?" "Not Mind, not Buddha," was the answer. "How do you teach a man who does not uphold either of these?" The Master said, "I would tell him, 'Not things.'" The monk again questioned, "If you met a man free from attachment to all things, what would you tell him?" The Master replied, "I would let him experience the Great Tao."

Another time a monk asked, "What was the meaning of Bodhidharma coming from the West?" "What is the meaning [of your asking] at this moment?" replied the Master.

A lay disciple, P'ang Yün, asked, "How is it possible that water without muscle or bones supports a vessel of ten thousand tons?" The Master replied, "There is neither water nor a vessel. Why are you talking about muscle and bone?"

One day the Master came to the assembly and kept silent for quite a while.[11] Po-chang rolled up the mat in front of his seat. Thereupon the Master left the assembly hall.

Po-chang once asked, "What is the meaning of Buddha's teaching?" The Master replied, "It is that upon which your life depends." When Po-chang was asked by the Master how he would teach Ch'an, he held up the *fu-tzu*. The Master further asked, "Is that all? Anything further?" Thereupon Po-chang put down the *fu-tzu*.

On another occasion a monk asked, "What can I do to be in accord with Tao?" The Master answered, "I have not been in accord with Tao."

A monk asked, "What is the meaning of Bodhidharma coming from the West?" The Master struck him, saying, "If I do not strike you, people all over the country will laugh at me."

After traveling far on foot a disciple returned to the Master and drew a circle on the ground in front of him. Then he stepped into the circle, made a bow, and stood quite still. The Master asked him, "Do you intend to be a Buddha?" "I do not know how to press my eyes."[12] The Master answered, "I am not as good as you are." The disciple made no further remark.

Têng Yin-fêng, another disciple, came to bid the Master goodbye. The Master asked him where he was going. He said that he was going to see Shih-t'ou [Master Hsi-ch'ien; *shih-t'ou* means "stone"]. Ma-tsu said, "Shih-t'ou is slippery." Têng Yin-fêng answered, "I am fully equipped with juggling instruments[13] which I can play with at any time." When he arrived at his destination he walked around the seat of Master Shih-t'ou once, shook his stick, and demanded, "What does this mean?" Shih-t'ou exclaimed, "Good heavens! Good heavens!" Têng Yin-fêng said nothing more, but returned home and reported this to Master Ma-tsu. The Master told him that he should go back to see Shih-t'ou and, if he should say "Good Heavens!" again, then Têng Yin-fêng should puff and whisper twice. Têng Yin-fêng returned to Shih-t'ou. He repeated what he had done before and asked again, "What does this mean?" Whereupon Shih-t'ou puffed and whispered twice. Têng Yin-fêng again took his departure without further words. He reported the incident to Ma-tsu, who said he had already warned him that Shih-t'ou was slippery.

A monk once drew four lines in front of Ma-tsu. The top line was long and the remaining three were short. He then demanded of the Master, "Besides saying that one line is long and the other three are short, what else could you say?" Ma-tsu thereupon drew one line on the ground and said, "This could be called either long or short. That is my answer."

A monk who lectured on Buddhism[14] came to the Master and asked, "What is the teaching advocated by the Ch'an masters?" Ma-tsu posed a counterquestion: "What teachings do you maintain?" The monk replied that he had lectured on more than twenty sūtras and śāstras. The Master exclaimed, "Are you not a lion?"[15] The monk said, "I do not venture to say that." The Master puffed twice and the monk commented, "This is the way to teach Ch'an." Ma-tsu retorted, "What way do you mean?" and the monk said, "The way the lion leaves the den." The Master became silent. Immediately the monk remarked, "This is also the way of Ch'an teaching." At this the Master again asked, "What way do you mean?" "The lion remains in his den." "When there is neither going out nor remaining in, what way would you say this was?" The monk

Illogical and Unconventional Approaches to Ch'an

made no answer but bid the Master good-bye. When he reached the door the Master called to him and he immediately turned his head. The Master said to him, "Then what is it?" The monk again made no answer. "What a stupid teacher this is!" the Master cried out.

The Governor of Hung-chou asked, "Master, should I eat meat and drink wine or should I not?" The Master replied, "To eat and drink is your blessing. Not to do it is also a blessing."

There were one hundred and thirty-nine disciples who received the Dharma from the Master and every one of them became a Ch'an leader in the district where he taught. Their teachings were transmitted from generation to generation. In the middle of the first month of the fourth year of the period of Chên-yüan [788] the Master climbed the Stone Gate Mountain in Chien-ch'ang, and as he was passing through the forest, he saw some level ground in the valley. He told his followers that his body would be buried in that ground in the following month. On the fourth day of the following month, he fell ill. Thereupon he bathed, and sitting cross-legged in silence, he died. In the middle of the Yüan-ho period [806–820] the posthumous title Ch'an Master of the Great Silence was bestowed upon him. His pagoda is called the Pagoda of Splendid Reverence.

NAN-CH'ÜAN P'U-YÜAN
(748–834)

"To Be a Buffalo Down the Hill"

(*From* The Transmission of the Lamp, *Chüan* 8)

CH'AN Master Nan-ch'üan P'u-yüan of Ch'ih-chou[16] was a native of Hsin-cheng in Cheng-chou.[17] His original surname was Wang. In the second year of the Chih-tê period [756–757] of the T'ang Dynasty he went to study under the Ch'an master Ta-hui of the Ta-wei Mountain. When he was thirty he went to the Sung Mountain[18] for his ordination. He began his studies with the ancient text of the *Four-Division Vinaya* and devoted himself to the refinements of disciplinary rules.[19] Later he visited various centers and listened to the lectures on the *Laṅkāvatāra* and *Avataṁsaka*[20] *Sūtras*. He also delved into the doctrine of the Middle Way given in the *Mādhyamika Śāstra*, the *Śata Śāstra*, and the *Dvādaśanikāya Śāstra*.[21] Thus he acquired a thorough discipline in Buddhist philosophy. Finally he came to Ma-tsu and studied Ch'an Buddhism with him, and achieved sudden enlightenment. He immediately freed himself from what he had previously learned[22] and obtained the joy of *samādhi*.

One day while Nan-ch'üan was serving rice gruel to his fellow monks, his master, Ma-tsu, asked him, "What is in the wooden bucket?"

Illogical and Unconventional Approaches to Ch'an

"This old fellow should keep his mouth shut and not say such words," remarked Nan-ch'üan.[23] The rest of the monks who were studying with him did not dare to raise any questions about the exchange.

In the eleventh year [795] of the period of Chên-yüan, Master Nan-ch'üan moved to Ch'ih-yang and built a small temple on the top of Mount Nan-ch'üan. He remained there for thirty years, never once coming down. At the beginning of the period of Ta-ho [827–835], Lu Hsüan, a provincial governor in Hsüan-ch'êng,[24] admired the spirit of the Master's Ch'an teachings. He and his supervisor from the Royal Court invited the Master to come down to the city to promote the learning of Ch'an, and both of these high officials assumed the position of disciple to the Master. Thereafter several hundred disciples gathered around him, and his teachings were widely disseminated. Master Nan-ch'üan came to be highly esteemed as a teacher of Ch'an.

One day Master Nan-ch'üan delivered a sermon, saying, "As soon as you talk about 'suchness,' it has already changed. The Buddhist master and monk of today should follow the path upon which other creatures proceed." Kuei-tsung remarked, "Even though man proceeds as a beast does, he would not receive a beast's retribution." The Master answered, "The rough eighth brother of Meng[25] behaves repeatedly like that."

Once Master Nan-ch'üan remarked, "In the middle of last night I gave Mañjuśrī and Samantabhadra[26] each twenty blows and chased them out of my temple." Chao-chou challenged him: "To whom have you given your blows?" The Master answered, "Could you tell me where Teacher Wang's[27] mistake was?" Chao-chou bowed and departed.

Once the Master planned to visit a village on the following day. During the night the God of Earth[28] informed the head of the village of the Master's coming, and consequently everything was prepared for his visit. When the Master arrived, he was surprised and asked, "You have prepared everything well. How did you know I was coming?" The village head replied that the God of Earth had informed him. Thereupon Master Nan-ch'üan proclaimed,

"Teacher Wang's achievement was not high enough; his mind was observed by the spirits and gods." A monk immediately asked him, "Master, as you are a man of great virtue, why should you be watched by spirits and gods?" Nan-ch'üan replied, "Offer a portion of food before the Earth God's shrine."

On one occasion the Master stated, "Ma-tsu of Kiangsi maintained that the Mind is the Buddha. However, Teacher Wang would not say it this way. He would advocate 'Not Mind, not Buddha, not things.' Is there any mistake when I say it this way?" After listening to this, Chao-chou made a bow and went away. Thereupon a monk followed him, saying, "What did you mean just now, when you bowed and left the Master?" Chao-chou replied, "Sir, you will have to ask the Master." The monk went to the Master and said, "Why did Ts'ung-shen [Chao-chou] behave that way a moment ago?" "He understood my meaning!" Nan-ch'üan exclaimed.

One day the Master came to the assembly holding a bowl in both hands. Huang-po,[29] the head monk, saw him coming but did not stand up. Master Nan-ch'üan asked him, "Dear abbot! When did you begin to teach Ch'an?" Huang-po answered, "Ever since the time of Dharmagahanābhyudgatarāja."[30] The Master replied, "Then you are still Teacher Wang's grandson! Go away!"

Another day Master Nan-ch'üan spoke to Huang-po thus: "There is a kingdom of yellow gold and houses of white silver. Who do you suppose lives there?"

"It is the dwelling place of the saints," replied Huang-po.

"There is another man.[31] Do you know in what country he lives?" asked the Master.

Huang-po folded his hands and stood still.

"You cannot give an answer. Why don't you ask Teacher Wang?" asked the Master.

Huang-po, in turn, repeated his master's question: "There is another man. Do you know in what country he lives?"

"Oh, what a pity this is!" said Nan-ch'üan.[32]

There was another time when the Master questioned Huang-po about the meaning of *dhyāna*[33] and *prajñā*. Huang-po answered,

Illogical and Unconventional Approaches to Ch'an

"During the twelve periods of the day I do not attach myself to anything."

"Is this not your own idea?" asked the Master.

"I do not dare to say so," answered Huang-po.

"You may put off payment for soybean milk, but who will pay the cost of the sandals of its carrier?" asked the Master.

Once the Master saw a monk chopping wood. He then knocked on a piece of wood three times. The monk laid down his ax and returned to the residential hall, while the Master returned to the lecture hall. After a while the Master went to the monks' hall and saw the monk sitting by his bowl and robe. The Master remarked, "What a deception!"

The monk retorted, "You returned to your room. What did you mean by that?"

The Master replied, "In the middle of last night a cow was lost, and at daybreak there was a fire."

Once the monks in the two wings of the monastery were disputing over the possession of a cat when the Master appeared on the scene. He took hold of the animal and said to the quarreling monks:

"If any one of you can say something to the point, he will save the life of this creature; if nobody can, it will be killed." Unfortunately, no one could, so the cat was killed. Later on, when Chao-chou came back, Master Nan-ch'üan told him about the incident that had taken place during his absence. At once Chao-chou took off a sandal and put it on top of his head, and then went away.

The Master said, "Had you been here a moment ago, you would have saved the animal's life."

One day Master Nan-ch'üan was sitting with Shan-shan by the fire in his chamber. Said the Master, "Do not point to the east or to the west, but go straight to what is fundamental."

Putting down the fire tongs, Shan-shan folded his hands and stood silently. The Master said, "Although you have reached such an answer, there is still a difference from the Tao maintained by Teacher Wang."

There was another monk who greeted the Master by folding his

NAN-CH'ÜAN P'U-YÜAN

hands and standing still. The Master said to him, "What a common manner this is!" On hearing this, the monk immediately unfolded his hands and placed his palms together. The Master said to him, "This is indeed too monklike." The monk made no answer.

When a monk was cleaning his bowl, Master Nan-ch'üan snatched it away from him. The monk stood empty-handed. The Master said, "The bowl is now in my hands. What is the use of muttering?" The monk made no answer.

Once when Master Nan-ch'üan went to the vegetable garden, he saw a monk there and threw a brick at him. When the monk turned his head to look, the Master lifted one of his feet. The monk said nothing, but when the Master returned to his room the monk followed him there and asked, "A moment ago you threw a brick at me. Did you not mean to give me some warning?" The Master said, "Then why did I lift my foot?" The monk made no reply.

Once Master Nan-ch'üan addressed the assembly: "Teacher Wang wants to sell his body. Who would like to buy it?" A monk stepped forward and said, "I want to buy it."

"He does not ask for a high price, nor does he ask for a low one. What can you do?" asked the Master. The monk made no answer.

Once Master Nan-ch'üan told Kuei-tsung and Ma-yü that he was going to take them with him to visit Nan-yang Hui-chung, the National Teacher. Before they began their journey, Nan-ch'üan drew a circle on the road and said, "As soon as you give a right answer we will be on our way." Thereupon Kuei-tsung sat down inside the circle and Ma-yü bowed in woman's fashion. The Master said to them, "Judging by this answer, it will not be necessary to go." Kuei-tsung complained, "What kind of mind is this?" But Master Nan-ch'üan called them both back, and they did not make their visit to Nan-yang.

Master Nan-ch'üan asked Shên-shan what he was doing. Shên-shan answered, "I am beating the gong."

"Do you beat it with your hand or with your foot?" pressed the Master.

"Master! Please, you answer it!" said Shên-shan.

"Remember it clearly; this question is put to an expert," replied Nan-ch'üan.

Illogical and Unconventional Approaches to Ch'an

An abbot came to bid good-bye to the Master, who asked him, "Where are you going?"

"I am going down from the mountain," was the answer.

"After you leave here, the first thing you should remember is not to slander Teacher Wang," said the Master.

"How would I dare to slander you?" said the monk.

The Master sneezed and said, "How much?" The monk left him immediately.

One day Master Nan-ch'üan spread ashes outside his doorway and closed the doors. Then he announced that if anyone could comment correctly, the door would be opened. A number of answers were given, but none of them satisfied the Master. Thereupon, Chao-chou cried out, "Good heavens!" and immediately the door was thrown open by the Master.

One evening when Master Nan-ch'üan was enjoying the moonlight, a monk asked him when one could be equal to the moonlight. The Master said, "Twenty years ago I attained that state." The monk continued, "What about right now?" The Master went immediately to his room.

Governor Lu Hsüan asked the Master, "I just came from Lu-ho. Is there another self of mine there?" The Master answered, "Remember it clearly; the question is put to an expert." Lu again said to him, "Master! Your teaching of Ch'an is beyond thought. Everywhere you go you uplift the world." The Master replied, "What we said a moment ago is all the Governor's affair."

Another day Lu said to the Master, "I also understand a little of Buddha's teachings." The Master asked, "Governor! What do you engage in during the twelve periods of the day?" Lu answered, "There is not even an inch of thread covering me." The Master said, "You are still at the bottom of the doorstep."[34] Later he continued, "Don't you see that the virtuous king does not recruit intellectuals as his officials?"

One day when the Master came to the assembly hall, Governor Lu said, "Master, please teach Dharma to all of us!"

"What do you want to talk about?" asked the Master.

"Don't you have any expedients for attaining enlightenment?" Lu continued.

"What is it that you want me to say?" asked the Master.

"Why should we have four modes of birth and six levels of reincarnation?"[35] asked the Governor.

"This is not what I teach," replied the Master.

Once Governor Lu together with Master Nan-ch'üan saw someone playing dice. Lu picked up the dice and asked, "How is it that one can let his luck decide whether things turn out to be this or that?"

"These are indeed dirty pieces of bone!"[36] said the Master.

The Governor then said, "There is a piece of stone in my house. Sometimes it stands up and sometimes it lies down. Now, can it be carved into the image of a Buddha?"

"Yes, it is possible," answered the Master.

"But is it impossible to do so?" countered the Governor.

"It is impossible! It is impossible!" exclaimed the Master.

Chao-chou asked, "Tao is not external to things; the externality of things is not Tao. Then what is the Tao that is beyond things?" The Master struck him. Thereupon Chao-chou took hold of the stick and said, "From now on, do not strike a man by mistake!" The Master said, "We can easily differentiate between a dragon and a snake, but nobody can fool a Ch'an monk."

Master Nan-ch'üan addressed the head of the monastery thus: "When Buddha stayed in Trayastriṃśāh for ninety days preaching the Dharma for his deceased mother, Udayana [King of Kauśāmbī] longed for Buddha. He asked Maudgalyāyana[37] three times to exercise his supernatural powers to transport an artist to where Buddha was, so that the artist could carve Buddha's image. It was said that the artist could carve only thirty-one characteristics of the Buddha.[38] Why could the remaining one, the Brahma voice, not be carved?" The head of the monastery asked, "What is the form of the Brahma voice?" The Master said, "What a grievous deceit!"

The Master asked the supervisor,[39] "What is the purpose of our working together today?" The answer was, "To turn the millstone." The Master stated, "As for the millstone, I'll let you turn it. But as for the axle, be sure not to move it." The supervisor uttered no word.

One day an elder monk asked the Master, "When we say, 'The

Illogical and Unconventional Approaches to Ch'an

Mind is the Buddha,' we are wrong. But when we say, 'Not Mind, not Buddha,' we are not correct either. What is your idea about this?" Master Nan-ch'üan answered, "You should believe 'The Mind is the Buddha' and let it go at that. Why should you talk about right or wrong? It is just the same as when you come to eat your meal. Do you choose to come to it through the west corridor, or by another way? You cannot ask others which is wrong."

When the Master was living in a small temple a monk came to visit him. Master Nan-ch'üan told the monk that he was going to the top of the hill, and asked the monk to have his own meal at lunchtime and then bring another portion up the hill for the Master. The monk, however, when he had had his lunch, broke his regular routine and went to bed. The Master waited for him on the hill, but the monk did not come. Eventually he returned to the temple and found the monk lying asleep. The Master lay down on the other side of the bed and went to sleep himself. Thereupon the monk got up and left. Some years later the Master recalled this, saying, "In the temple where I lived in my early years, there was a talented monk who came to visit me. I have not seen him since."

The Master once picked up a ball and asked a monk, "How do you compare that one to this one?" The answer was, "It is incomparable." The Master continued, "What difference did you see that made you say, That one is incomparable to this one?" "If you want me to tell you the difference that I see, you must put down the ball," answered the monk. The Master remarked, "I must admit you have one eye open to wisdom."

Governor Lu Hsüan spoke to the Master, saying, "Sêng-chao[40] is very strange indeed. He maintains that all things share the same root and that right and wrong are mutually identified." The Master pointed to the peony blossoms in the courtyard and said, "Governor! When people of the present day see these blossoms, it is as if they saw them in a dream." The Governor could not understand what he was saying.

Lu Hsüan asked, "Where is the residence of the Mahārāja-deva?" The Master answered, "If it is a *deva*, it would obviously not be bound to any earthly residence."[41] Lu Hsüan continued, "I have heard that the Mahārāja-deva dwelt in *pramudita*, the first stage."[42] The Master answered, "When one is transformed through the Selfhood of *deva*, one reveals the Selfhood of *deva*, and thus will be able to deliver the discourse on Absolute Truth."

When Governor Lu was about to return to his office in Hsüan-chêng, he came to bid the Master good-bye. The latter asked him, "Governor! You are going back to the capital. How will you govern the people?" The Governor replied, "I will govern them through wisdom." The Master remarked, "If this is true, the people will suffer for it."

Once Master Nan-ch'üan went to Hsüan-chêng. Governor Lu came out of the city gate to welcome him, and pointing to the gate, said, "Everybody here calls it Yung-mên, or the Gate of the Jar. What would you call it?" The Master said to him, "If I should say what I would like to call it, it would blemish your rule." Lu Hsüan further asked, "If the bandits should come into the town suddenly, what should we do?" The Master answered, "It is the fault of Teacher Wang." Lu Hsüan again asked, "What is the purpose of the many hands and eyes of the Bodhisattva of Great Compassion, Kuan-yin?" The Master answered, "Just as our nation employs you."

Master Nan-ch'üan arranged an assembly of chanting monks and provided food as an offering to his late master Ma-tsu. He asked the assembly if Ma-tsu would attend. None of the monks in the assembly ventured to reply until Tung-shan[43] said, "As soon as he has companions, he will come." The Master said, "Although you are very young, you are very worthy to be taught." Tung-shan answered, "You, Master, should not force an honorable man to be a slave."

When the Master was washing his clothes, a monk said, "Master! You still are not free from 'this'?" Master Nan-ch'üan replied, lifting the clothes, "What can you do to 'this'?"

The Master asked Liang-hsin, a monk, whether there is a Buddha in the kalpa of the void.[44] The monk answered, "There is." The Master asked, "Who?" "It is Liang-hsin!" the monk replied.

Illogical and Unconventional Approaches to Ch'an

"In what country do you live?" pressed the Master. The monk made no answer.

A monk inquired, "From patriarch to patriarch there is a transmission. What is it that they transmit to one another?" The Master said, "One, two, three, four, five!"

The monk asked, "What is that which was possessed by the ancients?" The Master said, "When it can be possessed, I will tell you." The monk said dubiously, "Master, why should you lie?" The Master replied, "I do not lie. Lu Hsing-chê[45] lied."

The monk asked, "During the twelve periods of the day what is the state of your mind?" The Master answered, "Why don't you ask Teacher Wang?" The monk replied, "I have asked him." The Master said, "Has he given you something to be the state of your mind?"

The monk asked, "What is that moment when the green lotus is not scattered and destroyed by the wind and fire?" The Master said, "What is it that is free from destruction when there is no wind or fire?" The monk made no answer. The Master stated, "Do not think of good and do not think of evil. Let us have, rather, that state when our mind is free from any thought and thus return to our original self." The monk commented, "There is no appearance that can be revealed."

Master Nan-ch'üan asked a Vinaya monk, "Please explain the sūtra to me, will you?" The monk answered, "If I explain the sūtra to you, you tell me about Ch'an. Thus you have my explanation." The Master said, "How could a golden ball be exchanged for a silver one?" The Vinaya monk said, "I do not understand." The Master said, "Suppose there is a cloud in the sky. Is it to be held there by driving nails or tied up with vines?" The monk asked, "Should there be a pearl in the sky, how would you fetch it?" The Master said, "Chop the bamboo and make it into a ladle, and we will use it to fetch the pearl from the sky." The monk challenged him: "How would it be possible to use the ladle in the sky?" The Master answered, "What do you suggest we do to fetch the pearl from the sky?" The monk then bid the Master good-bye, saying to him, "I am going to travel far. If anyone asks me what you are doing these days, I will not know how to answer." The Master replied, "You tell them that recently I have come to understand how to rush upon another." The monk said, "How is that?" The Master answered, "With one rush, both sides are destroyed."

A monk asked, "Where are one's nostrils before one is born?" The Master replied, "Where are one's nostrils after one has been born?"

Before the Master passed away, the head monk asked him, "Where are you going after your death?" The Master answered, "I am going down the hill to be a water buffalo." The monk continued, "Would it be possible to follow you there?" The Master said, "If you want to follow me, you must come with a piece of straw in your mouth."

Thereafter the illness of Master Nan-ch'üan was announced. On the twenty-fifth day of the twelfth month in the eighth year of the Ta-ho period, early in the morning, he told his disciples, "For a long time the stars have been blurring and the lamplight dimming; don't say that I alone have to come and go." After saying this, he passed away. He was then eighty-seven years of age and in the fifty-eighth year of his ordination. The year after his death his body was enshrined in a pagoda.

CHAO-CHOU TS'UNG-SHEN
(778–897)

"You See the Logs, But Not the Chao-chou Bridge"

(*From* The Transmission of the Lamp, *Chüan 10*)

CH'AN Master Ts'ung-shen of the Kuan-yin Monastery in Chao-chou[46] was a native of Ho-hsiang in Ts'ao-chou.[47] His original surname was Ho. During his boyhood he had his head shaved at the Hu-t'ung Monastery in his native town. Before he was ordained he visited Master Nan-ch'üan in Ch'ih-yang.[48] He arrived while Nan-ch'üan was lying down resting. Nan-ch'üan asked him:

"Where have you just come from?"

"I have just left Shui-hsiang."[49]

"Have you seen the standing image of Buddha?"

"What I see is not a standing image of Buddha, but a supine Enlightened One!"

"Are you your own master or not?"

"Yes, I am."

"Where is this master of yours?"

"In the middle of the winter the weather becomes bitterly cold. I wish all blessings on you, sir!"

At this, Nan-ch'üan decided that this visitor was promising and permitted him to become his disciple.

Chao-chou Ts'ung-shen

Some days later Chao-chou asked his master, "What is Tao?" Nan-ch'üan replied, "Everyday-mindedness is Tao."

"Is it possible to approach it?"

"If you intentionally approach it, you will miss it."

"If you do not approach it intentionally, how can you know it?"

Master Nan-ch'üan then explained to him, "Tao is not a matter either of knowing or of not-knowing. Knowing is a delusion; not-knowing is indifference.[50] When one has really attained Tao with non-intention,[51] one is as if in the great Void, free from obstruction and limitation. How can any assertion or negation be made?"

Hearing this, Chao-chou was awakened. Thereupon he went to the Liu-li Altar on Mount Sung, where he was ordained. Later he returned to Nan-ch'üan.

One day Chao-chou asked Nan-ch'üan, "Where should one rest after having attained Tao?"

"One should become a buffalo down the hill."

"Thank you for this instruction," said Chao-chou. Thereupon Nan-ch'üan remarked, "In the middle of last night the moonlight shone on the window."

One day when Chao-chou was serving as a scullion, he shut the door and let the kitchen fill with smoke. Then he cried for help to come put out the fire. When the monks came running, he called out, "If anyone says the right word, I'll open the door!" None of the monks uttered a word. However, Nan-ch'üan passed the lock through the window to Chao-chou, and he opened the door immediately.

Another time Chao-chou went to visit Master Huang-po [Huang-po Hsi-yün], who closed the door of his chamber when he saw him coming. Whereupon Chao-chou lit a torch in the Dharma Hall and cried out for help. Huang-po immediately opened the door and grabbed him, demanding, "Speak! Speak!" Chao-chou answered, "After the thief is gone, you draw your bow!"

Chao-chou went to the monastery of Master Pao-shou.[52] When Pao-shou saw him coming, he turned around in his seat. Chao-chou unfolded his sitting cloth and bowed. Pao-shou came down from his seat, and Chao-chou immediately left him.

Illogical and Unconventional Approaches to Ch'an

Chao-chou visited Yen-kuan[53] and said to him, "Watch the arrow!" Yen-kuan answered, "It is gone!" "It hit the target," said Chao-chou.

Chao-chou arrived at Chia-shan's[54] monastery and went to the Dharma Hall with a staff in his hand. Chia-shan asked him, "What is the staff for?" "To test the depth of the water," was the answer. Chia-shan said, "There is not a drop here. What can you test?" Chao-chou leaned on his staff and went away.

When Master Chao-chou was planning to go to Mount Wu-t'ai,[55] a monk from another school wrote a *gāthā*:

Wherever there is a green grove-covered mountain,
There is a place for studying Tao.
Why should we trudge far with our staff to Mount Ching-liang?[56]
Even though a golden lion [Buddha] appear from the clouds,
Looking at him squarely would not bring us luck.

Chao-chou asked, "What does it mean, 'looking squarely'?" The monk made no answer.

After Master Chao-chou visited Mount Wu-t'ai his teaching spread widely in North China. He was invited to stay in the Kuan-yin Monastery in his native town of Chao-chou. He came to the assembly and said:

"It is as if a transparent crystal were held in one's hand. When a foreigner approaches it, it mirrors him as such; when a native Chinese approaches it, it mirrors him as such. I take a stalk of grass and let it act as a golden-bodied one, sixteen feet high, and I take a golden-bodied one, sixteen feet high and let it act as a stalk of grass. Buddhahood is passion [*kleśa*], and passion is Buddhahood." During his sermon a monk asked him, "In whom does Buddha cause passion?"

"Buddha causes passion in all of us."

"How do we get rid of it?"

"Why should we get rid of it?" asked Chao-chou.

When Master Chao-chou was sweeping the floor, a visitor asked him, "How is it that even a great wise man like you is not free from dust?"

"The dust comes from the outside," was the Master's answer. On another occasion a monk asked him, "How could you find a speck of dust in such a pure and clean monastery?"

"Look, here is another one," answered the Master.

Someone was walking in the garden with the Master and saw a rabbit running away in fright. He asked, "How could the rabbit be frightened and run away from you, since you are a great Buddhist?" To this the Master replied, "It is because I like to kill."

A monk asked, "How can you recognize what is true before the blossoming of enlightenment?"

"It is blossoming now," replied the Master.

"Is it actual or true?" queried the monk.

"What is actual is true, and what is true is actual," remarked the Master.

"Who shares in this?"

"It is for me to share, and it is also for you to share."

"What if I do not accept your bribery?"

The Master pretended not to hear this and the monk uttered no further word. The Master said to him, "Go away!"

In the Kuan-yin Monastery the dharma ensign[57] was once broken down by the wind. A monk came to Chao-chou and asked, "What will this magic ensign turn into, a divine or a mundane thing?" The Master answered, "Neither mundane, nor divine." The monk further pressed, "What will it ultimately be?" The Master said, "Well, it has just dropped to the ground."

Once the Master asked an abbot, who gave lectures, on what sūtra he was speaking. The abbot answered that he was lecturing on *The Sūtra of Nirvāna*.[58] Then the Master said to him, "May I ask you the meaning of one section of the sūtra?" To this the monk consented. Thereupon the Master lifted one foot, kicked the air, and blew once through his mouth. He asked the monk, "What is the meaning of this?"

The monk replied, "There is no meaning like this in the sūtra."

"It means five hundred strong men are lifting a rock, and yet you say there is no meaning to it!"

When the assembly was attending the evening sermon Master

Chao-chou announced, "Tonight I am going to answer your questions. If you know how to ask questions, please step forward." Thereupon a monk came out of the group and bowed to the Master, who said, "Recently we discussed throwing away a brick and getting in return a piece of jade, but now we have got an unbaked brick."

A monk who was on his way to visit Mount Wu-t'ai met an old woman to whom he said, "Which way leads to Mount Wu-t'ai?"

"It's straight ahead," answered the old woman. The monk followed her instruction and went on accordingly. Whereupon the woman remarked, "He, too, goes off in that direction."

The monk later reported this happening to Master Chao-chou, who said to the monk, "I shall test this old woman." The next day the Master went out and asked the way to Mount Wu-t'ai. The old woman said, "It's straight ahead." The Master went as directed, and again the old woman said, "He, too, goes off in that direction." When the Master came back to the monastery he told his monks, "I have tested this old woman for you."

A monk asked, "If someone comes this way, will you greet him?"

"Yes, I will."

"If he does not come this way, will you still receive him?"

"Yes, I will."

"If someone comes this way you can greet him, but if he does not come this way, how can you possibly greet him?" the monk challenged.

"Stop! Stop! This should not be talked about. My teaching is subtle and beyond thought," declared the Master.

The Master, coming out of the monastery, met a woman who asked him where he lived. The Master answered, "In the *hsi* of the Eastern Monastery [Kuan-yin Monastery] of Chao-chou." The woman departed without another word.

When the Master arrived back at his monastery he asked his disciples what the character should be for *hsi*. Some said that it should be the character for "west," but others insisted that it should be the character for "stay." The Master remarked, "All of you are qualified to be severe judges at the court." Thereupon the disciples complained, "Why should you say such a thing?" The Master replied, "It is because you all know characters."

A monk asked, "What is the precious treasure in the bag?" The Master replied, "Shut your mouth!"

A monk who had just arrived at the monastery told the Master that since he had left Chang-an with a staff across his shoulder he had not hit anyone. The Master said to him, "That proves that the staff you carried was too short." The monk made no answer.

A monk drew a portrait of the Master and presented it to him. The Master said, "Tell me whether or not this picture resembles me. If it does, kill me with a single blow. If it does not, I will burn it immediately." The monk had no answer.

The Master was striking a flint for a light. He asked a monk, "I call this a light. What do you call it?" The monk did not say a word. Thereupon the Master said, "If you do not grasp the meaning of Ch'an, it is useless to remain silent."

A newly arrived monk was asked by the Master, "Where do you come from?"

"From the South."

"Buddhism is all in the South. Why should you come here?"

"How could Buddhism be divided into south and north?"

"Even though you come from Hsüeh-fêng[59] and Yün-chü,[60] you are still a one-sided lumber carrier!"

Master Chao-chou was asked by a monk, "Who is the Buddha?"

"The one in the shrine," was the answer.

"Isn't it a clay statue that sits in the shrine?" the monk went on.

"Yes, that is right."

"Then who is the Buddha?" the monk repeated.

"The one in the shrine," replied the Master.

A monk asked, "What is my own self?"

"Have you finished your rice gruel?" asked the Master.

"Yes, I have finished it," replied the monk.

"Then go and wash your dishes," said the Master.

When the monk heard this, he was suddenly awakened.

The Master came to the assembly and said, " 'As soon as you make the differentiation between right and wrong, you are confused

Illogical and Unconventional Approaches to Ch'an

and lose your mind.'[61] Is there anyone who wants to comment on this?" Lo-p'u, one of the monks, clacked his teeth together, and Yün-chü said, "It is not necessary." The Master commented, "Today somebody has found his real self."[62]

A monk asked the Master for a statement, and the Master simply repeated what he had said before. The monk then pointed to another monk standing by and said, "Look! This monk uttered such words." The Master silently accepted the challenge.

Once a monk came and asked the Master, "For a long time I have yearned to see the stone bridge of Chao-chou, but on arriving here I see nothing but a few old logs." To this Chao-chou answered, "You just see the logs; you fail to see the bridge of Chao-chou." "What is the Chao-chou bridge?" asked the monk. The Master said, "Cross over! Cross over!"

There was another monk who asked the same question and received the same answer. Persisting, he inquired again, "What is the Chao-chou bridge?" The Master said, "Horses pass over it, donkeys pass over it." The monk asked, "What are these logs?" The Master answered, "Each one of them carries a man across."

Hearing that an ordained monk sought an audience, the Master told his attendant, "Send this man away!" The attendant did as he was told, and the monk bowed and went away. Thereupon the Master said, "The monk entered the door, but the attendant was still outside."

The Master asked a monk who had come to visit, where he came from. The monk answered that he came from the South. The Master asked him, "Do the people in the South know that there is a Gate of Chao-chou here?" The monk said to him, "You must know that there is always someone who does not come through the gate." "The salt smuggler,"[63] said the Master.

A monk asked, "What is the meaning of Bodhidharma coming from the West?" The Master came down from his seat and stood beside it. The monk asked, "Is this your answer?" The Master said, "I have not said a word."

Master Chao-chou once asked his cook whether they would eat raw or cooked cabbage that day. The cook picked up a piece to show him. The Master commented, "Those who understand kindness are few, but those who are ungrateful are many."[64]

A monk asked, "Is there anyone cultivating himself in the kalpa of the void?"[65] The Master asked, "What is it that you call the kalpa of the void?" The monk explained, "It is that in which there is nothing." The Master replied, "This should be called cultivation. What is it that you call the empty kalpa?" The monk made no answer.

A monk asked, "What is the mystery in profundity?" The Master said, "How long have you been mystified?" The monk replied, "It has been a long time." The Master said, "If you had not met me, you would have been killed by mystery."

A monk asked, "Since all things return to One, where does this One return to?"

"When I was in Tsing-chou,[66] I had a robe made which weighed seven *chin*,"[67] replied the Master.

A monk asked, "At night one lives in the Tuṣita Heaven,[68] and in the daytime one descends to the continent of Jambūdvīpa.[69] Why shouldn't one reveal one's self like a mani gem[70] during the time between these two periods?" The Master asked, "What did you say?" The monk repeated his question. The Master stated, "Ever since Vipaśyin[71] gave his attention to this the wonder has not been achieved."

The Master once asked the chief administrator of the temple, "Where have you been?" The answer was that he had been setting birds free. The Master asked him, "Why should the ravens fly away?" The answer was, "Because they are afraid of me." "What do you mean by this?" challenged the Master. The chief administrator then asked him, "Why do the ravens fly away?" "Because someone has a murderous mind," the Master told him.

Holding a bowl in his hands, the Master said, "If you should see me thirty years from now, use this bowl for your offerings. If you do not see me, the bowl will be destroyed." A monk stepped out from the group and said, "Who dare say that he will see you after thirty years?" The Master thereupon destroyed the bowl.

A monk came to bid the Master good-bye and was asked where

Illogical and Unconventional Approaches to Ch'an

he was going. The monk replied that he was going to visit Master Hsüeh-fêng. The Master said, "If Hsüeh-fêng should ask you for some statements that I have recently made, what will you tell him?" The monk could not answer and asked the Master to help him. Thereupon Chao-chou told him, "When it is winter, speak cold; when it is summer, speak hot." The Master later asked the monk what he would say if Hsüeh-fêng asked him what the Ultimate is. The monk failed to respond. The Master told him, "Simply say that you yourself have come from Chao-chou and are not a verbal messenger." When the monk came to Hsüeh-fêng, he repeated what he had been told. Hsüeh-fêng said, "All that you say can only have come from Chao-chou." Master Hsüan-sha[72] heard this and commented, "Even the great Master Chao-chou was defeated without knowing it himself."

There was a monk who asked, "What is the one word of Chao-chou?" The Master answered, "I have not even half a word." The monk exclaimed, "Master! Are you not in existence?" The Master retorted, "I myself am not a word."

A monk asked, "How can one be a real homeless Buddhist?" The Master answered, "Live without fame; seek no gain."

A monk asked, "How can perfect purity be attained without a spot of defilement?" The Master answered, "The wanderer cannot stay here."

A monk asked, "What is the meaning of the Patriarch [Bodhidharma] coming from the West?" The Master struck the leg of his seat. The monk then again, "Is it not 'this'?" The Master said, "If it is, you take it away."

A monk asked, "What is the perfect symbol of *vairocana*?" The Master answered, "Ever since I left my home in my early days to be a Buddhist I have not been troubled by blurred eyesight." The monk persisted, "Then why don't you help people to see?" The Master replied: "I want you to see the *vairocana* for yourself."

There was a question: "Will you, Master, also go to hell?" The Master replied, "I will be the first one to go to hell."[73] The monk inquired, "Why should you, a great wise man, go to hell?" The Master replied, "If I do not go, who will be there to teach you?"

Once the Prince-General of Chen-ting came with his sons to the temple to visit the Master. Receiving his noted guests, the Master did not rise from his seat and asked the Prince, "Does Your Highness understand this?" The Prince said that he did not, and the Master chanted:

> "Ever since my younger days
> I have abstained from meat.
> Now my body is getting old.
> Whenever I see my visitors
> I have no strength left for coming down from the
>   Buddha-seat."

When he heard this the Prince esteemed Chao-chou even more. The next day he sent his general with a message for the Master. Chao-chou came down from his seat to receive him. Subsequently his attendant asked the Master, "Yesterday when you saw the Prince you did not move from your seat; then why did you step down from your seat today when you received the general?" The Master explained, "This is beyond your understanding. To receive the first-class visitor, one should remain seated; for the second-class visitor, one should step down; as for the third-class visitor, one should welcome him outside the temple gate."

The Master sent a *fu-tzu* to the Prince and told the messenger that if the Prince should ask about it, he should answer, "This is what I have used all my life, and I will never exhaust it."

The Master's teachings of Ch'an spread all over the country. People of that day called it the spirit of Chao-chou. Everyone respected and revered him.

On the second day of the eleventh month of the fourth year in the Ch'ien-ning period [894–897] of the T'ang Dynasty, Master Chao-chou lay down on his right side and passed away. He was one hundred and twenty years old. Posthumously he came to be known as the Great Master of Ultimate Truth.

P'ANG YÜN
(?–811)

Inner Harmony in Daily Activity

(*From* The Transmission of the Lamp, *Chüan* 8)

THE lay Buddhist P'ang Yün of Hsiang-chou[74] was a native of Heng-yang[75] in Hêng-chou. His courtesy name[76] was Tao-hsüan. His family had been Confucianists for generations. While he was still young he became aware of the entanglements of worldly passions and searched for truth. In the beginning of the Chên-yüan period [785–894] of the T'ang Dynasty he went to visit Shih-t'ou Hsi-ch'ien,[77] from whom he began to understand Ch'an through no-words. He became a good friend of Tan-hsia T'ien-jan[78] as well.

One day Master Shih-t'ou asked him, "What have you been doing with your days since you came here to see me?" P'ang Yün answered, "If you ask me my daily activity, there is nothing that I can speak of." He presented him with a *gāthā* which read:

> Daily activity is nothing other than harmony within.
> When each thing I do is without taking or rejecting,
> There is no contradiction anywhere.
> For whom is the majesty of red and purple robes?
> The summit of the inner being has never been defiled by
>   the dust of the world.

Supernatural power and wonderful functioning are found
In the carrying of water and the chopping of wood.

Shih-t'ou Hsi-ch'ien accepted this and said, "What do you want to be, a monk or a layman?" P'ang Yün answered, "I wish to be what I most admire." Therefore [choosing freedom] he did not have his head shaved or wear a monk's robe.

Later on P'ang Yün went to Chiang-hsi to visit Ma-tsu. At that time he asked Ma-tsu, "What kind of man is he who has no companion among all things?"

Ma-tsu answered, "When you swallow all the water in the West River in one gulp, I will tell you."

As soon as P'ang Yün heard this, he was suddenly aware of the essence of Ch'an. He remained with Ma-tsu and studied under him for two years. He wrote the following *gāthā*:

> I have a son who has never been married:
> neither has my daughter.
> We all come together and talk about no-birth.*

From this period on, when P'ang Yün expounded Ch'an, he was noted for his eloquence and his quick responses. People from all parts of the country admired him.

Once P'ang Yün went to listen to a lecture on the *Diamond Sūtra*. When he heard the lecturer declare, "There is no self and there are no others," he asked:

"Abbot! If you say there is no self and there are no others, then who is he who is giving the lecture, and who are they who are listening?" The abbot made no answer. P'ang Yün said to him, "Although I am a layman, I know how to entrust myself to Buddhism." The abbot asked him, "In that case, what is your interpretation?" Thereupon P'ang Yün made a *gāthā*:

> As there is no self and no others
> How can there be degrees of intimacy?
> You should not lecture from assembly to assembly,
> Since words do not lead directly to the Truth.
> *Prajñā* being likened to the diamond

---
* For an explanation of the last line, see the episode described on page 145 of the introduction.

Should be free from even a speck of dust.
The entire sūtra from beginning to end[79]
Is nothing but deceitful words.

When the abbot heard this, he was filled with admiration and pleasure. Wherever P'ang Yün went, most of the senior Buddhists and scholars came to hold discussions with him. He answered them directly and spontaneously, even as an echo, and his replies were beyond measurement and rules.

Sometime during the middle of the Yüan-ho period [806–820], he went north to Hsiang-chou and Han-chou. He stayed wherever he found himself. Sometimes he rested in the mountains accompanied by the birds and the deer. Other times he lived in town, either by the noisy market place or in a quiet residential district. For a time he lived in Tung-yen. Later he moved to a small house to the west of this city, always accompanied by his daughter, Ling-chao. He earned his living with bamboo work which his daughter sold for him. In the following *gāthā*, he summarizes his way of life:

> Let mind and the external world be as they are.
> There is neither actuality nor emptiness.
> If there is actuality, I do not care for it.
> Though there is a Void, I do not abide in it.
> I am neither a sage nor a great worthy,
> I am an ordinary man who fulfills his daily tasks.
> How simple are the Buddhist teachings!
> In the Five Aggregates lie true wisdom.
> All things are identified with the First Principle.
> The formless essence of things is not twofold.
> If you wish to be free from suffering and enter *bodhi*,
> I cannot tell you where the land of Buddha is.

When it came time for P'ang Yün to enter into *nirvāna*, he ordered his daughter to watch the movement of the sun and tell him when it was exactly noon. Ling-chao went out to look and returned immediately, saying that it was already noon but there was an eclipse of the sun. Thereupon P'ang Yün went out to take a look. Ling-chao immediately sat on her father's chair with her hands joined together and passed away. P'ang Yün smiled and said, "My daughter! Your way is the swift one!" He lived for seven days more. Yü Ti, the governor of Hsiang-chou, came to see him in his final illness. P'ang Yün said to him, "I pray you to hold all that is thought to be real as empty, and never to take that which is empty as being real. Farewell! The world is merely a shadow, an echo." When he had finished speaking, he laid his head upon the governor's leg and passed away. He left instructions that his body should be cremated and his ashes scattered upon the nearby lakes and rivers. Buddhist and layman alike deeply lamented his death. There was general agreement that P'ang Yün was Vimalakīrti in China. He left behind him some three hundred poems and *gāthās* for the world.

NOTES

1. The four alternatives are: being (Sanskrit *sat*, "is"); non-being (*a-sat*, "is-not"); both being and non-being (*sat a-sat*, "both is and is-not"); neither being nor non-being (*na sat naiv a-sat*, "neither is nor is-not"). They are discussed more fully in the introduction to Part I, pages 10–11.

2. In the Upanishads, Yājñavalkya's famous theory of *neti, neti* (not! not!) is twofold negation; the Middle Way goes beyond this to the hundredfold negation.

3. Now Kung-han, northwest of Ch'eng-tu in Szechwan Province.

4. The long tongue and the wheel-shaped marks are among the thirty-two characteristics ascribed to a Buddha.

5. Now the town of Pahsien, in Szechwan.

6. One of the famous five sacred Buddhist mountains of China, located north of Hengyang, Hunan Province.

7. The truth of Buddha, transmitted from master to enlightened disciple, is spoken of among Ch'annists, symbolically, as the mind-seal.

8. Northwest of Ch'ien-ou (Kienow) in Fukien Province.

9. Southwest of Nan-ch'ang in Kiangsi Province.

10. Southwest of Kanchow in Kiangsi Province.

11. *Liang chiu* commonly means "for a good while," but in the monastic tradition it means keeping silence for quite some time.

12. "To press the eyes" means to create illusion.

13. The original meaning of *kan-mu* is bamboo poles and wooden sticks. In this context it means the instruments used by jugglers.

14. Abbot Liang from Szechwan, who had received his enlightenment under Ma-tsu. When he left he said: "All that I have learned previously has

just melted away." He stayed thereafter in the Western Mountain of Hung-chou and never lectured again.

15. The lion, as king of the beasts and free from all fear, is often a symbol of Buddha.

16. Now Kuei-ch'ih (Kweichih), northeast of Anking, on the right bank of the Yangtze River in Anhwei Province.

17. Chengchow, west of K'ai-fêng in Honan Province.

18. Another of the five sacred Buddhist mountains, in northwestern Honan Province near Loyang; elevation over 7,800 feet.

19. According to the biography of P'u-yüan in *Biographies of the Eminent Buddhist Monks*, Sung Compilation, Chüan 11, Master Nan-ch'üan went to the Sung Mountain in 777 to study under the Vinaya master Hao of the Shan-hui Monastery and later was ordained there. He studied the text of the *Four-Division Vinaya*, which was Dharmagupta's version in sixty *chüan* translated by Buddhayasas into Chinese with a commentary by Fa-li (589–635) of the Jih-k'ung Monastery in Hsiang-chou. This is usually called "The Old Text of Hsiang-pu." Nan-ch'üan devoted himself to the study of the details and the refinement of the disciplinary regulations for Buddhist monks, such as the five *p'ien* and the seven *chü*. *P'ien* and *chü* are various infractions or sins demanding various punishments, such as expulsion from the order, confession before and absolution by the assembly, etc. Vinaya, from *vi-ni*, meaning "to train" or "to discipline," became the name of a school of Buddhism founded in China by Tao-hsüan (596–667) in the T'ang Dynasty. The emphasis of the school is on the rules of monastic discipline.

20. The *Avataṁsaka Sūtra* (*Hua-yen Ching*), which became the foundation of the Hua-yen School, basically lays stress on the doctrines of identity and interpenetration. Three translations of this sūtra were made in Chinese. The first translation, called *Chin Ching*, was by Buddhabhadra in A.D. 418–420. The second translation by Śikṣānanda in 695–699 is called *T'ang Ching*. The third was made by Prajñā in 796–797 and served as the last chapter of the two previous scripts. The Hua-yen School was founded in China by Tu-shun, who died in 640, and further expounded by Fa-tsang, who died in 712.

21. These three śāstras are the basic scripts of the Mādhyamika School, founded in India by Nāgārjuna in the second century A.D. They all were translated by Kumārajīva: the *Mādhyamika Śāstra*, corresponding to the Middle Way, in 409; the *Śata Śāstra*—the One Hundred Verses—in 404, and the *Dvādaśanikāya Śāstra*—concentrating on the Twelve Gates—in 408. Chi-tsang (549–623) founded the San-lun School when he was in the Chia-hsiang Monastery. The teaching of this school revolves around the doctrine of reducing reality to *śūnyatā* by the process of negation of negation.

22. *Wang chüan* means to forget the net once the fish has been caught. This expression originated in the *Chuang-tzu*, by the fourth-century (B.C.) Chinese philosopher Chuan Chou, a follower of Lao-tzu. Here it implies that Nan-ch'üan forgot all knowledge about Ch'an in achieving *samādhi*, which is the bliss arising from superconsciousness of mind.

23. It was apparent to everybody that it was rice gruel in the bucket. Nan-ch'üan saw that the Master was trying to trap him into answering on a relative plane, and replied instead as we see. This was not rudeness on Nan-

NOTES

ch'üan's part, but rather a statement that absolute reality cannot be expressed by words.

24. Southeast of Wuho, Anhwei Province.

25. Traditionally a rude man, proud of his unpolished manner and of his boldness in offending others.

26. According to tradition Mañjuśrī was a guardian of wisdom and Samantabhadra a guardian of law. The former is often placed on Śākyamuni's left and the latter on his right, symbolizing *prajñā* and *samādhi* respectively.

27. Nan-ch'üan often referred to himself as Teacher Wang, from his family name.

28. In Chinese literature and tradition, spirits or gods often appear in dreams to deliver messages, such as happened in the case of the village leader. The highest achievement of Ch'an should be free from this. Because his visit was predicted by the Earth God, Nan-ch'üan said that his achievement of Ch'an was not high enough. When the monk asked him why he was observed by the Earth God, Nan-ch'üan wished to cut off his disciple's intellectual pursuit. Hence his irrelevant answer.

29. Huang-po Hsi-yün (d. 850). See *The Lamp*, Chüan 9.

30. Refers to one of the Buddhas of a previous kalpa, or aeon.

31. I.e., the real self.

32. When Huang-po followed the Master's advice by repeating the question, he revealed that he did not understand that the "other man" was the real self. He was trapped in intellectual considerations.

33. The original meaning of the Sanskrit *dhyāna* was meditation, or concentration or tranquillity. *Dhyāna* originated in India in the Vedic Age, and was adopted by Buddhists throughout Asia. *Dhyāna* is sometimes used synonymously with *samādhi*, or absorption (*sammai* in Japanese, *san-mei* in Chinese). It is one of the essential approaches of Zen; as it is practiced in China and Japan, the awakening of *prajñā* is its object.

34. This was to say that Lu's understanding was not yet high enough for him to be able to make a correct answer. He had not yet come up to the door.

35. The four modes of birth are: from the womb, from the egg, from moisture, and through the transformation of forms. The six levels of reincarnation are: that of a spirit in hell, that of a bodiless ghost, that of an animal body, that of a malevolent spirit, that of a human form, and that of a deva on a high level of existence.

36. I.e., dice made from animal bone.

37. One of the ten chief disciples of Śākyamuni, specially noted for miraculous powers.

38. According to the Indian tradition there are thirty-two distinguishing physical characteristics of all great sages, including the Buddha, such as slender fingers, broad shoulders, a beautiful voice, etc.

39. *Wei-na* is the Chinese transliteration of *karmadana*, the duty-distributor, the second in command in a monastery.

40. Sêng-chao (384–414), one of the best disciples of Kumārajīva.

41. The Chinese text refers to "residence" as *ti-wei*, which means the position of the earth. And *"deva"* is referred to as a "Heavenly King." The

literal translation would be: If he is a Heavenly King, it is obvious that he is non-attached to the position of the earth.

42. *Pramudita*, the first stage of Mahāyāna Bodhisattva development, means joy at having overcome former difficulties and entering upon the path of Buddhahood.

43. Ch'an Master Tung-shan Liang-chieh. See *The Lamp*, Chüan 15.

44. *Kalpa* means aeon. More specifically, it refers to the period of time between the creation and the re-creation of the universe. This Great Kalpa is divided into four lesser kalpas: formation, existence, destruction, and void. The kalpa of the void is the last stage in the cycle.

45. Hui-nêng, the Sixth Patriarch.

46. In the southwestern Hopeh Province, near Shih-chia-chuang; called Ch'ao-hsien since 1913.

47. Now Ho-tse, east of Hsin-hsiang in southern Pingyuan Province.

48. Now Kuei-ch'ih (see note 16 above).

49. Shui-hsiang, the name of the monastery, means the Image of Buddha. Traditionally the first image of Buddha was made of sandalwood by Udayana, King of Kauśāmbī.

50. I.e., not yet differentiated as either good or bad; *wu-chi* in Chinese, *avyākrita* in Sanskrit

51. According to Chao-chou's *Dialogues* the Chinese text is *pu-nien*, or "non-intention." This coheres with the previous statement. However, the text of *The Lamp* is *pu-yi*, or "without doubt," which does not apply to his prior comment.

52. Ch'an Master Pao-shou Chao of Chen-chou, a disciple of Lin-chi I-hsüan.

53. Ch'an Master Yen-kuan Ch'i-an of Hang-chou, a disciple of Ma-tsu Tao-i. See *The Lamp*, Chüan 7.

54. Ch'an Master Chia-shan Shan-hui of Li-chou. See *The Lamp*, Chüan 15.

55. Another of the five sacred Buddhist mountains, near the northeastern border of Shansi Province; altitude 9,974 feet. Mañjuśrī is its patron saint, and it is much frequented by pilgrims.

56. Ching-liang was another name for Mount Wu-t'ai, at the time of the T'ang Dynasty.

57. *Dhvaja*, a stone Buddhist symbol indicating the power of the Bodhisattva to exorcise devils.

58. There are two versions of this sūtra, the Hīnayāna and the Mahāyāna, both of which have been translated into Chinese on several occasions. Numerous treatises have been written on them. The title *The Sūtra of Nirvāna* usually refers to the Mahāyāna version.

59. Ch'an Master Hsüeh-fêng I-ts'un. See *The Lamp*, Chüan 16.

60. Ch'an Master Yün-chü Tao-ying (d. 902), a disciple of Tung-shan Liang-chieh.

61. This quotation is from "Inscribed on the Believing Mind" by Sêng-ts'an, the Third Patriarch (d. A.D. 606).

62. The text reads *sang shen shih ming*, a colloquial expression of the time, meaning literally to lose one's body and life, but used by the Ch'an Buddhists to imply losing one's calculating mind and thereby finding one's real self.

NOTES

63. This refers to a salt peddler who evaded his taxes by not passing through the city gate.

64. In the idiomatic text of the original, Chao-chou stresses "understanding" here rather than "gratitude."

65. See note 44 above.

66. Now Chinan (Tsinan), capital of Shantung Province in northeast China.

67. Chinese measuring unit, usually sixteen ounces.

68. Tuṣita Heaven is the name of the fourth *devaloka* in the passion realm between the Yama and Nirmarati Heavens. Its inner department is the Pure Land of Maitreya, who was reborn there before descending to earth as the next Buddha.

69. Jambūdvīpa is one of the seven continents surrounding the mountain Meru.

70. The mani gem is a bright, luminous pearl, a symbol of Buddha and his doctrine.

71. Vipaśyin is the first of the seven Buddhas of antiquity.

72. Hsüan-sha Shih-pei (935–908), a disciple of Hsüeh-fêng I-ts'un. His teachings appear in *The Lamp*, Chüan 18.

73. *Mu-shang* means "the last to enter," in modern terms, but in T'ang dialect it meant "the first one to enter." In the fascicle of Fa-yen Wên-i, in *The Lamp*, the T'ang meaning of *mu shang* is used in denoting the first statement of "Contemplation on Identification and Unification."

74. Now Hsiang-yang (Siangyang), in northern Hupeh Province on the Han River.

75. A city east of Heng-shan in central Hunan Province.

76. The courtesy name is used as a form of address only by one's friends. Letters or documents require a formal name.

77. Shih-t'ou Hsi-ch'ien was the leading master in the Ch'an center in Hunan (South of the Lake), while Ma-tsu Tao-i was the leader in Kiangsi (West of the River). See *The Lamp*, Chüan 14.

78. A disciple of Shih-t'ou Hsi-ch'ien. See *The Lamp*, Chüan 14.

79. The beginning words of the sūtra are "Thus I have heard"; the concluding words, "In faith receive and obey."

Part V

Introduction
Inner Experience Illustrated in Three-Way Interplay

Kuei-shan Ling-yu (771–853)
Great Action and Great Potentiality

Yang-shan Hui-chi (814–890)
"An Excellent Swordsman"

Hsiang-yen Chih-hsien
Enlightened by One Stroke

Inner Experience Illustrated in Three-Way Interplay

The School of Kuei-yang, one of the five most famous sects of Ch'an Buddhism in China, was founded by Kuei-shan Ling-yu and his follower Yang-shan Hui-chi. Hsiang-yen Chih-hsien, another noted disciple of Master Kuei-shan and a brother monk of Yang-shan, was also important in the early history of the school. In Ch'an literature the dialogues between Kuei-shan and Yang-shan are considered typical of the question-and-answer method of instruction, with question and answer following one another even as the echo responds to the voice in the valley. The exchanges between Kuei-shan and Yang-shan are well known, but the three-way conversations between these two and Hsiang-yen are less so, though they eloquently illustrate the very highest level of interplay between their respective inner realities in complete freedom from attachment to things.

Let us look first at a dialogue between Master Kuei-shan and his disciple Yang-shan. Once Kuei-shan asked Yang-shan, "Where have you been?" Yang-shan replied, "I have just come from the field." Kuei-shan went on, "How many people are there?" Yang-shan thrust his hoe into the ground and stood there motionless. Said

Kuei-shan, "Today at the southern mountain a man worked at harvesting the rushes." Thereupon Yang-shan picked up his hoe and walked away.

When we first come to study the teachings of Kuei-shan, we notice that he often discusses the doctrines of *ta-chi*, or "the great potentiality," and *ta-yung*, or "the great action." Both doctrines are illustrated in the foregoing *kung-an*. When Yang-shan thrust his hoe into the ground, we note, he stood there motionless. He did not answer his master in words, but his inner understanding was nevertheless revealed through this very non-action. That is why Master Kuei-shan, in his remark about the farmer harvesting his crop, praised him for having reached such an advanced stage in his cultivation of Ch'an. But this flattering remark did not move Yang-shan in the least; his inner tranquillity, like the calmly reflecting mirror of a lake, remained undisturbed even after a stone was dropped into it. When Kuei-shan made his comment, Yang-shan picked up his hoe and walked away. According to conventional ideas, such behavior might well be considered rude, but a Ch'an disciple's concept of personal relationships is quite different. He has been taught to free himself from all entanglements with persons or things. His ultimate aim is the complete liberation of his own inner self, freedom from every sort of circumstantial fetters. Yang-shan demonstrated this capacity by picking up his hoe and walking away from his master, indifferent even to his praise, an inner self not shaken by either praise or criticism. This is action of a powerful sort.

On another occasion Yang-shan remarked to Kuei-shan that Po-chang had achieved the great potentiality, and Huang-po, the great action. However, we find that when either potentiality or action reaches its utmost, then both are simultaneously present and have become one and the same. The distinction is made here for convenience of discussion, but in reality it does not exist. When Huang-po considered the teachings of Ma-tsu, he recognized this synthesis and called it *ta-chi chih yung*, or "potentiality in action." This can be better understood if we look at a *kung-an* which was used in the process of selecting an abbot for the monastery on Mount Kuei.

Inner Experience Illustrated in Three-Way Interplay

Hua-lin, head monk in the temple, went angrily to Master Po-chang when he heard that Kuei-shan was to be appointed abbot on Mount Kuei. How could this be? he asked. Whereupon Po-chang said to him, "If you can correctly answer my question in front of the assembly, you will be appointed abbot." Po-chang then pointed to a pitcher and said, "Do not call this a pitcher. What, rather, should you call it?" Hua-lin answered, "It cannot be called a wooden wedge." Master Po-chang shook his head and turned to Ling-yu for an answer. Ling-yu kicked the pitcher over. Master Po-chang laughed and said, "Our head monk has lost his bid for Mount Kuei." Thus Ling-yu was selected to be the abbot in the new monastery.

From this *kung-an* it is quite clear that Hua-lin's answer was only on an intellectual level. He merely argued about the name of an object, revealing no depth of inner cultivation. Kuei-shan Ling-yu, however, did not take his answer from the relative plane. He did not declare that the pitcher should be called this or that. In knocking over the pitcher instead, he revealed his inner enlightenment.

Another illustration of great potentiality and great action occurring simultaneously is found in the fascicle of Po-chang. One day all the monks of the temple were working together in the fields. When the drum summoning them to dinner sounded, one of the monks threw up his hoe, and laughing heartily, started back toward the temple. Master Po-chang remarked, "What fine work this is! It is the way whereby the Goddess of Mercy enters Ultimate Reality."

The monk who laughed and threw up his hoe demonstrated thus his awakening to the truth of Ch'an. From the depths of his unconscious his potentiality suddenly manifested itself in a spontaneous action, just as Kuei-shan had revealed his potentiality in action by wordlessly knocking over the pitcher. Responses such as these do not aim at a display of intellectual superiority but reveal spontaneous enlightenment.

Sometimes Kuei-shan considered potentiality as separate from action, but what he mainly stressed was potentiality in action, *ta-chi chih yung*. Once when he complained that his disciples had not attained great action, one of his disciples, Chiu-fêng Tzu-hui, stepped out of the crowd and started to walk away. When Kuei-shan called to him, he proceeded straight ahead without even turning his head. Kuei-shan remarked, "This man is certainly qualified to be a man of Ch'an." His silent disappearance from the scene was his answer—a gesture of non-action. But to Kuei-shan the gesture was correct, a powerful action. It was, in fact, potentiality in action. Reality may be revealed through action or silence: thus both become great potentiality and great action.

From these remarks on great potentiality and great action, perhaps we can derive what Kuei-shan meant by *ti*, substance, and *yung*, function. The following *kung-an*, famous in Ch'an literature, appears in the fascicle of Kuei-shan. One day when the Master and Yang-shan were picking tea leaves, the Master said, "All day I have heard your voice as we picked tea leaves, but I have not seen you yourself. Show me your real self." Yang-shan shook the tea tree. The Master commented, "You have achieved the function but not the substance." When Yang-shan asked his Master what he himself had achieved, the Master remained silent. Thereupon Yang-shan commented, "You, Master, have achieved the substance but not the function."

What Kuei-shan and Yang-shan meant was that *ti*, substance, is formless and thoughtless, and yet through it reality is revealed. *Yung*, function, is the direct and free action manifesting absolute reality. In other words, *ti* is reality revealed in non-action, and *yung* is reality manifested in action. If the shaking of a tea tree manifests reality, then it is an instance of the great action, or *ta-yung*; if silence reveals reality, then it is an example of the great potentiality, or *ta-chi*. The essence of Ch'an may be experienced either in silence or in action.

We must note that the *ti* and *yung* discussed by Kuei-shan are not identical to those in the "three greatnesses" expounded by Aśvaghosa, the great Indian Mahāyāna philospher, in *The Awakening of Faith*. These three greatnesses are *ti*, substance; *hsiang*, appearance; and *yung*, function. But substance here implies appearance or form, and function implies activity. If we mistake these three greatnesses for merely intellectually intelligible concepts,

Inner Experience Illustrated in Three-Way Interplay

Ch'an slips away from us. Unless we ourselves experience what Kuei-shan and Yang-shan experienced, we will never be able to penetrate to the underlying truth.

To experience Ch'an in silence and in action is to progress in self-realization. A disciple's various levels of inner achievement may be recognized by his gestures and words, however irrelevant or irrational they may appear to one who is accustomed to more conventional communication. When we compare Hsiang-yen's three famous *gāthās*, we find they reveal successive stages in the progression of his inner enlightenment. In the *Recorded Dialogues of Ch'an Master Kuei-shan Ling-yu of T'an-chou* we learn that when Hsiang-yen was accidentally enlightened by the sound of a stone knocking against a bamboo tree, his brother monk Yang-shan, from Mount Kuei, went to the place where Hsiang-yen was staying, to test him. When Yang-shan arrived, Hsiang-yen recited the *gāthā* he had composed after his awakening:

> With one stroke, all previous knowledge is forgotten.
> No cultivation is needed for this.
> This occurrence reveals the ancient way
> And is free from the track of quiescence.
> No trace is left anywhere.
> Whatever I hear and see does not conform to rules.
> All those who are enlightened
> Proclaim this to be the greatest action.

Yang-shan did not accept this *gāthā*, remonstrating, "Herein you followed the sayings of the ancient masters. If you have really been awakened, speak from your own experience." Then Hsiang-yen composed a second *gāthā*:

> My poverty of last year was not real poverty.
> This year it is want indeed.
> In last year's poverty there was room for a piercing gimlet.
> In this year's poverty even the gimlet is no more.

Yang-shan made the following well-known comment on this *gāthā*: "You may have the Ch'an of Tathāgata,[1] but as for the Ch'an of the Patriarchs, you have not yet even dreamed of it." Hearing this, Hsiang-yen immediately uttered his third *gāthā*:

Inner Experience Illustrated in Three-Way Interplay

I have my secret.
I look at you with twinkling eye.
If you do not understand this
Do not call yourself a monk.

Yang-shan was much pleased with this third *gāthā* and went back to report to Master Kuei-shan, "I rejoice that brother Hsiang-yen has grasped the Ch'an of the Patriarchs."

These three *gāthā* reveal Hsiang-yen's inner experience on different levels. The first is an intellectual description of his awakening. Although he was truly enlightened, this *gāthā* is merely a conceptual product of his sudden awakening, not a direct revelation from the depth of his unconscious. In the second *gāthā*, Hsiang-yen refers to the absolute nothingness, or "poverty," as he puts it, using this as a metaphor for the emptiness which is usually achieved through meditation. Therefore Yang-shan called it the Ch'an of Tathāgata. But the third *gāthā* is different from the traditional approach. It is neither an intellectual description of the awakening, nor does it speak of the attainment of nothingness or emptiness. In other words, it is free from both verbal determination and the void. In the "twinkling eye" we have great action revealing great potentiality from the depths of true experience. Only those who have achieved the same level of experience can understand what Hsiang-yen meant. Yang-shan accepted this *gāthā* wholeheartedly.

Some years later, when Hsiang-yen was serving as abbot in Têng-chou, a monk came from Mount Kuei to visit him. He asked his visitor about Kuei-shan's recent teachings. The monk replied that on a recent occasion the question had been raised about the meaning of Bodhidharma coming from the West, a question which Kuei-shan had responded to by raising his *fu-tzu*. Hsiang-yen asked, "How did the fellow monks in the temple take this?" His visitor quoted: "Mind is illumined through matter and reality is revealed through things." Hsiang-yen did not approve of this interpretation since it was merely an intellectual response, not a revelation of the inner experience that is achieved through Ch'an. When the visitor requested Hsiang-yen's answer, Master Hsiang-yen lifted his *fu-tzu* even as Master Kuei-shan had done. From this *kung-an*, it is apparent that it had not been in vain that in earlier days Yang-shan had pressed Hsiang-yen for his third *gāthā*.

In connection with the various levels of awakening implicit in Hsiang-yen's *gāthā*-making, we might examine the story of his sudden enlightenment. One day when Hsiang-yen was still a disciple of Kuei-shan, the Master had said to him, "I do not want to ask what you have learned from your studies or what you remember from the sūtras and the śāstras. Simply tell me in one word what was your original being before your parents gave you birth and before you could discriminate among things." Hsiang-yen could not come up with an answer, and finally looked to his notes for help. But even from among the words of the well-known masters he was unable to formulate a reply, whereupon he set fire to all his notes and left his master.

In his solitary life, it happened that one day when he was weeding in the fields, a piece of stone he had dislodged struck a bamboo tree. The sound that this produced made him burst out laughing and unexpectedly opened him to a state of enlightenment.

In Hsiang-yen's case we have an example of enlightenment attained paradoxically in the abandonment of the search for Ch'an —the effect of the cultivation of non-cultivation. However, the conventional use of intellectual concepts to describe one's inner awakening can hardly be avoided. Although Hsiang-yen was enlightened, it was not until later that he was able to reveal his invisible potentiality directly from the depth of his unconscious in his third *gāthā*.

The story of Hsiang-yen's enlightenment and his three *gāthās* helps us to understand the way in which Ch'an is achieved. The progress of Yang-shan in the study of Ch'an is also a good illustration for those who strive toward the awakening of the mind. Yang-shan's achievement of Ch'an is well known, and he is famed as the cofounder of the School of Kuei-yang. Nevertheless his grasp of the truth was not at all as simple and as easy as it may appear. To understand a single *kung-an* on the meaning of Bodhidharma coming from the West, he had to go to three masters, one after the other, before he finally was awakened.

Inner Experience Illustrated in Three-Way Interplay

When Yang-shan was a boy attendant of Shih-shuang Hsing-k'ung in T'an-chou, he heard a monk ask the meaning of Bodhidharma coming from the West, and heard Master Shih-shuang's answer: "This question will be solved by one who can climb out of a well a thousand feet deep without even an inch of rope." Yang-shan failed completely to understand this reply. Some time later he went to study under Tan-yüan Chen-ying and put to him the question of the man getting out of the well without a rope. Master Tan-yüan replied, "Oh, what a fool! Who is in the well?" But Yang-shan still remained in the dark, gaining no insight into the truth. Finally he arrived at Mount Kuei and became a disciple of Kuei-shan Ling-yu. One day he put this same question to Master Kuei-shan. Kuei-shan cried, "Oh! Hui-chi [Yang-shan]!" Yang-shan replied, "Yes, Master!" "Here! He is out!" answered Kuei-shan. Therefore Yang-shan told his friends, "Under Tan-yüan I gained an understanding of the name, but it was under Kuei-shan that I reached an understanding of the substance." According to Dr. Suzuki's interpretation, the former understanding is philosophical, while the latter is inner awareness.

In this story of Yang-shan's awakening through the use of a *kung-an*, we see that to have one's mind opened and see the truth requires patience and effort in addition to one's inherent capacity. By the first master's irrelevant answer Yang-shan's mind was stirred, but he failed to see the point. Tan-yüan, the second master, tried to brush away his confusion and turn him toward the center of his being, but he was still trapped in a well of intellection and could not emerge. Finally Master Kuei-shan awakened him directly by calling out his name, thereby stirring up his initial consciousness, or *yeh shih*, in order to penetrate into the depths of his mind. Through a sudden awakening of the initial consciousness, the shell of the unconscious is often broken and the mind thereby opened.

Throughout *The Lamp* we find that masters such as Ma-tsu, Po-chang, Nan-ch'üan, Mu-chou, Yün-mên, and others often applied the same approach in order to open the minds of their disciples through initial consciousness. For instance, when the disciple made

Inner Experience Illustrated in Three-Way Interplay

a bow and started to leave, the master would suddenly call out his name. As soon as the man turned his head, the master would ask him, "What is it?" Whereupon the disciple was often awakened.

After Yang-shan had become an abbot he went back to visit Master Kuei-shan. On one occasion, he wished to point out to the Master what he understood about the initial consciousness. When he saw a monk passing by he suddenly called him by his name, and the monk immediately turned his head. Yang-shan said to the Master, "Here we have proof that initial consciousness is invisible and that nothing in it can be determined." According to *The Awakening of Faith* the mind is opened through this initial consciousness, which marks the very beginning of the emergence of the non-differentiated mind.

Both Yang-shan and Hsiang-yen, as we have seen, had to exhaust their intellectual pursuit in order to move toward the plane on which their masters stood. Ch'an had to be experienced; it could not be reasoned out. And it is not until we ourselves penetrate into the depth of the unconscious that we can appreciate the efforts made by Yang-shan and Hsiang-yen in their pursuit of Ch'an. We observe their progress up until the moment they abandon intellectual searching and are thrown open to a basic awakening.

In the history of Ch'an we have noted that the question is asked repeatedly as to the meaning of Bodhidharma coming from the West. In *Ch'an-lin Lei-chu*, or *Collection and Classification of Ch'an Materials*, we find some instances of the use of this pertinent question. It occurs frequently in other places in Ch'an literature. The answers to this *kung-an* vary widely. Chao-chou's answer was, "The cypress tree in the courtyard." Feng-yang Shan-chao's answer was, "The blue silk fan brings the cool breeze." Ling-shu Jü-min remained silent when he was approached with this question. Ma-tsu treated his questioner to a kick and knocked him down. When Hsüeh-fêng and Hsüan-sha were repairing a fence, the latter put the same question. Hsüeh-fêng merely shook the fence. When Yang-shan asked Kuei-shan the question, Kuei-shan's reply was, "A fine large lantern." This answer, for all its apparent difference, is as

Inner Experience Illustrated in Three-Way Interplay

relevant as the reference to the blue silk fan or any of the others because it leads directly to the ultimate truth of Ch'an. The fan, the lantern, the cypress tree must not be given symbolic interpretations, because to do so misses the point. Commenting on Kuei-shan's answer in terms of the lantern, Dr. Suzuki has this to say:

> The master when questioned may happen to be engaged in some work, or looking out of the window, or sitting quietly in meditation, and then his response may contain some allusion to the objects thus connected with his doing at the time. Whatever he may say, therefore, on such occasion is not an abstract assertion or one deliberately chosen for the illustration of his point.
>
> Wei-shan [Kuei-shan], for instance, questioned by Yang-shan, answered, "What a fine lantern is this!" Probably he was looking at the lantern at the moment, or it stood nearest to them and came in most convenient for the master to be utilized for his immediate purpose.[2]

After Kuei-shan's answer in terms of the lantern, Yang-shan tried to get his master's approval by displaying his own understanding on the intellectual level. He asked, "Is it not 'this'? " ("This" refers to Ch'an.) Kuei-shan immediately cut his stream of thought by asking him, "What is 'this'? " Yang-shan answered, "A fine large lantern." Master Kuei-shan said, "You really don't know."

Are we then to suppose that Yang-shan really did not know, despite his progress? When I was in Kyoto I discussed this problem with Rōshi Yamada Mumon, a distinguished Zen scholar and president of Hanazono University. His answer was that Ch'an masters often use these tactics of concealment and denial to test their disciples. He was convinced that Yang-shan really did know. Later in Kamakura, I asked Dr. Suzuki about the same point. His answer was the same: "This is the secrecy that the Zen masters frequently applied. Yang-shan really did know." For further proof of this interpretation we may look at a few older exchanges between Kuei-shan, Yang-shan, and Hsiang-yen.

Once when Yang-shan and Hsiang-yen were attending Master Kuei-shan, the Master remarked, "All Buddhas in the past, present, and future walk on the same path. From this path everyone finds his way to freedom. What is this way that leads everyone to freedom?" Kuei-shan turned his head to look at Hsiang-yen, saying, "Hui-chi [Yang-shan] is asking you a question. Why don't you answer him?" Hsiang-yen said, "If we are talking about the past, present, and future, I have no answer." Kuei-shan demanded, "Come! You must answer!" Thereupon Hsiang-yen made a bow and went away. Master Kuei-shan turned to Yang-shan and said, "Hsiang-yen has made his answer. Do you agree with him?" Yang-shan replied, "I do not agree with him." Kuei-shan asked, "Then what is your answer?" Yang-shan also made a bow and went away. Seeing this, Master Kuei-shan laughed heartily and commented, "They are just like milk mixed with water."

Yang-shan answered in the same manner as Hsiang-yen. Nevertheless, when Master Kuei-shan asked him if he agreed with the answer given by Hsiang-yen, Yang-shan said that he did not. But actually Hsiang-yen's answer was correct and Yang-shan knew it. Likewise, when Kuei-shan heard Yang-shan's answer in terms of the lantern, he seemed not to accept his disciple's words, but actually he perceived that Yang-shan really did know. When we read the fascicle of Fa-yen Wên-i in Part VI, we will find that this master also often appears to disagree with the answers of his disciples even when it is apparent that they are correct: when interrogated by such a disciple as to what answer he himself would have given, the master repeats the very words which have just been offered him and apparently rejected by him. Accordingly, we may deduce that mere verbal denial by a master does not necessarily signify rejection of the answer. Such denials may be indirect or concealed recognition of the disciple's awakened mind, a mind far beyond those trained in dualistic dialectics.

Perhaps one more illustration of Kuei-shan's denials will make the subtleties of his approach clearer to us. One day Master Kuei-shan said to Yang-shan and Hsiang-yen, "In the middle of the winter the weather becomes bitterly cold. But this happens every year. Can you tell me who is its mover?" When Yang-shan heard this he folded his hands in front of his chest, paced a few steps,

Inner Experience Illustrated in Three-Way Interplay

and then stood still. The Master remarked, "I know you cannot answer my question." Then Hsiang-yen came forward and said, "I can answer it." Master Kuei-shan said, "What is your answer?" Hsiang-yen paced a few steps with his hands folded in front of his chest and then he also stood still. Master Kuei-shan thereupon announced, "It is unfortunate that Hui-chi [Yang-shan] could not understand my question." But this verbal denial is quite clearly not a disparagement of Yang-shan's reply.

Oftentimes we find that Yang-shan used silence as his answer. Sometimes he stood still, sometimes he departed from his questioner without a word. Often he used significant gestures. According to Kuei-shan, such silent answers can be as powerful as a sharp sword, as illustrated in the following story.

A monk asked Master Yang-shan, "Would the *dharmakāya* also know how to expound the teachings of Buddhism?" The Master answered, "I cannot tell you, but somebody else can." The monk asked, "Where is the one who can tell?" Master Yang-shan silently pushed forward a pillow. Kuei-shan's comment on this was, "Hui-chi is engaging in swordplay."

Yang-shan's swordplay was applied not only in answering his disciples; he had long practiced it in answering his fellow monks when he was still a disciple himself under Kuei-shan. An instance of this is his response to the statement of the head monk at Mount Kuei: "On the tips of a hundred million hairs a hundred million lions reveal themselves." Yang-shan asked whether the lions revealed themselves on the front of the hairs or on the back. The head monk replied, "When the lions reveal themselves, we do not say whether it is on the front or on the back." Yang-shan's answer was to depart in silence, at which Master Kuei-shan remarked, "Now the lion is chopped off at the middle!"

Yang-shan's silent departure was a form of "swordplay" which chopped the head monk off at the middle. Because it was the head monk who had first mentioned the lion, Master Kuei-shan referred to him sarcastically as "the lion." Actually, this kind of interplay appears frequently in the School of Kuei-shan. In the *Amalgamation of the Essentials of the Lamps*, Chüan 5, we have a clear illus-

Inner Experience Illustrated in Three-Way Interplay

tration of such swordplay between Master Kuei-shan and Yang-shan.

Yang-shan asked Master Kuei-shan, "When the great action is taking place, how do you determine it?" Master Kuei-shan immediately came down from his seat and went to his chamber. Yang-shan followed him and entered the room. Kuei-shan said to him, "What was it you asked me?" Yang-shan repeated the question. Kuei-shan said, "Don't you remember my answer?" Yang-shan said, "Yes, I remember it." Kuei-shan then pressed him further: "Try to say it to me." Yang-shan immediately left the room. Silent departure from one's questioner, as applied by both Kuei-shan and Yang-shan, may be a revelation of the great potentiality. Inner reality is revealed through silence. Such silence may be as powerful as "swordplay."

The teaching of Kuei-shan not only stressed *kung-an* training to achieve mind-awakening but also emphasized meditation as the path to illumination. In the *Ts'ung-yung Lu*, or *Records of Serenity*, Kung-an 32, Hung-chih Cheng-chio relates that in the middle of the night Yang-shan achieved *samādhi* during meditation. All of a sudden he felt that mountains, rivers, fields, monasteries, people, all things, even he himself, did not exist. It was as if his mind were in a world of transparent emptiness. The next morning he reported this to Master Kuei-shan, who told him that when he himself was studying under Master Po-chang Huai-hai, he had had a similar experience of illumination. However, Kuei-shan warned those who practiced meditation that though they might reach a high level of spiritual achievement, there would still be a basic delusion which could not be entirely eliminated.[3] This point is also taken up in the fascicle of Kuei-fêng Tsung-mi, where he says:

> I went to the mountain to practice *samādhi* identified with *prajñā*. During two separate stays I spent a total of ten years there, keeping myself in the state of cessation of thought; the inevitable remaining passions continue to rise up and disappear in the realm of quiescent wisdom.

Freeing themselves from the remaining delusions is what the Buddhists are deeply concerned about. Kuei-shan's method of

Inner Experience Illustrated in Three-Way Interplay

gaining complete liberation comprises more than meditation. In his works we read the following:

> When the approach to enlightenment is like the swift thrust of a sword to the center of things, then both worldliness and holiness are completely eliminated and Absolute Reality is revealed. Thus the One and the Many are identified. This is the Suchness of Buddha.

Kuei-shan's "swift thrust of a sword to the center of things" is illustrated by his own answer to Po-chang when the latter was choosing the candidate for abbot of Mount Kuei. The "great action" of kicking over the pitcher demonstrated Kuei-shan's inner tranquillity, free from affirmation and negation, worldliness and holiness. Thus what is revealed with him is the "Suchness of Buddha," entirely free from delusion.

In the fascicle of Yang-shan, we find that he maintains the same attitude toward the practice of meditation and freedom from it as did his master, Kuei-shan. He advises beginning students of Ch'an that although a man of exceptional capacity and intuitiveness might become totally enlightened in a moment, those who are less talented should be content in their meditations and pure in thought, for the pursuit of sudden enlightenment would leave them entirely lost. At the same time, he warns that to remain in emptiness is also far from correct. He particularly points out the difference between *hsin wei*, "the level of concentration on the void," and *jen wei*, "the level of absolute freedom." On the level of concentration on the void, one is still attached to it and cannot set oneself free. But when one reaches the level of absolute freedom, one is liberated from both the void and the non-void. In the *Records of Serenity*, Kung-an 32, these two levels are commented upon as stages of inner cultivation. We have an illustration in the *Diagrams of the Twelve Stages of Cow Herding*, by Ch'ing-chü Hao-sheng.[4] At the diagram of the sixth stage, the author remarks:

> When the level of concentration on the void is gradually attained, one will feel that he is free from delusion. Although he keeps himself pure and rejects the impure, his mind is not

Inner Experience Illustrated in Three-Way Interplay

yet completely pure—it is as a sword that has cut through mud and remains uncleaned.

In the diagram, the cow is shown as still being pulled by the halter. At this stage one cannot be certain of one's achievement: hence, the cow is drawn half white and half black. In the diagram of the twelfth stage we have the following comment:

> When one reaches *jen wei*, or the level of absolute freedom, he is truly free. His mind and body are non-attached to anything. There is absolutely no gain and no loss. This mystery is the way of non-differentiation. If one tried to say even one word about it, he would miss the point.

When we are clear as to the difference in achievement between the level of concentration on the void and the level of absolute freedom, we can understand the "swordplay" so much emphasized in the works of the masters of the School of Kuei-yang. When we encounter the various *kung-an* on swordplay in Kuei-shan, Yang-shan, and Hsiang-yen, we can then see the great potentiality in action. This is the manifestation of the level of absolute freedom, as will be evident in the following fascicles.

KUEI-SHAN LING-YU
(771–853)

Great Action and Great Potentiality

(*From* The Transmission of the Lamp, *Chüan* 9)

CH'AN Master Kuei-shan Ling-yu of T'an-chou[6] was a native of Chang-ch'i in Fu-chou.[7] His original surname was Chao. When he was fifteen he left his parents and became a monk. In the Chien-shan Monastery in his native town, he studied under the Vinaya master Fa-ch'ang and had his head shaved. Later he was ordained at the Lung-hsing Monastery in Hang-chou,[8] where he devoted himself to the study of the sūtras and vinayas of both the Mahāyāna and the Hīnayāna. At the age of twenty-three he traveled to Kiangsi, where he visited Master Po-chang Huai-hai. As soon as the master saw his visitor he gave him permission to study in the temple, and thereafter Kuei-shan became Po-chang's leading disciple.

One day Kuei-shan was attending Master Po-chang, who asked him:

"Who are you?"

"I am Ling-yu."

"Will you poke the fire pot and find out whether there is some burning charcoal in it?" said Po-chang.

Kuei-shan did so, and then said, "There is no burning charcoal."

Master Po-chang rose from his seat. Poking deep into the fire pot, he extracted a small glowing piece of charcoal which he showed to Kuei-shan, saying, "Is this not a burning piece?"

At this, Kuei-shan was awakened. Thereupon he made a profound bow and told Po-chang what had happened. However, Po-chang explained:

"The method that I used just now was only for this occasion. It is not the usual approach. The Sūtra says, 'To behold the Buddha-nature one must wait for the right moment and the right conditions. When the time comes, one is awakened as from a dream. It is as if one's memory recalls something long forgotten. One realizes that what is obtained is one's own and not from outside one's self.' Thus an ancient patriarch said, 'After enlightenment one is still the same as one was before. There is no mind and there is no Dharma.'[9] One is simply free from unreality and delusion. The mind of the ordinary man is the same as that of the sage because the Original Mind is perfect and complete in itself. When you have attained this recognition, hold on to what you have achieved."

During this period, Dhūta[10] Ssu-ma came from Hunan to see Master Po-chang. The Master asked whether it was possible for him to go to Mount Kuei. The Dhūta answered that Mount Kuei was extremely steep, but that despite this one thousand five hundred devotees could gather there. However, the Dhūta said that it would not be a good preaching place for Master Po-chang. The Master asked why he said that. The Dhūta pointed out that Master Po-chang was a gaunt man of ascetic habits, while Kuei was a mountain of flesh, warm and sensuous, and that if he should go there, he could expect fewer than a thousand disciples. Po-chang asked him whether he thought that among his students there might be one suitable to act as abbot on the mountain. Dhūta Ssu-ma told him he would like to see all his disciples one by one. Po-chang thereupon sent for the head monk. The Dhūta ordered him to cough deeply once and pace several steps, and afterward announced that this monk was not qualified for the post. Po-chang sent for Ling-yu, who was the business supervisor of the temple. As soon as he saw him the Dhūta announced, "Here we have the right man to be the Master of Mount Kuei!"

The same night Po-chang called Ling-yu to his chamber and

Inner Experience Illustrated in Three-Way Interplay

told him, "Mount Kuei will be a splendid place to carry forth the teaching of our school and to extend enlightenment to the generation to come."

When the head monk, Hua-lin, heard of this decision he complained to Po-chang, pointing out that he was the head monk and deserved the appointment. How could Ling-yu rightfully be appointed abbot of Mount Kuei? Po-chang said to him:

"If you can make an outstanding response in front of the assembly, you shall receive the appointment." Po-chang then pointed to a pitcher and said to him, "Do not call this a pitcher. What, instead, should you call it?" Hua-lin answered, "It cannot be called a wooden wedge." Master Po-chang did not accept this, and turned to Ling-yu, demanding his answer. Ling-yu kicked the pitcher and knocked it over. Master Po-chang laughed and said, "Our head monk has lost his bid for Mount Kuei." Ling-yu subsequently was sent to be abbot of Mount Kuei.

Mount Kuei had formerly been an inaccessible region. The rocks were steep and high, and no one lived there. Only monkeys could be found for companions and only chestnuts were available as food. When people at the foot of the mountain heard that Master Ling-yu was living there they assembled to build a monastery for him. Through General Li Ching-jang's recommendation the Royal Court granted the title Tung-ching to the monastery. Often the Prime Minister, Pei Hsiu, came to the Master to ask questions about the meaning of Ch'an, and from this period onward devotees from all over the country journeyed to Mount Kuei.

One day Master Kuei-shan Ling-yu came into the assembly and said:

"The mind of one who understands Ch'an is plain and straightforward without pretense. It has neither front nor back and is without deceit or delusion. Every hour of the day, what one hears and sees are ordinary things and ordinary actions. Nothing is distorted. One does not need to shut one's eyes and ears to be non-attached to things. In the early days many sages stressed the follies and dangers of impurity. When delusion, perverted views, and bad thinking habits are eliminated, the mind is as clear and tranquil as the autumn stream. It is pure and quiescent, placid and free from attachment. Therefore he who is like this is called a Ch'annist, a man of non-attachment to things."

During an assembly period a monk asked whether the man who has achieved sudden enlightenment still requires self-cultivation. The Master answered, "If he should be truly enlightened, achieving his original nature and realizing himself, then the question of self-cultivation or non-cultivation is beside the point. Through concentration[11] a devotee may gain thoughtless thought. Thereby he is suddenly enlightened and realizes his original nature. However, there is still a basic delusion,[12] without beginning and without end, which cannot be entirely eliminated. Therefore the elimination of the manifestation of karma, which causes the remaining delusion to come to the surface, should be taught. This is cultivation. There is no other way of cultivation. When one hears the Truth one penetrates immediately to the Ultimate Reality, the realization of which is profound and wondrous. The mind is illuminated naturally and perfectly, free from confusion. On the other hand, in the present-day world there are numerous theories being expounded about Buddhism. These theories are advocated by those who wish to earn a seat in the temple and wear an abbot's robe to justify their work. But reality itself cannot be stained by even a speck of dust, and no action can distort the truth. When the approach to enlightenment is like the swift thrust of a sword to the center of things, then both worldliness and holiness are completely eliminated and Absolute Reality is revealed. Thus the One and the Many are identified. This is the Suchness of Buddha."

Yang-shan asked, "What was the meaning of Bodhidharma coming from the West?"

The Master answered, "A fine large lantern."

"Is it not 'this'? "

"What is 'this'? "

"A fine large lantern," Yang-shan said.

"You do not really *know*."

One day the Master said to the assembly, "There are many people who experience the great moment, but few who can perform the great function." Yang-shan went with this statement to the abbot of the temple at the foot of the mountain and asked him its meaning. The abbot said, "Try to repeat your question to me." As Yang-shan began to do so, the abbot kicked him and knocked him down. When Yang-shan returned and repeated this to the Master, Kuei-shan laughed heartily.

The Master was sitting in the Dharma Hall when the treasurer monk of the temple beat upon the "wooden fish,"[13] and the assistant cook threw away the fire tongs, clapped, and laughed loudly. The Master said, "In our temple, too, we have people like this. Call them here so that I can ask them what they are doing." The assistant cook explained, "I did not eat gruel and I was hungry. So I am very happy." The Master nodded his head.

Once when all the monks were out picking tea leaves the Master said to Yang-shan, "All day as we were picking tea leaves I have heard your voice, but I have not seen you yourself. Show me your original self." Yang-shan thereupon shook the tea tree.

The Master said, "You have attained only the function, not the substance." Yang-shan remarked, "I do not know how you yourself would answer the question." The Master was silent for a time. Yang-shan commented, "You, Master, have attained only the substance, not the function." Master Kuei-shan responded, "I absolve you from twenty blows!"

When the Master came to the assembly, a monk stepped forward and said to him, "Please, Master, give us the Dharma." "Have I not taught you thoroughly already?" asked the Master, and the monk bowed.

The Master told Yang-shan, "You should speak immediately. Do not enter the realm of illusion."

Yang-shan replied, "My faith in reality is not even established."

The Master said, "Have you had faith and been unable to establish it, or is it because you never had faith that you could not establish it?"

Yang-shan said, "What I believe in is Hui-chi. Why should I have faith in anyone else?"

The Master replied, "If this is the case, you have attained arhatship."[14]

Yang-shan answered, "I have not even seen the Buddha."

The Master asked Yang-shan, "In the forty volumes of the *Nirvāna Sūtra*, how many words were spoken by Buddha and how many by devils?"

Yang-shan answered, "They are all devils' words."

Master Kuei-shan said, "From now on, no one can do anything to you."

Yang-shan said, "I, Hui-chi, have simply seen the truth in this one instant. How should I apply it to my daily conduct?" The Master replied, "It is important that you see things correctly. I do not talk about your daily conduct."

Once when Yang-shan was washing his clothes, he lifted them up and asked the Master, "At this very moment, what are you doing?" The Master answered, "At this moment I am doing nothing." Yang-shan said, "Master! You have substance, but no function." The Master was silent for a while, then picked up the clothes and asked Yang-shan, "At this very moment, what are you doing?" Yang-shan replied, "At this moment, Master, do you still see 'this'?" The Master said, "You have function, but no substance."

One day the Master suddenly spoke to Yang-shan, "Last spring you made an incomplete statement. Can you complete it now?" Yang-shan answered, "At this very moment? One should not make a clay image in a moment." The Master said, "A retained prisoner improves in judgment."

One day the Master called for the manager of the temple, who came. The Master said, "I called for the manager of the temple. Why should you come here?" The manager made no answer. Thereupon the Master sent an attendant to summon the head monk. When the head monk appeared the Master said, " I called for the head monk. Why should you come here?" The head monk, too, made no answer.

The Master asked a newly arrived monk what his name was. The monk said, "Yüeh-lun [Full Moon]." The Master then drew a circle in the air with his hand. "How do you compare with this?" he asked. The monk replied, "Master, if you ask me in such a way, a great many people will not agree with you." Then the Master said,

"As for me, this is my way. What is yours?" The monk said, "Do you still see Yüeh-lun?" The Master answered, "You can say it your way, but there are a great many people here who do not agree with you."

The Master asked Yün-yen, "I have heard that you were with Master Yüeh-shan for a long time. Am I correct?" Yün-yen said he was right, and the Master continued, "What is the most distinctive aspect of Yüeh-shan's character?" Yün-yen answered, "*Nirvāna* comes later." The Master pressed, "What do you mean, *nirvāna* comes later?" Yün-yen replied, "Sprinkled water drops cannot reach it." In turn Yün-yen asked the Master, "What is the most distinctive feature of Po-chang's character?" The Master answered, "He is majestic and dignified, radiant and luminous. His is the soundlessness before sound and the colorlessness after the pigment has faded away. He is like an iron bull. When a mosquito lands upon him it can find no place to sting."

The Master was about to pass a pitcher to Yang-shan, who had put out his hands to receive it. But he suddenly withdrew the pitcher, saying, "What is this pitcher?" Yang-shan replied, "What have you discovered from it, Master?" The Master said, "If you challenge me in this way, why do you study with me?" Yang-shan explained, "Even though I challenge, it is still my duty to carry water for you in the pitcher." The Master then passed the pitcher to him.

During a stroll with Yang-shan, the Master pointed to a cypress tree and asked, "What is this in front of you?" Yang-shan answered, "As for this, it is just a cypress tree." The Master then pointed back to an old farmer and said, "This old man will one day have five hundred disciples."

The Master said to Yang-shan, "Where have you been?" Yang-shan answered, "At the farm." The Master said, "Are the rice plants ready for the harvest?" Yang-shan replied, "They are ready." The Master asked, "Do they appear to you to be green, or yellow, or neither green nor yellow?" Yang-shan answered, "Master, what is behind you?" The Master said, "Do you see it?" Then Yang-shan picked up an ear of grain and said, "Are you not asking about *this*?"

The Master replied, "This way follows the Goose-King in choosing milk."[15]

One winter the Master asked Yang-shan whether it was the weather that was cold or whether it was man who felt cold. Yang-shan replied, "We are all here!" "Why don't you answer directly?" asked the Master. Then Yang-shan said, "My answer just now cannot be considered indirect. How about you?" The Master said, "If it is direct, it flows with the current."

A monk came to bow in front of the Master, who made a gesture of getting up. The monk said, "Please, Master, do not get up!" The Master said, "I have not yet sat down." "I have not yet bowed," retorted the monk. The Master replied, "Why should you be ill-mannered?" The monk made no answer.

Two Ch'an followers came from the assembly of Master Shih-shuang to the monastery of Master Kuei-shan, where they complained that no one there understood Ch'an. Later on everyone in the temple was ordered to bring firewood. Yang-shan encountered the two visitors as they were resting. He picked up a piece of firewood and asked, "Can you make a correct statement about this?" Neither made an answer. Yang-shan said, "Then you had better not say that no one here understands Ch'an." After going back inside the monastery, Yang-shan reported to Master Kuei-shan, "I observed the two Ch'an followers here from Shih-shuang." The Master asked, "Where did you come upon them?" Yang-shan reported the encounter, and thereupon the Master said, "Hui-chi is now being observed by me."

When the Master was in bed Yang-shan came to speak to him, but the Master turned his face to the wall. Yang-shan said, "How can you do this?" The Master rose and said, "A moment ago I had a dream. Won't you try to interpret it for me?" Thereupon Yang-shan brought in a basin of water for the Master to wash his face. A little later Hsiang-yen also appeared to speak to the Master. The Master repeated, "I just had a dream. Yang-shan interpreted it. Now it is your turn." Hsiang-yen then brought in a cup of tea. The Master said, "The insight of both of you excels that of Śāriputra."[16]

Once a monk said, "If one cannot be the straw hat on top of

Mount Kuei, how can one reach the village that is free from forced labor? What is this straw hat of Mount Kuei?" The Master thereupon stamped his foot.

The Master came to the assembly and said, "After I have passed away I shall become a water buffalo at the foot of the mountain. On the left side of the buffalo's chest five characters, *Kuei-shan-Monk-Ling-yu*, will be inscribed. At that time you may call me the monk of Kuei-shan, but at the same time I shall also be the water buffalo. When you call me water buffalo, I am also the monk of Kuei-shan. What is my correct name?"

The Master propagated the teachings of Ch'an for more than forty years. Numerous followers achieved self-realization, and forty-one disciples penetrated to the final profundity of his teaching. On the ninth day of the first month of the seventh year [853] of Ta-chung of the T'ang Dynasty, the Master washed his face and rinsed his mouth and then seated himself and, smiling, passed away. This was sixty-four years after he was ordained. He was eighty-three years old. He was buried on Mount Kuei where he had taught. His posthumous name, received from the Royal Court, was Great Perfection, and his pagoda was called Purity and Quiescence.

YANG-SHAN HUI-CHI
(814–890)

"An Excellent Swordsman"

(*From* The Transmission of the Lamp, *Chüan 11*)

CH'AN Master Yang-shan Hui-chi of Yüan-chou[17] was a native of Huai-hua in Shao-chou.[18] His original surname was Yeh. When he was fifteen years old he wanted to leave home and become a Buddhist monk, but his parents would not permit it. Two years later he cut off two fingers and knelt down and put them before his parents, begging their permission. He swore he would seek for the proper Dharma in order to express his gratitude for their labors in bringing him up. Thereupon he went to Ch'an Master T'ung of the Nan-hua Monastery to have his head shaved. Before he was ordained he traveled widely all over the country.

First he visited Tan-yüan, by whom he was awakened and where he grasped the essence of Ch'an. Later, when he came to Kuei-shan Ling-yu, his understanding had become profound. On his arrival Master Kuei-shan asked him:

"Are you your own master or not?"

"I am."

"Where is your own master?"

Thereupon Yang-shan walked away from the west of the hall to the east and stood there. Kuei-shan recognized immediately that he

Inner Experience Illustrated in Three-Way Interplay

was an unusual man and immediately decided to teach him. When Yang-shan asked, "Where is the abiding place of the real Buddha?" Kuei-shan replied:

"Imagine the wonder of no-thought and trace it back to the infinity of the light of the spirit. While thoughts are exhausted and return to their source, nature and appearance are ever abiding. Reality and events are no longer differentiated. Therein is the real Buddha of Suchness."

Hearing this Yang-shan was suddenly enlightened, and thereafter he served Master Kuei-shan.

Later Yang-shan went to Chiang-ling[19] and was ordained there. He participated in the summer assembly and devoted himself to the study of the Vinaya-Pitaka.[20] Afterwards he visited Yen-t'ou.[21]

During his interview with the latter, Yen-t'ou lifted his *fu-tzu*, whereupon Yang-shan unfolded his sitting cloth. Then Yen-t'ou lifted the *fu-tzu* again and put it behind him. Yang-shan folded up his sitting cloth, and throwing it over his shoulder, went out. Later Yen-t'ou said to him, "I do not agree with the gesture of putting down your sitting cloth, but I do agree with your taking it away."[22]

Yang-shan asked Shih-shih,[23] "What is the difference between Buddha and Tao?" Shih-shih answered, "Tao is like an unfolding hand; Buddha is like a clenched fist." When Yang-shan left, Shih-shih saw him to the outer door and called after him, "Do not stay away forever; I pray you will come back again."

Wei-chou went to Kuei-shan asking him for a *gāthā*. He was told, "Handing you the teachings in person would mark me as an ignorant man. How can I teach you through writings?" Thereupon Wei-chou went to Yang-shan and asked him for a *gāthā*. Yang-shan drew a circle on paper, remarking, "To know through thinking is secondary; to know through not-thinking is tertiary."

One day Yang-shan went with Kuei-shan to the fields to help him with the plowing. Yang-shan asked, "How is it that this side is so low and the other side is so high?"

Kuei-shan replied, "Water can level all things; let the water be the leveler."

Yang-shan said, "Water is not reliable, Master. It is just that the high places are high and the low places are low."

Kuei-shan assented.

There was a patron who sent some silk to Master Kuei-shan. Yang-shan asked him, "Master, you have received a great gift. What will you do to return his favor?" Kuei-shan showed him by striking his own seat.[24] Yang-shan commented, "Master! How can you use the things belonging to all people for yourself?"

Kuei-shan suddenly asked Yang-shan, "Where have you been?" Yang-shan said, "I have just come from the fields." Kuei-shan went on, "How many people were there?" Yang-shan thrust his hoe into the ground and stood there. Kuei-shan said, "Today at the southern mountain there was one who harvested rushes." Yang-shan picked up his hoe and went away.

When Yang-shan was herding cows at Mount Kuei the head monk said, "On the tips of a hundred million hairs a hundred million lions reveal themselves." Yang-shan did not comment upon this. Later when he was with Kuei-shan the head monk approached and greeted him. Yang-shan referred to his earlier statement: "Was it not you who said a while ago that on the tips of a hundred million hairs a hundred million lions reveal themselves?" The head monk acknowledged that this was so. Yang-shan asked, "When the lions reveal themselves, are they on the front of the hairs, or on the back?" The head monk replied, "When the lions reveal themselves, we do not say whether it is on the front or on the back." Upon hearing this Yang-shan went out immediately. Kuei-shan remarked, "Now the lion is chopped off at the middle."

The head monk in the monastery of Kuei-shan lifted his *fu-tzu* and said, "If anyone makes a correct answer I'll give this to him." Yang-shan said, "If I make a correct answer, will it be given to me?" The head monk replied, "What you need is a correct answer; then you shall have it." Thereupon Yang-shan grasped the *fu-tzu* of the head monk and went away with it.

One day when it was raining the head monk said to Yang-shan, "It is a good rain, Teacher Chi!"

Yang-shan asked him, "What is good about it?"

The head monk could not give an answer.

Yang-shan volunteered, "I can answer."

The head monk put the question to him, and Yang-shan pointed at the rain.

Once when Kuei-shan and Yang-shan were taking a walk together, a crow dropped a red persimmon in front of them. Yang-shan took it, washed it, and gave it to Kuei-shan. The latter asked him, "Where did you get this?" Yang-shan answered, "This is bestowed on you for the inspiration of your virtue." Kuei-shan said, "Your efforts, too, should not be in vain," and he gave half the fruit to him.

When Yang-shan was washing his clothes Master Tan-yüan came to him and asked, "What are you doing at this very moment?"

Yang-shan replied, "Where can one see this very moment?"

Yang-shan stayed at Mount Kuei for about fifteen years all together. His words were respected and his fellow disciples deeply revered him. After he had received the mind-seal from Master Kuei-shan he led a group of disciples to Mount Wang-ma. Conditions there proved to be unsuitable, and the group later moved to Mount Yang [Yang-shan]. Many followers gathered about him.

Master Yang-shan came into the assembly and told the audience:

"Every one of you should turn his own light inward and look at the Self within. Do not try to remember my words. Ever since the beginningless past you have walked away from your own light and entered into darkness. It is evident that false thinking is deeply rooted in you, and it is very hard to dig out. Many means have been contrived to rid you of your coarse imagination, but they are all like distracting a child with a yellow leaf to stop his crying. What is the use of that? But my teaching is like a shop which offers all sorts of merchandise besides mere gold and jade. The merchandise is sold according to demand. I should like to say that Shih-t'ou has a shop dealing only in pure gold. In my shop I handle all kinds of wares. When a man comes to me for rat excrement, he will get it; when he wants genuine gold, I shall hand that to him."

When the Master ceased speaking a monk stepped forward and said, "As for rat excrement, I do not want it. Please, Master let me have the pure gold."

The Master said, "One who bites the point of an arrow and then tries to open his mouth will never understand." The monk made no reply.

The Master went on, "When a man cries out 'Things for sale!' he will do business; but when he does not call out his wares he will have no dealings. If I reveal Ch'an only in its genuine form, no one will be able to go along with me, not to speak of a group of five or seven hundred. But if I talk of Ch'an in this way and that, people will strive for it and collect whatever words I have left. This is just like fooling a child with an empty hand, for there is nothing real in it at all. Although I tell you where enlightenment abides, do not try to locate it with your conscious mind but sincerely cultivate the depth of your original nature. The insight into past, present, and future mortal conditions and their related miracles is not necessary at all because these are only the fringes of reality. What you need now is to be aware of mind and to reach to the source of things. Do not bother about anything else. Just strike toward the Source. In later days you will realize the truth of this yourself. If you have not yet reached the Source, even though you force yourself to learn it, you will never achieve it. Have you not heard what Master Kuei-shan said? 'When both worldliness and holiness are completely eliminated, Absolute Reality is revealed. Thus the One and the Many are identified. This is the Suchness of Buddha.'"

A monk asked, "What is the distinguishing mark of a patriarch?" The Master used his hand to draw a circle in the air and then wrote the character *fu* [Buddha] in it. The monk made no comment.

The Master asked the head monk, "What is that moment when one thinks neither good nor evil?" The monk replied, "That moment on which my life depends." The Master continued, "Why do you not ask me to answer the question?" The head monk replied, "During that moment, we would not see you, Master!" The Master said, "You cannot successfully advance my teaching of Ch'an."[25]

Master Yang-shan returned to Kuei-shan to see his master, who asked him, "You are now called a wise man. How do you discriminate among the students who come to you from far and wide? How can you tell if they have learned their teachers' lessons and whether they are Ch'annists or of another school? Can you tell me this?" The Master answered, "Hui-chi [i.e., himself] has his ways of testing. When I interview devotees who come to me from different parts of the country, I lift my *fu-tzu* and ask them, 'In your monastery do you talk about "this" [i.e., Ch'an]?' In addition, I ask, 'As to *"this,"* what would your old masters say?' " Kuei-shan exclaimed, "You have the 'teeth and claws' that were used by the early Ch'an masters!" He then inquired further, "To all beings on this great earth, initial consciousness is invisible and nothing of it can be grasped. How then do you know whether such a thing exists?" The Master answered, "Hui-chi has a way of demonstrating this." To a monk who happened to be passing by as they conversed the Master called out, "Sir!" The monk responded by turning his head. And Yang-shan said to Kuei-shan, "This is the initial consciousness that is invisible and of which nothing can be grasped." Kuei-shan praised him: "This is just as when even one drop of lion's milk dissipates and drives off six pints of donkey's milk!"[26]

The Prime Minister Cheng Yü asked, "How is it when one enters *nirvāna* without casting off his passions?" The Master lifted his *fu-tzu*. The Prime Minister said, "It is not necessary to use the word 'enter.' " The Master said, "The word 'enter' is not for Your Highness."

The Master asked a monk where he came from. The monk answered, "From Yu-chou."[27] The Master said, "I was just hoping for some news from Yu-chou. What is the price of rice there?" The monk answered, "When I came from over there I unexpectedly passed through the center of the market. I stepped on the bridge and broke it." The Master silently assented.

The Master saw a monk coming toward him and lifted his *fu-tzu*. The monk said, "Ho!" The Master said, "To utter a 'Ho' is not nothingness. Tell me where is my mistake." The monk said, "You, Master, should not depend upon objective means to reveal the truth to the people." The Master immediately struck him.

The Master asked Hsiang-yen,[28] "What have you seen recently, brother monk?"

Hsiang-yen replied, "I cannot tell you." But he made a *gāthā*:

My poverty of last year was not real poverty.
This year it is want indeed.
In last year's poverty there was room for a piercing gimlet.
In this year's poverty even the gimlet is no more.

The Master said, "You have the Ch'an of Tathāgata, but you do not have the Ch'an of the Patriarchs."

Kuei-shan wrapped up a piece of mirror and sent it to Yang-shan, who, when he received it, held up the mirror before the assembly and said:

"Let us speak of this! Is it Kuei-shan's mirror or is it Yang-shan's? If there is someone who can give a correct answer, it will not be smashed into pieces." No one was able to answer, and the mirror was smashed.

The Master asked his brother monk Shuang-fêng what he had recently learned. Shuang-fêng answered, "According to what I understand, there is no single truth that can be considered adequate." The Master replied, "Your understanding is still limited to objective conditions." Shuang-fêng went on: "As for me, that is just the way I am. How about you?" The Master said, "How is it you do not know there is no single truth that is adequate?" When Kuei-shan heard of this, he commented, "One word of Hui-chi causes the people of the world to be in doubt."

A monk asked, "Would *dharmakāya* [the essence of all beings] also know how to expound the teachings of Buddhism?" The Master answered, "I cannot answer you, but somebody else can." The monk asked: "Where is the one who can answer?" The Master pushed forward his pillow. When Kuei-shan heard of this, he remarked, "Hui-chi is engaging in swordplay."

While the Master was sitting with his eyes closed a monk came upon him and silently stood near him. The Master opened his eyes and drew a circle, then wrote the word "water" in it. He looked at the monk, did not utter a word.

When the Master was carrying a staff in his hand a monk came to him and asked, "Where did you get this?" The Master turned it over and held it at his back. The monk said nothing.

Inner Experience Illustrated in Three-Way Interplay

Once the Master asked a monk what he knew besides Buddhism. The monk said that he understood the divination techniques in *The Book of Changes*. The Master lifted his *fu-tzu* and asked, "Which one among the sixty-four hexagrams[29] is this one?" The monk was unable to reply. The Master answered for him, "It is Lei-t'ien Ta-chuang [the great potentiality of thunder and lightning] and now it is transformed into Ti-ho Ming-i [the destruction of earth-fire]."

The Master asked a monk what his name was. The monk answered, "Ling-t'ung [spirit-penetration]." The Master said, "Now please enter the lantern." The monk replied, "I have entered it already."

A monk spoke to the Master as follows: "The ancients often said that when one sees form one finds mind, and that the seat of meditation is an objective form. Please point out to me the mind beyond the form." The Master said, "Where is the seat of meditation? Please point it out to me." The monk did not answer.

A monk asked, "Who is the teacher of *vairocana* [godhead]?" The Master cried out, "Ho!" The monk asked, "Who is your teacher?" The Master replied, "Don't be rude."

When the Master was talking to a monk a bystander said, "He who speaks is Mañjuśrī; he who is silent is Vimalakīrti." The Master said, "Are you one who is neither silent nor speaking?" The monk remained silent. The Master said, "Why don't you reveal your spiritual power?" The monk replied, "If I should reveal my spiritual power, I am afraid you would place me in a school other than Ch'an." The Master said, "From what I see of your background, you do not have the insight of Ch'an."

A question was asked: "How great is the distance between heaven and hell?" The Master used his staff to draw a line upon the ground.

When the Master was staying in the Kuan-yin Temple, he put up a notice that while he was reading the sūtras no one should ask him questions. Subsequently a monk came to greet the Master and observed that he was reading the sūtras. So he stood by the Master's side and waited. The Master put away his sūtra and asked the monk, "Do you understand?" The monk said, "I do not read the sūtras. How can I understand?" The Master answered, "Later on you will understand."

A monk queried, "The School of Ch'an maintains the theory of sudden enlightenment. How does one attain sudden enlightenment?"

The Master replied, "To attain sudden enlightenment is very difficult. If a student of Ch'an is a man of great capacity and profoundly intuitive, he may grasp a thousand things in a moment and thus become totally enlightened. However, a man of such capacity is hard to find. Therefore the ancient sages said that those of lesser talents should content themselves with their meditations and be pure in thought, for if they aimed at sudden enlightenment they would be entirely lost."

The monk went on: "Besides these, is there any other way that you can help me to be enlightened?"

The Master remarked, "Asking whether or not there is another way to achieve enlightenment creates a disturbance in your mind. May I ask where you come from?"

The monk said, "Yu-chou."

The Master asked, "Do you still think of that place?"

The monk answered, "Yes, I often do."

The Master asked, "In that place the people and horses are very numerous in the buildings and in the parks. When you recollect them, do you still recall how many were there?"

The monk replied, "When I try to recollect this, I see nothing at all."

The Master said, "What you understand is still limited by objective conditions. If you want to achieve a level of concentration upon the void only, this is the answer. But if you want absolute freedom, this is not a correct answer.* Your understanding of experience is still in the initial stage of Ch'an. Later on you may earn a seat in the monastery and wear a robe. Watch for what will come to you then."

* See the introduction to Part II, "Interfusion of Universality and Particularity," pages 41–57.

Inner Experience Illustrated in Three-Way Interplay

The monk made a deep bow and left.

The Master stayed first at Mount Yang and then moved to the Temple of Kuan-yin. In his contacts with the outside world and in his teachings he set for his pupils the model for the School of Ch'an. Several years before he passed away he predicted his death in the following *gāthā*:

> My age, a full seventy-seven.
> Even now I am fading away.
> Rising and falling
> Let nature take its course.
> In my two arms I hold my bended knee.

The Master entered *nirvāna* in Mount Tung-ping in Shao-chou. He was seventy-seven, as he said in his *gāthā*, and he passed away embracing his bended knee. The Royal Court bestowed on him the posthumous title of Great Master of the Penetration of Wisdom, and his pagoda was called Subtle Light. Later his pagoda was moved to Mount Yang.

HSIANG-YEN CHIH-HSIEN

Enlightened by One Stroke

(*From* The Transmission of the Lamp, *Chüan 11*)

CH'AN Master Hsiang-yen Chih-hsien[30] of Têng-chou[31] was a native of Tsing-chou.[32] When he tired of conventional living with his family, he left his parents' home and went to visit Buddhist centers to study Ch'an. He stayed at the Ch'an monastery on Mount Kuei. Master Kuei-shan Ling-yu recognized in him the capacity to become a great Buddhist and undertook to awaken him.

One day Kuei-shan said to Hsiang-yen, "I do not want to ask what you have understood from your studies and what you have remembered from the sūtras and śāstras. Just tell me in a word what your original being was before your parents gave you birth and prior to your capacity to discriminate things. I want to register you as my disciple." Hsiang-yen did not know how to reply. After he had deliberated for some time, he said a few words in which he attempted to express his ideas, but all that he said was rejected by Kuei-shan. Hsiang-yen then implored Kuei-shan to tell him the correct answer. Master Kuei-shan replied, "Whatever I say is according to what I see. It will not benefit your insight."

Hsiang-yen was disappointed and returned to the monks' hall, where he reviewed all his notes but found nothing that would serve as a suitable answer. Finally he exclaimed, "There is no hunger which can be satisfied by pictures of food painted on paper!" Thereupon he burned all his notes and memoranda and declared to himself, "In this life I shall never again study Buddhism. I shall be a plain homeless monk wandering the roads. I shall torment my mind no longer with such studies." Then he wept and bid good-bye to Master Kuei-shan.

When he arrived at the tomb of National Teacher Nan-yang Hui-chung,[33] he built a hut nearby and stayed there. One day when he was weeding, a piece of rock which he had dislodged struck a bamboo tree. The sound it produced made him suddenly burst out laughing and quite unexpectedly opened his mind to a state of enlightenment. He returned to his hut, washed himself, put his things in order, and then burned incense and bowed in the direction of Kuei-shan's abode. He exclaimed, "Master! Your kindness is beyond even that which my parents showed to me. If on that day you had spoken openly to me, how could this have happened?" Then he made a *gāthā*:

> With one stroke, all previous knowledge is forgotten.
> No cultivation is needed for this.
> This occurrence reveals the ancient way
> And is free from the track of quiescence.
> No trace is left anywhere.
> Whatever I hear and see does not conform to rules.
> All those who are enlightened
> Proclaim this to be the greatest action.

The Master [Hsiang-yen] came to the assembly and said, "The Tao is attained by one's inner awakening; it does not depend upon words. Look at the invisible and boundless. Where can you find any intermittence? How can you reach it by the labor of the intellect? It is simply the reflection of illumination, and that is your whole daily task. Only those who are ignorant will go in the opposite direction."

A monk asked, "What is the realm of Hsiang-yen's mind?"

The Master replied, "Plants and trees are not abundant."

The monk then asked, "What is *saindhava*?"[34]

The Master knocked on his seat and said, "Come here to this side!"

The monk asked, "What is learning at this moment?"

The Master turned his fan around and showed it to him, saying, "Do you see this?" The monk made no reply.

A monk asked, "What is 'the meal of the right livelihood'?"[35]

The Master made as if he were picking up food with his fingers.

He was asked, "What is the invisible inward power received with commandments during ordination?"[36]

The Master replied, "I will tell you when you return to being a layman."

A monk asked, "What is the one word that can bring us together beyond the world of sense?"

The Master replied, "It is just like myself before I became the abbot of Hsiang-yen. Can you say where I was then?"

The monk said, "I do not dare say where you were then."

The Master replied, "Your mind is just like that of an illusionist, full of passion."

A monk asked, "What occurs when the sages are not admired and one's own spirit is not regarded as important?"

The Master replied, "All functions cease and none of the thousand enlightened men are held in esteem." Just then Shu-shan,[37] who was in the assembly, complained, "What kind of words are these?" The Master asked who had spoken and the answer came from the audience, "Shu-shan." The Master said to him, "You do not agree with what I said a moment ago?"

"That is correct, sir!"

"Can you say something more relevant to the truth?"

"Yes, I can."

"Please try it now."

"If you want me to tell you, you have to make a bow to me as to a teacher." Immediately the Master came down from his seat and bowed to Shu-shan. He repeated his question and Shu-shan replied, "Why don't you say that you cannot esteem the ancients, and also respect your own spirit?"

The Master replied, "Even though you have a certain understanding, you will suffer from illness for thirty years. When you live in the mountain forest you will lack wood for fuel; when you stay by the side of a river you will lack water to drink. Remember this!"

Later when Shu-shan was living the monastic life, everything came about exactly as the Master had predicted. He recovered from his illness, in fact, after he had suffered for twenty-seven years. He said to himself, "What Hsiang-yen predicted about my suffering for thirty years came true, and I was only able to avoid three years of it." Whenever he ate he must have had to put aside a few grains of rice from his bowl to remind himself of what Hsiang-yen had said.

A monk asked, "What is a word before it is said?"

The Master replied, "I answered you the moment before you asked the question."

The monk went on, "What is this moment?"

The Master replied, "It is the same as the moment you asked the question."

A monk asked, "What is that direct approach to the Source to which Buddha would give his seal of approval?"

At this, the Master threw away his staff and walked out with his hands empty.

A monk asked, "What is the general idea of Buddhism?"

The Master replied, "The frost came early this year, so we did not have a good harvest of buckwheat."

A monk asked, "What is the meaning of Bodhidharma coming from the West?"

The Master put his hand into his cloak, withdrew it in the form of a fist, which he opened as if he were disclosing something to the questioner. The monk knelt down and put out both hands as if to receive something. The Master asked him, "What is this?" The monk made no answer.

A monk asked, "What is Tao?"

The Master answered, "A dragon is singing in the decaying woods."

The monk went on, "I do not understand this."

The Master said, "The eyes in the skull."

A monk requested, "Please say something beyond the four alternatives and the hundredfold negation."

The Master answered, "One should not talk to the skilled hunter about what is forbidden by Buddha."

One day the Master spoke to the assembly thus: "Imagine a man hanging over a precipice a thousand feet high. There he is holding on to a branch of a tree with his teeth. Neither his hands nor his feet give him any support. Now let us imagine someone coming to him and asking, 'What is the meaning of the First Patriarch coming from the West?' If this man should try to answer he is sure to fall and kill himself, but if he makes no answer it will be said that he has ignored his questioner. What ought he to do?"

The monk Chao stepped forward from the assembly and said, "Let us not discuss the man who is hanging from a tree, but the moment just before he got hung up there." The Master smiled but made no answer.

The Master asked a monk where he came from. He replied that he came from Kuei-shan. The Master asked what statement Kuei-shan had made recently. The monk replied that another monk had asked him about the meaning of the Patriarch coming from the West and Master Kuei-shan had held up his *fu-tzu* in response. When Master Hsiang-yen heard this, he asked what Kuei-shan's disciples understood by this gesture. His brother monks agreed, said the monk, that it meant that mind is illumined through matter and reality is revealed through things. The Master said, "Their understanding is all right as far as it goes. But what is the good of being so eager to theorize?" The monk asked him how he would have explained the gesture. The Master held up his *fu-tzu*.

Whenever the Master taught his disciples, his words were direct and simple. He left more than two hundred *gāthās* and hymns, compositions that are spontaneous reflections of situations as they arose, with neither rhythm nor rhyme. They were widely admired throughout the country. After he passed away, the posthumous title of Great Master of the Succession of Light was bestowed upon him.

Inner Experience Illustrated in Three-Way Interplay

NOTES

1. *Tathāgata*, in this case, means both "so-come" and "so-gone," i.e., into *nirvāna*, or the Void.
2. Suzuki, *Essays in Zen Buddhism*, Series II, p. 215.
3. See note 12 below.
4. According to the *Amalgamation of the Sources of the Five Lamps*, Chüan 20, Ch'an Master K'uo-an Shih-yuan of Liang-shan created the *Ten Pictures of Cow Herding* and the attached commentaries. The *Records of the Source Mirror*, Kung-an 32, state that Ch'an Master Ch'ing-chü Hao-sheng composed the *Diagrams of the Twelve Stages of Cow Herding* with the attached commentaries, or "hymns."
5. The Chinese character *Kuei* is a phonetic contraction of *ku* and *wei*, according to the most recent and best edited dictionary of Chinese, published by the Chung-hua Book Company in Shanghai in 1947. *Kuei* is indicated as a similar contraction of the original Chinese words by R. H. Mathews in his well-known *Chinese-English Dictionary*. However, in both the *K'ang-hsi Dictionary* and the *Chung-hua Dictionary*, which are very commonly used by the Chinese people in the present day, the pronunciation is given as *chui*, which suggests a phonetic contraction of *chü* and *wei*. Ancient dictionaries, such as *Kuang-yün* by Lu Fa-yen (completed in 601) and *Chi-yün* by Tin Tu (completed 1039), record the pronunciation as *chui*, which was certainly the common pronunciation before the Sung Dynasty.
6. Now Changsha, capital of Hunan Province.
7. Foochow, now the capital of Fukien Province.
8. Hangchow, now the capital of Chekiang Province, on the Western Lake and near the Chien-t'ang River.
9. In the available Ch'an literature we find these lines as part of a *gāthā* by the Fifth Patriarch in India. See *The Lamp*, Chüan 1.
10. A *dhūta* was a Buddhist monk who traveled, begging his meals, as part of the purification from material desires.
11. In *Ta-chih-tu Lun* we read: "The beginner concentrates on *yuan chung* (centers of concentration), such as the space between the eyebrows, the middle of the forehead, or the tip of the nose." The word *yuan* here means concentration. In common usage it carries the meaning of causation. *Ta-chih-tu Lun* (*Mahāprajñāpāramitopadeśa*) is a one-hundred-fascicle commentary on the *Mahāprajñāpāramitā Sūtra*, attributed to Nāgārjuna, and translated by Kumārajīva.
12. *Vāsanā*, or force of habit, in the Ālayavijñāna doctrine. In Mahāyāna Buddhism, delusion is threefold: (1) active at present, (2) innate, (3) through force of habit. One may eliminate the first and second, but the third delusion tends to remain. Those who achieve only Śrāvakas—being merely hearers—cannot rid themselves of it. Those who achieve Pratyaksa-Buddha, or the middle conveyance, may in part rid themselves of it. But only Buddha can eliminate all of it.
13. A block of wood with the inside hollowed out. It is beaten with a stick to announce meals or to accompany the chanting of the sūtras, and is said to keep the monks' minds awake as a fish in water is always awake.

14. An *arhat* is an enlightened, saintly man, the highest type or saint in Hīnayāna, as the Bodhisattva is in Mahāyāna.

15. The Goose-King symbolizes the Bodhisattva, who drinks the milk and leaves the water contained in the same vessel. See *Chinese Dictionary of Buddhism*, p. 460.

16. One of the ten finest disciples of Buddha, whose wisdom is considered the greatest of all.

17. Now I-ch'un, in western Kiangsi Province. Mount Yang, or Yang-shan, is located south of the town.

18. Now Chü-chiang (Kükong), in northern Kwangtung Province.

19. A town on the northern bank of the Yangtze River in Hupeh Province.

20. Vinaya-Pitaka is one of the three divisions of the Buddhist Canon, or Tripitaka. It covers Buddhist discipline and monastic rules.

21. Yen-t'ou Ch'üan-huo (828–887). See *The Lamp*, Chüan 16.

22. When Yang-shan put down his sitting cloth and unfolded it as a gesture of reverence to Yen-t'ou, it indicated that he was not yet free from his master. Taking away the sitting cloth, on the other hand, revealed a negation of attachment to the Master. In the first gesture he was not yet his own master, so Yen-t'ou did not approve. The second gesture received Yen-t'ou's approbation because it showed Yang-shan had become his own master.

23. Shih-shih Shan-tao. See *The Lamp*, Chüan 14.

24. Striking the seat and remaining silent symbolized the Master's inner enlightenment. If the patron was prepared to accept this, it would be the Master's return gift to him.

25. The head monk's replies are still on the intellectual plane. He tries twice to explain verbally what he knows about Ch'an instead of directly revealing his inner experience. This indicates that he has not yet grasped Master Yang-shan's teachings.

26. The milk of the lion symbolizes the mind of *bodhi*, which is so powerful that it can cast off all confusions and passions. Kuei-shan's praise indicates that Yang-shan possesses the mind of *bodhi*.

27. Now Cho-hsien, in central Hopeh Province.

28. Hsiang-yen Chih-hsien, the translation of whose fascicle follows this one. Hsiang-yen and Yang-shan were the two outstanding disciples of Kuei-shan Ling-yu.

29. The *I Ching*, or *Book of Changes*, is a famous text for divination. Each of the sixty-four hexagrams expounded is a combination of two trigrams. This work was translated into German by Richard Wilhelm and then into English by Cary F. Baynes, with a foreword by Carl G. Jung, for publication in 1950 by Bollingen Foundation.

30. The dates of Hsiang-yen's birth and death are not known. His approximate period, however, can be derived from the fact that he was a student of Kuei-shan (771–853) and a younger brother monk of Yang-shan (814–890) and hence must have lived in the ninth century. Before 847 the Royal Prince Kuang studied under him.

31. Now Tenghsien, near the southern border of Honan Province.

32. Now Lin-tzu, in central Shantung Province.

Inner Experience Illustrated in Three-Way Interplay

33. Nan-yang Hui-chung (677–744) was one of the leading disciples of the Sixth Patriarch, Hui-nêng. He stayed in the Tang-tzu Valley of P'o-yai Mountain in Nan-yang for more than forty years and was buried there on his death.

34. *Saindhava* signifies the four necessities of a traveling monk: salt, cup, water, horse.

35. Earning money to maintain oneself is not considered a state free from cravings; begging for food indicates purity of mind. Such is the "meal of the right livelihood" according to Buddhism.

36. *Avjñapti áila* in Sanskrit.

37. Shu-shan K'uang-jen. See *The Lamp*, Chüan 17.

Part VI

Introduction
The Six Phenomena and the Void

FA-YEN WÊN-I (885–958)
"One Got It, the Other Missed"

YUNG-MING YEN-SHOU (904–975)
"From the Womb of a Cow an Elephant Is Born"

The Six Phenomena and the Void

One of the five schools of Ch'an Buddhism in China was the Fa-yen School, so called from the posthumous name of Master Wên-i of the Ch'ing-liang Monastery in Chin-ling. The school was established in the tenth century and was the last one of the five. Chin-ling was then the capital of Nan-t'ang, whose third king took the title Chiang-nan Kuo-chu, or Sovereign of the South Yangtze Kingdom. Chin-ling is now called Nanking, and is the most important cultural and political center in east and southeast China. Master Fa-yen had many disciples, forty-three of whom had their sermons recorded in *The Lamp*. One of his noted disciples, T'ien-t'ai Tê-chao, became National Teacher of the Wu-yüeh Kingdom, and another distinguished non-Chinese disciple, Tao-fen Hui-chu, served as the National Teacher of Sila, part of present-day Korea.

The most famous disciple of Master Fa-yen, three generations removed, is Yung-ming Yen-shou, a great scholar of Buddhism, who compiled the *Ts'ung-ching Lu*, or *Records of the Source Mirror*. When we study the history of the Fa-yen School, we notice that after Yung-ming Yen-shou the transmission gradually becomes obscure. It is not entirely unfounded to assume that the adoption of

The Six Phenomena and the Void

Pure Land training by Ch'an Buddhists caused the disappearance of the Fa-yen School and even of Ch'an Buddhism in China. To trace this trend of gradual obscuration, we have here translated the fascicle of Yung-ming Yen-shou.

In the Lin-chi School we find such basic principles of philosophy as *ssu liao chien*, or the Four Processes of Liberation from Subjectivity and Objectivity, and in the Ts'ao-tung School we find the basic principle *wu wei p'ien chêng*, the Five Relations Between Particularity and Universality, maintained by Tung-shan Liang-chieh. In the following poem Fa-yen expounds "the meaning of the six phenomena according to the Hua-yen School":[1]

As held by Hua-yen the meaning of the six phenomena is this:
Within identity there is yet difference.
To take the difference would differ from identity:
It would mean to entirely misunderstand the idea of all Buddhas.
All Buddhas further maintain that both universality and
    particularity
Are without either identity or difference.
When one enters into the realm of universality
The opposites are disregarded.
To disregard opposites is to do away with names.
Thus it is quite obvious that all forms are free from
    reality and appearance.

In his discussions, Fa-yen did not evidence any particular interest in the metaphysical structure of the Hua-yen School, but was greatly concerned to drive home the doctrine of the basic relationship between reality and appearance, or the One and the Many. Understanding of this brings freedom from such dichotomy.

When Yung-ming Tao-chien visited Master Fa-yen, the Master asked him, "Aside from meditation, what sūtra do you study?" Tao-chien answered, "I read the Hua-yen sūtra." After a short discussion Tao-chien did not know what to answer. Thereupon the Master said that Tao-chien could ask him the same question and he would give the answer to it. Then Tao-chien took up the question: "Does the Void contain the six phenomena?" The Master immediately responded, "Void." Tao-chien was awakened, and he jumped with joy. After he had made a bow to express his heartfelt gratitude, the Master asked him, "How did you become enlightened?" Tao-chien repeated, "Void."

The Master's answer "Void," though merely a repetition of the word used by Tao-chien, penetrated directly to the center of the disciple's being. No further intellectual pursuit was possible; instead, his inner vitality broke through the shell of his consciousness and he became enlightened. Many other such examples can be found in the teachings of Fa-yen. For instance, he once asked Hsiu-shan Chu to interpret the ancient saying, "If there is slight difference, it will make as great a separation as between heaven and earth." Hsiu-shan Chu replied, "If there is a slight difference, it will make as great a separation as between heaven and earth." Master Fa-yen commented, "If this is your understanding, how can you get the point?" Hsiu-shan Chu asked him for his own interpretation. Master Fa-yen immediately repeated, "If there is a slight difference, it will make as great a separation as between heaven and earth." The Master's repetition does not carry any intellectual meaning in words; it simply serves as a key to open the lock. Hsiu-shan Chu's first repetition of the Master's statement is also important. It stopped any further intellectual pursuit, thus stirring up the inner vitality of the earnest devotee. The Master's repetition broke through the wall of consciousness and thus opened the learner's mind.

There is another well-known illustration of Fa-yen's use of repetition to awaken the devotee. Hsuan-tsê told Master Fa-yen that when he was with his first teacher, he learned that to seek Buddhahood would be just as if Ping-ting T'ung-tzu were to ask for fire. He explained that Ping-ting T'ung-tzu was the god of fire; this god's asking for fire would be like being oneself a Buddha and seeking Buddha. Fa-yen remarked that his understanding was completely off the track. Hsuan-tsê was extremely offended and left the temple. But when he came back to the Master and asked for another statement, to Hsuan-tsê's surprise the Master said, "Ping-ting T'ung-tzu asks for fire." This immediately awakened Hsuan-tsê.

The repetition method was frequently applied by Ch'an masters of later days. *In Records of Pointing at the Moon*, Chüan 25, is described the awakening of Ts'ui-yen K'ê-chen, who was a disciple of the great eleventh-century master Tz'u-ming and very proud of it. Once when he was at another temple for the summer session, he felt like discussing Ch'an with a friend, who realized that Ts'ui-yen's understanding was not thorough. Therefore the friend picked up a broken tile, put it on top of a rock, and said, "If you can say a word on this that leads to Ch'an, you will truly be a disciple of Tz'u-ming." Ts'ui-yen looked at the tile and the rock from this side and that, seeking for an answer. His friend rebuked him harshly, "Have done with deliberation! You missed the very moment for a real answer. This proves that you are still immersed in illusion and have not yet even dreamed of what Ch'an is." Ts'ui-yen was ashamed and quickly returned to Master Tz'u-ming, who loudly condemned him, saying that in pursuing the study of Ch'an one should not leave in the middle of the summer session. Ts'ui-yen told the Master why he had come back to him. Tz'u-ming immediately asked him, "What is the essential idea of Buddhism?" To this Ts'ui-yen said, "No clouds are gathering on the mountain peak, but there is the moon casting itself into the middle of the waves." Tz'u-ming stared at him angrily and cried out, "An old hand like you to have such a view! When do you expect to grasp the meaning of Ch'an?" Ts'ui-yen was terrified and begged the Master to tell it to him. Tz'u-ming said to him, "You put the question to me!" Thereupon Ts'ui-yen repeated the question. Master Tz'u-ming thundered, "No clouds are gathering on the mountain peak, but there is the moon casting itself into the middle of the waves." Upon hearing this, Ts'ui-yen was suddenly enlightened. His awakening took place through his master's repetition of the answer he himself had made.

Among Fa-yen's famous *kung-an* the following may be said to express the essence of Ch'an Buddhism. Once before a meal, when all the monks had gathered for instruction, the Master pointed at the bamboo screens, and two monks went to roll them up. The Master remarked, "One got it, the other missed." The commentator Tung-ch'an Ch'i had this to say:

The Six Phenomena and the Void

Some would say that neither of these monks understood what the Master meant, but just went and rolled up the screen. Others would say that one of them got the Master's idea—he got the point, while the other did not—he missed the point. Do you think this interpretation correct? You know that one cannot possibly interpret the *kung-an* in that way. How then do you understand the *kung-an*?

In the *Records of Serenity* T'ien-tung Chen-chio wrote:

> A pine trunk is always straight;
> Thorny brambles are bent crooked.
> The legs of a crane are long;
> The feet of a duck are short.
> So is it true with the ancients:
> They care not for either success or failure.

Wang-sung commented that in this poem T'ien-tung has pointed out to us that by nature cranes' legs are long and ducks' feet are short. The "long" cannot be considered something excessive nor the "short" something lacking. Therefore to lengthen the short or shorten the long would cause either one distress. The same is true of human activities. Opposites are natural phenomena. Success and failure, white and black, life and death are natural products of human activities, and we ought to accept them for what they are. When we understand this, we transcend the dichotomy and are free from it. As long as we are trapped in the dichotomy, we cannot become enlightened. Therefore it is important for us to be careful lest we get trapped and thus miss our goal—our real self. Thus Master Fa-yen would warn his disciples: "You must grasp the absolute moment and watch what is coming to you. To lose the moment and miss the chance is to waste time in mistaking the visible for the invisible."

To open up his disciples' minds, Fa-yen often used abrupt negation which pulled out the intellectual roots of a question and threw them away. For instance, when Fa-yen was asked, "What is the first principle?" he answered, "If I should tell you, it would become the second principle." On another occasion he was asked, "What are non-dual words?" His answer was, "How could you possibly add any more?" For as soon as one says something, it is already dual. Rooting out intellection leads to the right answer—the opening of the mind.

Fa-yen also used the approach of opposites maintained by the Sixth Patriarch, Hui-nêng. For instance, when "being" is questioned, the answer should be non-being, or vice versa. This leads to enlightenment through the Middle Way. Once when Fa-yen was asked, "What is the moon?" his answer was, "Finger." When he was asked, "What is the finger?" his answer was, "Moon." When the question was about *dharmakāya*, his answer was *nirmānakāya*. This, however, is not intellectual play, but is used as a dam to stop the life current, forcing it back to seek deeper levels within. To an earnest learner who seeks the Truth day and night, such a verbal dam may become a decisive factor in turning the tide of his search inward to the very depth of his being, thus bringing about his enlightenment.

Yung-ming Yen-shou was the third-generation successor of the Fa-yen School. We find that some of his teachings of Ch'an recorded in *The Lamp* are similar to those of Fa-yen Wên-i, the founder of the school. When we examine the teachings of Fa-yen, we find that he would pull out the intellectual roots of the questioner through contradiction, negation, and opposites. When we read the fascicle of Yung-ming, we realize that he also applied these approaches. A monk once came to Master Yung-ming and asked why, when he had been at the monastery for so long, he still did not understand the spirit of Yung-ming's teaching.

"You should understand what is not to be understood," the Master answered.

"How can I understand what is not to be understood?" pressed the monk.

"From the womb of a cow an elephant is born; in the middle of the blue sea red dust is blown up," replied the Master.

In the following illustration a remark of Yung-ming's comes very close to what was said by Fa-yen on the occasion of the two monks rolling up the screen. In *Records of Pointing at the Moon*, Chüan 25, it says: "Two monks came to visit the Master [Yung-ming]. The Master asked the first visitor, 'Have you visited here before?' The answer was, 'Yes, I have.' Then the Master asked the second monk whether he had been here before. The second monk answered that he had not. Thereupon the Master made this remark: 'One got the point, the other missed it.' " In human activities, whether it be the mere rolling up of a screen or the seeking of the Truth from a master, all values are relative. What both Fa-yen and Yung-ming taught was an understanding of the subtlety of opposites. It is through this understanding that one will transcend the dichotomy and therewith be free from attachment to all things.

When we study the teachings of Yün-mên Wên-yen we shall learn that swiftness and suddenness characterized his style. He left his questioner no chance for reasoning, but immediately cut through his entanglements and confusions. The following case shows that in comparison to Fa-yen's methods, Yün-mên's style is of greater effectiveness.

In the fascicle of Ch'an Master Fêng-hsien Shen of Chin-ling, in *Records of Pointing at the Moon*, Chüan 21, it is related that one day, Fêng-hsien went with another monk, Ming, to visit Master Fa-yen. These visitors were disciples of Yün-mên. They came forward and asked:

"We have heard that you, Master, once said, 'There are three divisions in material existence [*rūpa*].' Is this correct or not?"

"Yes, it is correct," replied Master Fa-yen.

"The sparrow hawk flew across Sila," remarked the visitors, and after saying this they immediately went back into the group.

The King, who happened also to be present at the time, did not approve of the remark made by the two visitors from Yün-mên. He therefore invited them to dispute Ch'an with Master Fa-yen again on another occasion. The next day a tea party was prepared. After tea was served, a box full of silk and a sword were brought out. The King announced that if his visitors asked correct questions on Ch'an, they would get the silk as a reward. If not, they would only have the sword. When Fa-yen ascended his dharma chair, Fêng-hsien came forward and asked:

"Today the King granted us the opportunity to ask you a question. Do you agree to this, sir?"

"Yes, I agree," replied Fa-yen.

The Six Phenomena and the Void

"The sparrow hawk flew across Sila," remarked the visitor from Yün-mên.

As soon as he had made this remark, he took the box of silk and went back to the crowd. As the crowd began to scatter, Fa-têng (later Fa-yen's successor in the Ch'ing-liang Monastery), the officer monk on duty, struck the bell and called back the two visitors. He asked them:

"I hear that you both come from Master Yün-mên. Can you give us some special *kung-an* to discuss?"

Fêng-hsien stated, "The ancient said, 'The white egrets swoop down to the fields just like a thousand flakes of snow. The golden oriole perches on the tree just like a branch of blossoms.' How do you interpret this?"

Fa-têng was about to make a comment, but the visitor struck the dharma seat once and rejoined the crowd.

This story illustrates the difference in the methods of teaching of the Ch'an masters Fa-yen and Yün-mên. We may recall the dialogue that took place when Tung-shan Shou-ch'u first visited Master Yün-mên. What Tung-shan said were true facts, but they were all on the relative plane and were not "living words," as Tung-shan himself stated later. Here, Fa-yen's answer and Fa-têng's attempt to comment were not in the spirit of Yün-mên; therefore the visitors from Yün-mên did not accept them as correct.

Let us refer back to our discussion of Yung-ming. From Yung-ming's fascicle in *The Lamp* we learned that the Master recited the *Lotus Sūtra* many thousand times. He sought enlightenment mainly by *nien-fu*, or reciting Buddha's name, a practice of the Pure Land School. Yung-ming said, "Those who devote themselves to Ch'an and neglect the Pure Land will fail, nine out of ten, to attain enlightenment; but those who devote themselves to the practice of Pure Land will, without exception, have their awakening. Those who practice Ch'an and Pure Land at the same time will be at their best; they will be like tigers wearing horns." After Yung-ming many Ch'an masters followed the idea that the devotee must practice Pure Land in order to grow horns. This caused the discontinuation of the School of Fa-yen as well as the disappearance of

The Six Phenomena and the Void

Ch'an Buddhism in China. *Nien-fu* in Pure Land and the *kung-an* in Ch'an have each contributed to enlightenment, but when they are practiced at the same time, the results, as shown by Yung-ming's disciples, are rather discouraging. *The Lamp* records the names of only two of Yung-ming's disciples, who however did not make any contributions in sermons. After that, no one is mentioned as succeeding the great Master Yung-ming Yen-shou, whose teachings were so widely acknowledged. Thousands might have benefitted by reciting Buddha's name, but none of them has left a single word to enrich the teachings of Ch'an. The horns have destroyed the tiger! This certainly was not what Master Yung-ming intended.

FA-YEN WÊN-I
(885-958)

"One Got It, the Other Missed"

(*From* The Transmission of the Lamp, *Chüan* 24)

C H'AN Master Wên-i of the Ch'ing-liang Monastery in Sheng-chou[2] was a native of Yu-hang.[3] His original surname was Lu. When he was seven years old, he shaved his head and became the disciple of Ch'an Master Ch'üan-wei, of the Chih-t'ung Temple in Hsin-ting. At the age of twenty he was ordained in the K'ai-yüan Monastery in Yüeh-chou.[4] During that time the Vinaya master Hsi-chio was expounding Buddhism in the Yü-wang Monastery in Mei-shan of Ming-chou.[5] Wên-i went there to listen to his lectures and to seek the deep and abstruse meaning of Buddhism. At the same time, he also studied the Confucianist classics and made friends with scholars and literary men. Master Hsi-chio thought as highly of Wên-i as Confucius had of Tzu-yu and Tzu-hsia.[6]

However, when he suddenly had the urge to seek the truth of Ch'an, Wên-i immediately gave up all other pursuits, and taking up his staff, went traveling to the South. When he reached Fu-chou,[7] he joined the Ch'ang-ch'ing Hui-leng[8] congregation. Although his mind was not yet free from seeking, many people esteemed him very highly.

Not long afterward Wên-i set out again with his friends across the Lake.[9] Hardly had they started on their journey when a rainstorm began. The streams overflowed and flooded the land. Thereupon Wên-i and his companions took lodging temporarily at the Ti-ts'ang Monastery in the western part of the city of Fu-chou. While he was there, Wên-i took the opportunity to visit Lo-han Kuei-ch'en,[10] who asked him:

"Where are you going, sir?"

"I shall continue my foot travels along the road."

"What is that which is called foot travel?"

"I do not know."

"Not-knowing most closely approaches the Truth."

Wên-i was suddenly awakened. Hence he and his companions, Ch'ing-ch'i Hung-chin and others, four in all, determined to be disciples of Lo-han Kuei-ch'en, and they consulted him freely in order to clear their doubts. They all gained a deep understanding of Ch'an, and one after another went through the ceremony of *shou-chi*.[11] Later, they were all to become the leading masters in their localities.

When they were ready to leave, Wên-i planned to stay and build a hut for himself in Kan-chê Chou, but Ch'ing-ch'i and the other companions persuaded him to join them in visiting the monasteries south of the Yangtze River. When they arrived at Lin-ch'uan,[12] the governor invited Wên-i to be the abbot of the Ch'uing-shou Monastery. On the opening day, before the tea ceremony was completed, the audience were already gathered around his seat. The director of the monks[13] came up to him, saying, "All the audience are already gathered around your seat." Master Wên-i replied, "They really want to see the truly wise man." A moment later the Master walked up to his seat and all the audience made a deep bow. Then the Master said, "Since you all have come here, it is impossible for me not to make some remark. May I point out to you a way to truth which was given by our ancients? Be careful!" After saying this, he immediately left the seat.

At that moment a monk came forward and bowed to the Master. The Master said, "You may ask me a question!" But just as the monk was about to ask the question, the Master said, "The

The Six Phenomena and the Void

abbot has not yet begun his lecture, so no question will be answered."

When the monk Tzü-fang came from the Ch'ang-ch'ing Monastery, the Master recited to him the *gāthā* written by Master Hui-leng of that monastery and then said, "What is that among all manifestations by which the solitary One is revealed?" Tzü-fang lifted his *fu-tzu*. The Master remarked, "How can you understand Ch'an in such a way?" Tzü-fang persisted, "What is your idea?" The Master retorted, "What do you call all manifestations?" Tzü-fang said, "The ancients never tried to disregard all manifestations." The Master replied, "Among all manifestations the solitary One is revealed. Why should you speak of disregarding them or not?" Tzü-fang was suddenly enlightened and wrote a *gāthā* accepting the Master's instructions.

From that time on, members of all the other congregations who had some understanding of Ch'an came to the Master. When they first arrived, they would be bold and self-confident, but as they were awakened by the Master's subtle words, they would begin to respect and believe in him. His visitors often exceeded one thousand in number.

Once when the Master came before the congregation, he let his disciples stand for a long time, and finally said:

"If your gathering should be dismissed [without a word], what is your opinion on whether or not Buddha's teaching is still implied? Try to tell me! If Buddha's teaching is not implied, why should you come here? Even if there is an implication of the Buddhist teaching, there are many gatherings in the city, so why should you come here?

"Every one of you may have read *Contemplations on Returning to the Source, Explanations of a Hundred Mental Qualities, Treatise on the Avataṁsaka Sūtra, Nirvāna Sūtra,* and many another. Can you tell me in which of these teachings you find the absolute moment? If there is such a moment, please point it out to me. Are there no words in these sūtras which indicate this absolute moment? [If there are such words,] what have they to do with the absolute moment? Thus, when subtle words are retained in the mind, they cause anxiety; when Ultimate Reality exists before the eyes, it is manifest in the objective condition of names and forms. How can this manifestation take place? If Ultimate Reality is manifest in objective conditions, how then can objective conditions be traced back to the Ultimate Reality? Do you understand? What is the use if you only read the sūtra without understanding this?"

A monk asked, "How can you reveal yourself so as to identify with Tao?"

The Master answered, "When did you reveal yourself and not identify with Tao?"

Question: "What is the senselessness of the six senses?"

The Master's answer: "Your family group."

The Master then said, "What is your understanding? Don't say, when you ask what such a question means, that you have not obtained it. Tell me the senselessness of the six senses. Are eyes and ears senseless? If what is fundamental exists within you, how can you say that you have not obtained it? The ancients said that when you want to keep away from what you are hearing and seeing, you attach yourself to what you are hearing and seeing; when you want to keep away from names, you attach yourself to names. Even when one reaches the fourth of the four *dhyānas*[14] after innumerable years, once one gives up this practice all that one has achieved is lost. This is due to one's ignorance of fundamental reality. Through gradual cultivation, it takes at least three rebirths and at most sixty kalpas [to become a Śrāvaka[15]]. Also, it takes at least four rebirths and at most a hundred kalpas [to become a Pratyeka[16]]. The practice continues even through the three endless periods for the achievement of Buddhahood. According to the ancients, this cultivation is still not as good as 'One Thought,'[17] which emerges from no-birth and is far beyond the achievements of the learning of the Three Vehicles [Śrāvakayāna, Pratyekabuddhayāna, Bodhisattvayāna]. Our ancients also pointed out that in the absolute moment the waving of a finger perfects what eight thousand ways can achieve, or eliminates the three endless periods. All this should be carefully examined. If one would follow this way, how much effort one must put into it!"

The Six Phenomena and the Void

A monk asked, "As for the finger, I will not ask you about it. But what is the moon?"[18]

The Master said, "Where is the finger that you do not ask about?" So the monk asked, "As for the moon, I will not ask you about it. But what is the finger?"

The Master said, "The moon!"

The monk challenged him, "I asked about the finger; why should you answer me, 'the moon'?"

The Master replied, "Because you asked about the finger."

The Prince of Nan-t'ang[19] esteemed the Master's teaching and invited him to stay in the Ch'an monastery of Pao-en, and bestowed upon him the title of Ch'an Master Ching-hui. The Master came to the assembly and said, "The ancients said, 'I will stand here until you see it.' Now I would like to sit here until you see it. Do you think that this is the Truth, too? Which of these statements is closest to the Truth? Try your judgment."

Monk: "The bell has just struck and your audience is gathered together, Master! Please be 'this'!"

Master: "How can the audience match your understanding?"

Question: "What is the spirit of the ancient Buddhas?"

Master: "Where have you not seen enough?"

Question: "During the twelve periods of a day, what should one do, so that one will immediately identify himself with Tao?"

Master: "The mind of discrimination creates artificiality and falsity."

Question: "According to tradition the ancients transmitted their robes to their successors. What kind of man should be considered a successor?"

Master: "Where did you see that the ancients transmitted their robes?"

Question: "The worthies and sages of ten quarters all have entered the Source. What is the Source?"

Master: "It is where the worthies and sages all have entered."

Question: "What is the man who has approached Ultimate Reality like Buddha?"

Master: "For convenience we call him Buddha."

Question: "What is he who is free from what he hears and sees?"

Master: "All of you! Monks! Please tell me whether this monk can still be free from what he hears and sees? Those who understand what this question drives at will have no difficulty in becoming free from what is heard and seen."

Question: "What is the direct way to obtain Buddha's wisdom?"

Master: "There is nothing more direct than this question."

Question: "What is that which, like a plant of good omen,[20] never fades away?"

Master: "Deceptive talk."

Monk: "We all are gathered together here. Please clear up our doubts at once."

Master: "Discuss it in the dormitory; discuss it in the tea hall."

Question: "What is it when clouds scatter and the sun is seen?"

Master: "This is really deceptive talk."

Question: "What should be esteemed by monks?"

Master: "If there is anything that a monk esteems, he should not be called a Buddhist monk."

Question: "Among manifold forms of appearance, what is the pure essence of things?"

Master: "All are."

Question: "When manifestations all come at once, what do you think about that?"

Master: "Is it an eye or not?"

Monk: "My entire being is fully equipped with integrity; please engage me in a decisive battle."

Master: "Your integrity has been defeated by yourself."

Question: "What is the Mind of the ancient Buddha?"

Master: "It is that from which compassion, sympathy, joy, and limitless indifference flow out."

Monk: "It is said that a chamber which has been dark for one hundred years can be made light by a single lamp. What is this single lamp?"

Master: "Why should you talk about one hundred years?"

The Six Phenomena and the Void

Monk: "What is the real Tao?"

Master: "The first vow to put it into action. Also, the second vow to put it into action."

Monk: "What is the ground of Absolute Truth?"

Master: "If there should be a ground, it would not be Absolute Truth."

Monk: "How can the Truth be established?"

Master: "This still has nothing to do with it."

Monk: "Who is the ancient Buddha?"

Master: "Even right now there is nothing that is disliked."

Monk: "What should one do during the twelve periods of the day?"

Master: "Tread firmly with each step."

Monk: "How can the ancient mirror reveal itself before it is uncovered?"

Master: "Why should you reveal it again?"

Monk: "What is the subtle idea of all Buddhas?"

Master: "It is what you also have."

Question: "The ancient teachings state that from the origin of non-abiding, all things are established. What is the origin of non-abiding?"

Master: "Forms rise from that which has no substance; names come from that which has no name."[21]

Monk: "The robes left by the deceased monk are auctioned by other monks. Who is going to auction a patriarch's robe?"

Master: "What kind of robe of the deceased monk do you auction?"

Monk: "What happens when a vagrant returns to his native place?"

Master: "What is there to offer?"

Monk: "There is not a thing."

Master: "How about his daily supplies?"

The Master later stayed in the Ch'ing-liang Monastery. He came before the assembly and said:

"We Buddhists should be free to respond to whatever comes to us according to the moment and the cause. When it is cold, we respond to nothing else but cold; when it is hot, we respond to nothing else but heat. If we want to know the meaning of the Buddha-nature, we must watch the absolute moment and cause. In the past as well as at present there have been many means to enlightenment. Have you not read that when Shih-t'ao understood what was in the *Treatises of Sêng-chao:* 'To unify ten thousand things into one's self is to be a sage indeed,' he immediately said that a sage has no self, yet nothing is not himself. In his work *Contemplation on Identification and Unification [Ts'an Tung Ch'i]*, he first[22] points out that the mind of the Buddha in India cannot go beyond this. In this treatise he further expounds this idea. You, monks, need to be aware that all things are identified with yourself. Why? Because in this world not one isolated thing can be seen!"

The Master also said to the assembly, "You must not waste your time. A moment ago I told you that you must grasp the absolute moment and watch what is coming to you. If you lose the moment and miss the chance, you just waste your time and mistake what is formless for form.

"O monks, to take what is formless for form means losing the absolute moment and missing a chance. Just tell me whether it is correct to take the form for the formless. O monks, if you try to understand Ch'an in such a way, your efforts will be sadly wasted, because you are madly pursuing two extremes. What is the use of this? You should simply keep on doing your duty, follow what will come to you, take good care of yourself, and be careful."

Question: "What is the spirit of the Ch'ing-liang Monastery?"

Master: "When you go to other places, just say you are on the way to Ch'ing-liang."

Question: "How can you be free from all things?"

Master: "What is obstructing you?"

Question: "What can we do with day and night?"

Master: "Idle talk."

Question: "How is it when one sees one's body as illusion? How is it when one sees one's mind as illusion also?"

Master: "Is it necessary to be in such a condition?"

Question: "To identify oneself with reality immediately, one should speak non-dual words. What are non-dual words?"

The Six Phenomena and the Void

Master: "How can you add any more?"

Question: "What is the essence of things [*dharmakāya*]?"

Master: "It is the body of transformation [*nirmānakāya*]."

Question: "What is the first principle?"

Master: "If I should tell you, it would become the second principle."

The Master asked Hsiu-shan Chu,[23] "There is a saying: 'If there is a slight difference, it will make as great a separation as between heaven and earth.' How do you understand this?"

Hsiu-shan Chu said, "If there is a slight difference, it will make as great a separation as between heaven and earth."

Master: "If your understanding is like this, how can you get the point?"

Hsiu-shan Chu: "What then is your understanding?"

Master: "If there is a slight difference, it will make as great a separation as between heaven and earth."

Immediately Hsiu-shan Chu made a deep bow.

The Master and Ch'an Master Wu-k'ung were sitting by the fire. The Master picked up an incense spoon and asked, "If you do not call this 'an incense spoon,' what do you call it?"

Wu-k'ung replied, "An incense spoon!"

The Master did not approve of his answer. However, more than twenty days later Wu-k'ung realized what the Master really meant.

Once before a meal, the monks came to attend upon the Master. The Master pointed to the bamboo screens. Two monks went to roll up the screens. The Master said, "One got it, the other missed."

Some time ago, when Yün-mên asked a monk where he came from, the monk answered that he came from Kiangsi. Yün-mên said, "Have the old masters in Kiangsi stopped talking in their sleep?" The monk made no answer. Later on a monk [Fa-yen's disciple] referred to this episode and asked the Master, "What was the meaning of it?" The Master said, "Such a great master as Yün-mên was examined by this monk."

The Master asked another monk where he came from. The monk answered, "From the temple [where Ch'an is being taught now]." The Master asked, "Did you identify consciously or unconsciously?" The monk made no answer.

The Master ordered a monk to fetch some earth to fill up the lotus flowerpot. When the monk did so, the Master asked him, "Where did you get the earth, from the east side of the bridge or from the west side?" The monk replied, "I got the earth from the east side of the bridge." The Master asked him then, "Is this true or false?"

The Master asked a certain monk where he came from. The monk answered that he came from the Pao-en Monastery. The Master then asked him, "Are all the monks there well?" The monk answered, "Yes, they are all well." The Master said, "Go there and have a cup of tea."

Another time the Master asked a monk where he came from. The answer was that he came from Szu-chou, where he had visited the holy image of Ta-sheng. The Master asked, "Will Ta-sheng's image be carried out of the enshrined pagoda this year?" The monk answered, "Yes, it will." The Master then said to another monk who stood nearby, "Can you tell me whether he has been to Szu-chou or not?"

The Master once questioned the abbot Pao-tzu, saying, "The ancients said that neither mountain nor river could be an obstruction, because light penetrates everywhere. What is this light that penetrates everywhere?"

The abbot said, "The sound of the beating of the gong from the east side."

The Master pointed to a bamboo tree and asked a monk, "Do you see it?"

"Yes, I do."

"Is it that the bamboo tree comes to your eyes, or rather do your eyes go to it?"

The monk answered, "Neither is the case."

There was a certain scholar who presented a painted scroll to the Master. The Master looked at it and said,

"Is it that your hand is skillful, or rather that your mind is skillful?"

The scholar said, "My mind is skillful."

The Six Phenomena and the Void

The Master said, "What is your mind?"

The scholar had no answer.

A monk asked, "Where is the shadow of the moon?"

The Master answered, "Luxuriantly displaying themselves are ten thousand things."

The monk asked, "What is the real moon?"

The Master answered, "Ten thousand things display themselves luxuriantly."

The Master converted those who came under his influence in Chin-ling and presided three times over the great Buddhist center there. He taught Ch'an day and night. During that time the great monasteries in other places followed the Master's teachings, and his admirers in other countries came from far distances to visit him. Thus through him Master Hsüan-Sha's[24] teachings prospered south of the Yangtze River. He attuned himself to the "great function" by following the nature of things. He removed obstacles in the learners' minds and illumined the darkness. Devotees from all places came to him to present what they understood, while others bowed to him asking for enlightenment. The Master's remedies all met with good response. Those who followed the Master's directions and were enlightened thereby were innumerable.

On the seventeenth day of the seventh month in the fifth year of the Hsien-tê period [951–959] of the Chou Dynasty, the Master announced his illness. The Prince of the Kingdom came to console him. On the fifth day of the following month the Master had his head shaved and took a bath. Then he bid good-bye to his disciples and seated himself with his legs crossed. He passed away, and his visage was very lifelike. His age was seventy-four; it was fifty-four years after he had been ordained. At his funeral procession all the monasteries in the lower section of Chin-ling offered sacrifices. The high officials, from Li Chieh-hsün down, all wore mourning and proceeded to his pagoda in Tan-yang of Kiang-ning.[25] His posthumous name was Great Ch'an Master of the Dharma-Eye and his pagoda was called Beyond Form. His earliest disciples, Tê-chao in T'ien-t'ai, Wên-sui, Hui-chü, and others, fourteen men all together, were esteemed highly by the King and the princes. The latest disciples, forty-nine in all, such as Lung-kuang and T'ai-ch'in, expounded Ch'an and each taught in his own place. Their fascicles are also found in *The Lamp*. Because of his disciples' works and teachings, the Master was called Leading Master of Subtle Enlightenment. Also bestowed on him was the posthumous title Great Leading Master of Stored Wisdom. His sermons, given at three centers, *gāthās*, hymns, eulogies, inscriptions, comments, and other items numbered several hundred thousand words. Students of Ch'an copied them, and they were widely disseminated throughout the country.

YUNG-MING YEN-SHOU
(904–975)

"From the Womb of a Cow an Elephant is Born"

(*From* The Transmission of the Lamp, *Chüan 26*)

CH'AN Master Chih-chio of the Yung-ming Monastery on the Hui-jih Mountain in Hang-chou[26] was a native of Yü-hang.[27] His name was Yen-shou and his original surname was Wang. From early childhood on he believed in the teachings of Buddhism. When he reached the age of twenty he began to abstain from meat and only took one meal a day. He read the *Lotus Sūtra*[28] at exceedingly great speed, as if he were glancing at seven columns at a time, and in about sixty days he could recite the entire text. It was said that a number of sheep were inspired by his reading and kneeled down to listen to him. When he was twenty-eight he served as an officer under the general who guarded Hua-t'ing.[29] Later Master Ts'ui-yen[30] came to stay at the Lung-ts'ê Monastery and spread the teachings of Ch'an far and wide. King Wen-mo of Wu-yüeh[31] realized Yung-ming's devotion to Ch'an and sympathized with the strong faith that he had in Buddhism. Therefore the King released him from government service and let him become a Buddhist monk. Yung-ming went to Ts'ui-yen and became his disciple. In the temple he worked as a laborer and did all kinds of service for the other monks, entirely forgetting himself. He never wore silken fabrics, and when he ate he never took two dishes. He consumed only vegetables as his daily diet, and covered himself with a coarse cotton robe as his regular dress. Thus he passed his days and nights.

Later he went to the T'ien-t'ai Mountain[32] and meditated under the peak of T'ien-chu for ninety days. Little birds made their nests in the pleats of his robe. Later on he went to visit the National Teacher Tê-chao,[33] who esteemed him highly and personally transmitted the essence of Ch'an to him. The National Teacher told him that because he had a spiritual affinity with the King he would make the works of Buddhism flourish. It was secretly foretold[34] that Yung-ming would achieve Buddhahood in the future.

Master Yung-ming first stayed at Mount Hsüeh-t'ou in Ming-chou.[35] Many disciples came to listen to him. One day the Master said to the assembly:

> "Here in Hsüeh-t'ou Mountain
> A rapid waterfall dashes down thousands of feet.
> Here nothing stays,
> Not even the tiniest chestnut.
> An awesome cliff rises up thousands of feet
> With no space for you to stand.
> My disciples, may I ask:
> Where do you proceed?"

A monk asked, "A path lies in the Hsüeh-t'ou Mountain. How do you tread it?"

The Master replied:

> "Step by step the wintry blossom is born;
> Each word is crystal clear as ice."

In the first year of the Chien-lung period [A.D. 960] King Chung-i invited him to be the first abbot of the new monastery in the Ling-yin Mountain.[36] and in the next year promoted him to be abbot of the famous Yung-ming Monastery, as the successor of the first

The Six Phenomena and the Void

abbot Ts'ui-yen. His followers numbered more than two thousand.

A monk asked, "What is the profound essence of the teaching in the Yung-ming Monastery?"

The Master answered, "Put more incense in the burner."

The questioner said, "Thank you for revealing it to me."

The Master said, "Fortunately, I had nothing to do with the matter."

The Master made the following *gāthā*:

To know the essence of the teaching here in the Monastery of Yung-ming,
Imagine that a lake lies in front of the door.
When the sun shines upon it, a bright light is reflected.
When the wind blows, the ripples rise.

The questioner asked, "I have been at the Yung-ming Monastery for so long. Why should I still not understand the spirit of your teachings?"

The Master answered, "You should seek understanding from what you cannot understand."

The questioner continued, "How can I gain understanding from what I cannot understand?"

The Master answered, "From the womb of a cow an elephant is born; in the middle of the blue sea red dust is blown up."

The questioner asked, "There is nothing that one can attain even though one learns to be a Buddha or a patriarch; there is also nothing that one can attain even by going through the Karma of Six Courses.[37] What is this that one cannot attain?"

The Master said, "Nothing can come out of what you asked."

The questioner asked, "I heard from you that all Buddhas and their teachings came out of this *sūtra*. What is this *sūtra*?"

The Master answered, "Eternally revolving unceasingly, it is neither the meaning nor the sound."

The questioner asked, "How do I receive and retain it?"

The Master answered, "If you want to receive and retain it, you have to listen to it with your eyes."

The questioner asked, "What is the great perfect mirror?"
The Master said, "A broken earthen pot."
The Master stayed for fifteen years in the Yung-ming Monastery, which was the center for Ch'an training, and taught his disciples, who numbered about one thousand and seven hundred. In the seventh year of the K'ai-pao period [A.D. 974] he went to the T'ien-t'ai Mountain and ordered that the commandment of Bodhisattva be given to the general public. He gave food at night to the ghosts and gods as a sacrifice. In the morning, he set many captive birds and fish free. He spread flowers three times a day and three times a night.

In addition to all these activities, he recited the *Lotus Sūtra* thirteen thousand times, compiled one hundred volumes of the book *Records of the Source Mirror*, and wrote poems, *gāthās*, and songs, about ten thousand words in all. These writings spread widely outside the country. When the King of Korea read the writings of the Master, he sent his special envoy to present a letter in which the King humbly took the position of a disciple of the Master. The King's envoy also brought him a robe woven of gold thread, counting beads made of purple crystal, and a golden pot, etc. Thirty-six monks from Korea were ordained by the Master; they returned to their native land to preach, and each became the leader of his own district.

During the twelfth month of the eighth year of the K'ai-pao period [975], the Master announced his sickness. On the morning of the twenty-sixth day of the same month he burned incense and bid good-bye to his followers. Then he sat with his legs crossed and passed away. On the sixth day of the first month of the next year his body was buried on Mount T'ai-tzu. His age was seventy-two. It was then forty-two years after he had been ordained. The Emperor T'ai-tsung of Sung bestowed upon his temple the name of Ch'an Monastery of Everlasting Tranquillity.

The Six Phenomena and the Void

NOTES

1. See *Recorded Dialogues of Ch'an Master Wên-i of the Ch'ing-liang Monastery in Chin-ling*, in *Taishō shinshū daizōkyō*, Vol. 47, p. 591.
2. Now the city of Nanking in Kiangsu Province; formerly, also called Chin-ling. (Chin-ling is used later in this fascicle.)
3. A town near Hangchow in northern Chekiang Province.
4. Now Shao-hsing in northern Chekiang Province.
5. A town to the east of Yin-hsien, (formerly called Ning-po), in northeastern Chekiang Province.
6. Tzu-hsia is the courtesy name of Pu-shang, and Tzu-yu the courtesy name of Yen-yen. Both were disciples of Confucius, and both were especially learned in literature.
7. Foochow, the capital of Fukien Province.
8. Ch'ang-ch'ing Hui-leng (854–932) was a disciple of Hsüeh-fêng I-ts'un. See *The Lamp*, Chüan 18.
9. The Lake of Pan-yang, one of the five great lakes in China. The Yangtze River flows into it in northern Kiangsi Province. To the southwest of the Lake were many noted Ch'an Buddhist monasteries.
10. Lo-han Kuei-ch'en (867–928) was a disciple of Hsüan-sha Shih-pei. See *The Lamp*, Chüan 21.
11. In Sanskrit this ceremony is called *vyākarana*, which means being told that one will become a Buddha.
12. A town in northern Kiangsi Province.
13. A monk was appointed as director by the government to administer monastic affairs and act as supervisor of all the monks in the area.
14. *Asañjñisattvah*, the fourth of the four *dhyānas*. "The first dhyāna is an exercise in which the mind is made to concentrate on one single subject until all the coarse affective elements are vanished from consciousness except the serene feelings of joy and peace. But the intellect is still active; judgment and reflection operate upon the object of contemplation. When these intellectual operations too are quieted and the mind is simply concentrated on one point, it is said that we have attained the second dhyāna, but the feelings of joy and peace are still here. In the third stage of dhyāna, perfect serenity obtains as the concentration grows deeper, but the subtlest mental activities are not vanished and at the same time a joyous feeling remains. When the fourth and last stage is reached, even this feeling of self-enjoyment disappears, and what prevails in consciousness now is perfect serenity of contemplation." (See Suzuki, *Essays in Zen Buddhism*, Series I, pp. 81–82.)
15. A Śrāvaka is one who attains enlightenment by listening to Buddhist teachings.
16. A Pratyeka is a self-enlightened Buddha.
17. "One Thought" is an absolute state of mind in which no discrimination takes place. To view all things in One Thought is to go beyond relative empirical consciousness and to cut off all entanglements in order to reach absolute oneness of knower and known through sudden awakening.
18. This refers to a famous statement: "The finger is that which points at the moon, but it is not the moon."

NOTES

19. The Prince is Li-yü, the last ruler (937–975) of Nan-t'ang, the kingdom south of the Yangtze River.

20. A Chinese legend says that certain rare plants in the remote mountains live a thousand years and bring good luck.

21. The quotation is from *Pao-tsang Lun*, or *The Treatise of the Precious Treasury*, by Sêng-chao (384–414).

22. In T'ang dialect *mu shang* means "the first," as the quotation here used is the beginning of the treatise. In contemporary language, however, it means "the last."

23. Ch'an Master Shao-hsiu of Lung-shi Mountain in Fu-chou (Foochow), Kiangsi Province. See *The Lamp*, Chüan 24.

24. Hsüan-sha Shih-pei (835–908). See *The Lamp*, Chüan 18.

25. A town southeast of Nanking in Kiangsu Province.

26. Hangchow, now the capital of Chekiang Province.

27. A town in northern Chekiang Province west of Hangchow.

28. Also called *Miao-fa Lien-hua Ching*, or *The Lotus of the Wonderful Law*, as translated by W. E. Soothill.

29. Now Sung-chiang (Sungkiang), a town in southern Kiangsu Province near the border of Chekiang Province.

30. Ts'ui-yen Ling-ts'an of Ming-chou. See *The Lamp*, Chüan 18.

31. One of ten kingdoms during Wu Tai, or The Epoch of the Five Dynasties (895–978), Wu-yüeh comprised Chekiang, southern Kiangsu, and northern Fukien provinces.

32. T'ien-t'ai Mountain is in northern Chekiang Province.

33. T'ien-t'ai Tê-chao (901–972), the leading master of the second generation of the Fa-yen School. See *The Lamp*, Chüan 25.

34. *Shou chi*; see note 11 above.

35. Now the city of Ning-po in northeastern Chekiang Province.

36. Near Hangchow on the Western Lake in Chekiang Province. At the foot of the mountain the Ling-yin Temple was first built during the period of Hsien-ho (326–334).

37. The Karma of Six Courses: *narka-gati* (hell), *peeta-gati* (hungry ghosts), *tiryagyonti-gati* (animals), *asura-gati* (spirits), *menusya-gati* (human existence), *deva-gati* (deva existence).

Part VII

Introduction
"The Swiftness and Steepness"—a Forceful Means to Enlightenment

Hsüeh-fêng I-ts'un (822–908)
"Not To Blind Any Man's Eye"

Yün-mên Wên-yen (?–949)
"The Mountain Is Steep; the Clouds Are Low"

Tung-shan Shou-ch'u (?–990)
"Living Words and Dead Words"

"The Swiftness and Steepness"—a Forceful Means to Enlightenment

Hsüeh-fêng is distinguished for his diligent devotion to Ch'an. He sought the Truth many years as a peripatetic monk.[1] He visited Master Tung-shan Liang-chieh in Mount Tung nine times and Master T'ou-chih Ta-t'ung in Mount T'ou-chih three times. He often carried a ladle with him on his pilgrimages and served as cook at the places he stayed. Through long years of discipline, during which he performed the most despised and difficult labors, he penetrated deeply into the essence of Ch'an, far beyond any merely intellectual attainment. His asceticism and patience are rarely matched in all of Ch'an literature.

At the suggestion of Tung-shan Liang-chieh he went to study under Tê-shan Hsüan-chien, the noted "Master of the Thirty Blows." At that time he met Yen-t'ou Ch'üan-huo and Ching-shan Wên-ch'ü, and the three became close friends. Later among his disciples were numbered Yün-mên Wên-yen, Hsüan-sha Shih-pei, Ts'ui-yen Yung-ming, and Ch'ang-ch'ing Hui-leng, all leading masters in Ch'an history whose teachings are recorded in *The Lamp*.

The main emphasis of Hsüeh-fêng's teachings was to reveal what Ma-tsu called the "ordinary mind," or everyday-mindedness.

"The Swiftness and Steepness"—a Forceful Means to Enlightenment

In the records we have of Hsüeh-fêng he does not use this expression, which had become well known through the teachings of Ma-tsu, Nan-ch'üan, and Chao-chou, but in his teachings and his *kung-an* he constantly had recourse to this basic Ch'an tenet.

Once Hsüeh-fêng came before the assembly and said, "In a southern mountain there is a turtle-nosed serpent. You monks must have a good look at this creature." Ch'ang-ch'ing, Yün-mên, and Hsüan-sha were in the assembly. Ch'ang-ch'ing stepped forward and said, "In this hall someone will lose his body and his life [find his real self] today." Yün-mên threw his staff down in front of Hsüeh-fêng and made a gesture as of fear at discovering the serpent. Hsüan-sha said, "Brother Ch'ang-ch'ing's answer has some substance to it. However, I would not say it thus, but would ask why we should refer to the southern mountain."

This *kung-an* is among the strangest and most ambiguous. It is assuredly difficult to interpret. The key to understanding it is to realize that the serpent is simply a serpent, nothing else, just as the real self within us is simply that and nothing strange or esoteric. If we examine any serpent, we note that its head is like a turtle's. It is only the explicit statement to this effect that makes the creature sound strange. Thus, again, we must realize that the "real self" is simply ordinary mind and nothing strange at all.

The *Supplement to the Transmission of the Lamp*, Chüan 28, records a conversation that Master Hui-yüan (d. 1176) of the Ling-yin Monastery once had with Emperor Hsiao-tsung of the Sung Dynasty concerning the *kung-an* of the turtle-nosed serpent:

Hui-yüan: "A famous disciple of Master Kuei-shan once made a *gāthā*:

> "There is a turtle-nosed serpent in the pool of
>   Fang-shui Monastery.
> If you approach it with intention you will be
>   laughed at.
> Who can pull out this serpent's head?"

Emperor: "You have recited only three lines. What is the fourth line?"

Hui-yüan: "The author's idea was to wait for someone to complete it."

Indeed, two hundred years passed and the *gāthā* was still incomplete until Yüan-ching (d. 1135), elder monk of the Ta-sui Monastery, completed it thus: "After you pull the serpent's head out of the pool, there is still a turtle-nosed serpent there all the same!"

The serpent symbolizes real self, or everyday-mindedness. Chao-chou, as we know, once asked Master Nan-ch'üan whether everyday-mindedness can be approached. Nan-ch'üan replied, "If you intentionally approach it, you will miss it." It is when one obtains non-intentional mind that one is freed from limitations and obstructions. When the mind is thus freed one can reflect spontaneously whatever occurs to him. Yüan-wu K'êch'in, for example, later completed the unfinished *gāthā* another way: "Yün-mên's cake and Chao-chou's tea." The answer is not limited by the terms of the question but relies upon what is within, the unstained ordinary mind, not distorted by intellectual reasoning or logical analysis.

When a monk told Master Hsüeh-fêng that he had come from the Monastery of Spiritual Light, the Master asked, "In the daytime we say sunlight, in the evening we say lamplight. What is spiritual light?" The monk could not answer, so the Master answered for him: "Sunlight, lamplight." The enlightened man sees sunlight and lamplight as being spiritual too. As the Ch'annists would say, when one has not been enlightened one sees a mountain as a mountain and a river as a river—but when one is enlightened one still sees a mountain as a mountain and a river as a river. What has changed is not external; rather, it is one's own self and one's way of confronting reality. Thus, the ordinary mind is the spiritual mind.

The following story illustrates this point very well. Once an elderly lady in Mount Ching invited three Ch'an masters to tea. She brought three cups and a teapot on a tray, set it before them, and said, "He who possesses spiritual power and demonstrates it with regard to this tea may drink it." The guests, dumbfounded by the lady's challenge, could make no response. The lady immediately filled the cups with tea and went away without a word.

The pouring of the tea is an ordinary action, with nothing ex-

"The Swiftness and Steepness"—a Forceful Means to Enlightenment

ceptional or strange about it. But it is this action unspoiled by the artificial interference of thought that reveals spiritual potentialities. It is the action of everyday-mindedness, and is like a stream gushing forth from a fountain. The spontaneity, directness, and sincerity flow undiverted and cannot be mistaken for anything else. This can only be realized by those who have reached the profoundest depths of the Truth.

In Hsüeh-fêng's own experience we have an illustration of this kind of achievement. Once before he was completely enlightened, he told his brother monk Yen-t'ou that he had some understanding of the teaching of matter and Void, or *rūpa* and *śūnyatā*, from Master Yen-kuan. Yen-t'ou declined to accept this kind of intellectual apprehension. Hsüeh-fêng went on to explain that he had had his awakening after reading Tung-shan Liang-chieh's *gāthā* about crossing a river. The *gāthā* identifies the real self thus:

> He is the same as me,
> Yet I am not he!

Yen-t'ou, however, denied the validity of Hsüeh-fêng's experience of self-realization through this *gāthā*.

Hsüeh-fêng spoke of another incident that contributed to his awakening: "When I asked Master Tê-shan whether I could share the experience that the ancient masters knew, he struck me, and I was just like a bucket whose bottom had just dropped out." Yen-t'ou uttered a warning "Ho!" and asked, "Don't you know that what comes from without is not as good as what is produced within? If you were revealing your experience of Ch'an, everything that you said or did would flow directly from the center of your innermost being, which in turn would embrace and penetrate the entire universe." Upon hearing this, Hsüeh-fêng suddenly was truly enlightened and made a deep bow to Yen-t'ou. This incident came later to be known as "the Achievement of Enlightenment in Ao-shan," which was the village where the conversation took place. Hsüeh-fêng's later teachings had their roots in this experience.

Hsüeh-fêng became the leading master in southeast China.

Once a monk asked him, "How is it to be silent and free from dependence?" Hsüeh-fêng answered, "It is still troubled." The monk continued, "How is it when it is not troubled?" The Master replied, "A boatman swiftly leaving Yang-chou." The name of the port city Yang-chou simply happened to come to the Master's mind, and the important thing is that he spoke with spontaneity and intentionlessness.

In his teaching Hsüeh-fêng also used physical blows, as did many other Ch'an masters. For example, a monk once left Hsüeh-fêng and went to visit Master Ling-yen. He asked the latter, "Before the Buddha was born, what was he?" Master Ling-yen lifted the *fu-tzu*. Again the monk asked, "After the Buddha was born, what was he?" The Master again lifted his *fu-tzu*. The monk was puzzled by this and returned to Hsüeh-fêng, repeating the circumstances of the interview. Hsüeh-fêng said, "Repeat the questions to me now, and I will answer you." The monk repeated his first question. Hsüeh-fêng lifted his *fu-tzu*. Then the monk repeated his second question. The Master put down his *fu-tzu*. The monk bowed, and thereupon Hsüeh-fêng struck him sharply.

Later, Hsüan-sha, commenting on this episode, said, "I will tell you a parable. This monk's trouble may well be likened to that of a landowner who sells all his land, but continues to hold on to one tree in the center of his estate." In other words, the monk was not yet completely free. So Master Hsüeh-fêng struck him, to knock him free, as it were, of his last entanglement.

Striking was used for many purposes. Sometimes it was punitive and sometimes not. For the uninitiated the two are indistinguishable, but the enlightened know the difference. Once Hsüeh-fêng held up his *fu-tzu* and said, "This is for those who are inferior." A monk asked, "What would you do for those who are superior?" The Master lifted his *fu-tzu*. The monk objected, "But that is for those who are inferior!" and the Master struck him. Hsüeh-fêng's action seems to be identical each time he lifts the *fu-tzu*, but in fact it is quite different. The first time he raised it, it was to threaten those who did not have understanding and deserved a blow as punishment. The second time, it was symbolic of the great action,

"The Swiftness and Steepness"—a Forceful Means to Enlightenment

spontaneous and free, meaningless, and intentionless, having neither subject nor object. This great action, derived from the center of Hsüeh-fêng's innermost being, serves as the answer usually given by Ch'an masters.

There is a story that Chao-chou sent a *fu-tzu* as a gift to a patron prince, saying that he had used it all his life without exhausting it. The usage which he referred to was its life as a symbol of that which is beyond time and space. As Niu-t'ou Fa-yung once said, "The moment when the mind is in action is the same moment when no-mind acts." From no-mind emerges the great action, in its total freedom from objectivity and subjectivity, as Hsüeh-fêng here demonstrates so well.

The great action cannot be adequately defined or explained, as we have seen in our discussion of the fascicle of Kuei-shan Ling-yu. That which can be defined or explained falls within the realm of knowledge. Though our words are dealing with Ch'an, our explanations are something *about* Ch'an and do not reach the heart of the matter. The Ch'an masters taught directly, not through the explication of principles but through the great action. This is notably true of the teachings of Hsüeh-fêng. He strongly opposed the intellectual approach with its verbal approximations. He once quoted the famous statement—or rather, theoretical solution—of Hui-nêng, the Sixth Patriarch, concerning a problem which had arisen. Two monks were disputing whether it was the wind that moved the banner or the banner that moved the wind. Hui-nêng's statement on the subject has become a classic of Ch'an literature: "It is neither the wind nor the banner that moves. It is your mind that moves." It was, indeed, by this statement that Hui-nêng was identified as the Sixth Patriarch and his life in seclusion ended, as he became known to the outside world.[2] Between the Sixth Patriarch and Hsüeh-fêng, however, were two centuries, and much progress in the development and teaching of Ch'an. About the Sixth Patriarch's classic statement Hsüeh-fêng had this to say: "Such a great patriarch! He had a dragon's head but a snake's tail. He should receive twenty blows!" This was not irreverence but a way of saying that mind-awakening should rely upon self-realization, not on brilliant theories.

"The Swiftness and Steepness"

However, Hsüeh-fêng himself was not entirely free from the deficiency for which he criticized the Sixth Patriarch, as we see in the following story from the fascicle of Hsüan-sha Shih-pei in *The Lamp*: Hsüeh-fêng said to Hsüan-sha, "If the width of the world were one foot, then the ancient mirror [*śūnyatā*, or Void, or Absolute Reality] would also be one foot wide." Hsüan-sha pointed to the stove and asked, "How wide is this stove?" Hsüeh-fêng answered, "It is as wide as the ancient mirror." Hsüan-sha, greatly disappointed, said, "Our old master's feet have not yet touched the ground." In other words, Master Hsüeh-fêng's reply was an intellectual and superficial one, which had not emerged from the source of his being. The identification of reality and appearance was a basic principle of Buddhism handed down from very ancient times. Hsüeh-fêng refers to this basic principle by analogy. The mirror in his analogy stands for reality, the world, appearance. Where there is appearance there is reality. Hsüeh-fêng's analogy, therefore, is still rooted in intellection. Hsüan-sha skillfully tested him by asking the width of the stove. Unfortunately Hsüeh-fêng did not detect the trap and replied intellectually, and this is why Hsüan-sha criticized him.

On another occasion Master Hsüeh-fêng said to the assembly: "If you want to grasp this experience [Ch'an], your mind should be like the ancient mirror. When non-Chinese stand before it, non-Chinese are reflected in it; when Chinese stand before it, Chinese are reflected in it." Hsüeh-fêng's idea here is that the Ch'annist's mind should be free from all distortion, seeing things exactly as they are. However, this too is an intellectual analogy, far from the freedom of thoughtlessness, and Hsüan-sha again challenged him, "Suppose the mirror is broken, what then?" Hsüeh-fêng answered, "Then both the non-Chinese and the Chinese disappear." Once again, Hsüan-sha had trapped him in a logical answer and revealed a master "whose feet have not yet reached the ground."

Hsüeh-fêng, however, did use successfully a number of approaches to awaken the minds of his students without intellectual discussion. As we have previously illustrated, he used blows in the manner of Lin-chi, Tê-shan, and others. He also used the method

"The Swiftness and Steepness"—a Forceful Means to Enlightenment

of calling out the questioner's name to stir his initial consciousness, or *yeh-shih*, in the manner of Nan-ch'üan and Yang-shan. When a monk by the name of Ch'uan-t'an asked, "In the short grass of a level clearing there is a herd of deer. How can you shoot the leader of the herd?" the Master immediately called Ch'uan-t'an's name. "Yes, Master!" he responded. Hsüeh-fêng then said to him, "Go there and have a cup of tea!" What the monk Ch'uan-t'an wanted to know was how to find his real self among the crowd of his multiple selves. This speaking of deer and the leader of the herd is symbolic and basically conceptual in approach. But conceptual search reaches the real self because self-realization is a non-conceptual process. The calling of one's name, on the other hand, stirs the initial consciousness directly and opens one's mind. We have seen this approach before in the dialogues of Kuei-shan and Yang-shan. Hsüeh-fêng applied this well-known method effectively.

In the ideal dialogue between the Ch'an master and his disciples, there is absolute freedom. Sometimes the master's answer negates and at other times it affirms, but at times it does neither. For example, when a monk asked, "Is there any difference between the teaching of the Patriarchs and that of the Buddha?" Master Wu-tsu Fa-yen replied, "When you cup water in your hands it reflects the moon; when you gather flowers your robe absorbs the fragrance." Such an answer neither negates nor affirms. When the same question was put to Master Hsüeh-fêng, he responded similarly. His answer was, "The roaring thunder shakes the ground, but nothing is heard inside the chamber." This is typical of what Tung-shan Shou-ch'u later referred to as "living words."

Ch'an Master Yün-mên Wên-yen was a disciple of Hsüeh-fêng and founder of the school that bears his name. Yün-mên was the name of the monastery where he propounded his teachings, and in time, with the spread of his fame, his friends and followers referred to him as Yün-mên. In *The Lamp*, no fewer than fifty-one fascicles are devoted to the sermons of his disciples. Among his most outstanding followers were Tung-shan Shou-ch'u, Tê-shan Yuan-mi, Hsiang-lin Ch'eng-yüan and Chih-mên Kuang-tsu. Tung-shan

Shou-ch'u is generally considered the finest of his followers.

In the *Blue Cliff Records,* there are one hundred *kung-an* selected from the records of the Ch'an masters. Fourteen of these are from Master Yün-mên. And in the well-known *Records of Serenity,* there are eight *kung-an* selected from Yün-mên's works. The former script was used by the Lin-chi School as its text for the study of Ch'an, and the latter was the basic text for the Ts'ao-tung School.

According to Liao-yüan Fu-yin, who was a friend of Su T'ung-p'o, the great poet of the twelfth century, Yün-mên was an eloquent lecturer, his sermons moving with force and fluency, "like showers of rain." He never permitted his listeners to take notes. "What is the good of recording my words and tying up your tongues?" he is said to have cried as he chased away those who wanted to memorize his sayings. As a matter of fact, those dialogues of the Master which have come down to us were recorded by his attendant Hsiang-lin Ch'eng-yüan, who dressed himself in a paper robe and recorded the Master's words on it surreptitiously.

In the following lines the Master hints at the spirit of the teachings:

> How steep is Yün-mên's mountain!
> How low the white clouds hang!
> The mountain stream rushes so swiftly
> That fish cannot venture to stay.

The height and steepness of Yün-mên's mountain give us a feeling of solitude and freedom. The swift movement of the stream keeps it pure. This swiftness and steepness are characteristic of Yün-mên's style and were forceful attributes in bringing about his disciples' enlightenment. When a monk asked him, "Who is the Buddha?" his answer was, "Excrement!"[3] Yün-mên was not making disparaging remarks about the great spiritual leader here. Rather, he was making a dramatic attempt to nullify all religious dogma, which is only a hindrance to the total realization of one's own Buddha-nature. This intention can be seen even more clearly in another statement of his

"The Swiftness and Steepness"—a Forceful Means to Enlightenment

concerning Buddha. It is said of Śākyamuni that when he was born he exclaimed, "Above the heavens and below the heavens, I alone am the Honored One!" Yün-mên's comment on this was that if he had been there when Śākyamuni made such a statement, he would have killed him on the spot and thrown his body to the dogs. His unconventional and forthright efforts to free his disciples from attachment to any religious dogma whatsoever illustrate his strength and freedom—rushing waters and lofty mountains.

Yün-mên is particularly noted for his one-word answers, which later came to be known as the One-Word Gate. This single word pierced like a sword to the heart of reality, unobstructed by the usual dichotomy of thesis and antithesis. Once Yün-mên and two other Ch'an masters each attempted to express their understanding of Ch'an. The first one said, "A man who is a highway robber has an evil mind, full of treachery." The second one said, "Aren't they getting crowded?" Yün-mên exclaimed, *"Kwan!"* Kwan means a gate on a frontier pass, but the literal meaning of the word has nothing to do with the answer. It was merely a monosyllabic exclamation, forceful and solid as a falling rock. On another occasion, when he was asked what the straight pass to the Yün-mên Mountain was, his answer was *"Ch'in!"* The literal meaning of *ch'in* is "intimacy." Another time, when asked what the "sword of Yünmên" was, his answer was *"Tsu"*—literally, "ancestor." Obviously there is no logical relationship between these answers and the questions put to him. These abrupt exclamations exploded the dynamite, shocking listeners, as it were, into deeper awareness of the inner realm from which his response had emerged; pure and powerful living beyond mind—again the rushing waters and the lofty mountains.

Once when Master Yün-mên was asked what the eye of the true Dharma was, he said, *"P'u!"* P'u literally means, "everywhere." In the *Collection and Classification of Ch'an Materials,* Chüan 10, there is a *gāthā* concerning this answer, written by Tung-shan Hsiao-ts'ung during the Sung Dynasty:

> What ordinarily does the word *p'u* mean?
> One must look at its lightning!

"The Swiftness and Steepness"

If you try to understand by reasoning,
Ah, you are patching a boil with a piece of flesh!

Rather, one must be struck by the swift lightning of *p'u* and become illuminated instead of analyzing its meaning separately from ourselves. It is only then that one actually experiences the power of the word.

Yün-mên was enlightened by Master Mu-chou (Chên Tsun-su) and was sent later to Hsüeh-fêng I-ts'un, for whom he served a time as head monk. When he first came to Mu-chou to seek the Truth, he was repeatedly turned away. He went to see the Master on three consecutive days and was put out unceremoniously each time. The third day, he managed to sneak in but was caught by Mu-chou, who urged him, "Speak! Speak!" As Yün-mên was about to say something, the Master pushed him out and slammed the door on him, breaking one of his legs. Apparently this intense pain awakened him instantaneously. It is, of course, futile to attempt to find a rational explanation for this rough treatment accorded by Master Mu-chou to his eager disciple.

Mu-chou, as we know, was head monk in the monastery of Huang-po when he suggested to Lin-chi that he ask Master Huang-po questions. Lin-chi went to Huang-po three times and received blows each time. Here we find the same method that was adopted by Mu-chou to enlighten Yün-mên when he sought the Truth from him. It was not until the door had been shut on Yün-mên for the third time, and he had suffered intense physical pain, that he was awakened. Similarly, Lin-chi was not awakened until after he had left the monastery in despair, traveling on foot to Master Ta-yü to seek help from him. Later on, when Master Yün-mên had become the author of the forceful *"Kwan!"* we are reminded of Lin-chi, whose exclamatory "Ho!" was applied with like authority. These comparisons suggest that the better we understand one of these masters, the better we will understand the other.

The Ch'an Buddhist says, "I lift a finger and the whole universe moves along with it." If one understands this saying intuitively, one will be awakened to the Truth as Chü-shih was by Master T'ien-lung. The "finger" here is a symbol of absolute solitude. When the

"The Swiftness and Steepness"—a Forceful Means to Enlightenment

eager learner penetrates into this absolute solitude, he is instantly dispatched into the inner profundity. For the same purpose Yün-mên held up his staff, saying, "I have often told you that the numberless Buddhas, past, present, and future, the twenty-eight Patriarchs in India, and the six Patriarchs in China are all disputing the truth of Buddhism on the tip of a staff." A later commentator remarked, "As soon as one understands the staff, one has completed the study of Ch'an." Likewise, as soon as one understands the finger, one enters absolute solitude and is enlightened. However, for a better understanding of these techniques, we shall do well to remind ourselves of the underlying philosophical principle of "universality in particularity" (*p'ien chung cheng*), which was put forth by Tung-shan Liang-chieh as one of the five relationships between the two polarities. The Hua-yen School expressed this principle as "One in Many." With this in mind, for example, the meaning of the following passage in the fascicle of Yün-mên becomes clear:

> Among the old masters there were quite a few who transmitted to us their teachings, which are helpful. For example, Master Hsüeh-fêng said, "The entire great earth is nothing but yourself." Master Chia-shan said, "Find me on top of a hundred blades of grass and recognize the king in the noisy market place." Master Lo-p'u said, "When you hold a grain of dust, you are holding the great earth in your hand. A hairy lion, all of it, is you." Take these sayings and reflect on them again and again. After days, years, you will find your entrance.

When we read the fascicle of Yün-mên we may wonder why on the one hand the Master repeatedly warned his disciples not to look for words from the old masters, because they were merely laughingstocks, and why on the other hand he himself spoke so extensively on Ch'an and indeed referred so often to the sayings of the great masters of the past. However, such apparent contradictions are resolved if we look closely at his words: "He may speak all day but not carry a word in his mouth. He eats and dresses every day, yet it is as if he has neither tasted a grain of rice nor covered himself with so much as a thread."

Yün-mên also maintained that if you talk about Ch'an and have found your way to freedom in talking, then what you say *is* Ch'an. Thus he continued to speak even though, as he constantly pointed out, the true achievement of Ch'an depends upon one's inner awareness.

Now let us briefly examine the teachings of Tung-shan Shou-ch'u, the greatest of Master Yün-mên's followers. As we have seen, Yün-mên was strongly against those who depended upon their masters' sermons, and yet he maintained that there were words which went beyond words. This, he said, is like eating rice every day without any attachment to a grain of rice. The same is true of Master Tung-shan. He defined two kinds of words: "If there is any rational intention manifested in words, then they are dead words; if there is no rational intention manifested in words, then they are living words."

When Tung-shan went to visit Master Yün-mên, his answers were not accepted by the Master because his words were not living words, as we have noted. Let us look at this dialogue between Yün-mên and Tung-shan:

"Where have you come from recently?"
"From Ch'a-tu."
"Where were you during the summer?"
"I was in the Pao-tzu Monastery in Hunan."
"When did you leave there?"
"In the eighth month of last year."
"I absolve you from thirty blows!"

The next day Tung-shan went to question Yün-mên, saying, "Yesterday you were pleased to release me from thirty blows, but I do not know what my fault was."

"Oh, you rice-bag! This is the way you wander from the west of the River to the south of the Lake!"

What Tung-shan had offered in reply to Yün-mên's question were logical answers but not living words. After he had been enlightened and became a master himself his words were quite different, as we may see in the following exchange:

A monk asked him, "Before mind exists, where are things?"

"The Swiftness and Steepness"—a Forceful Means to Enlightenment

Tung-shan answered, "The lotus leaves move without a breeze, so there must be fish swimming by."

Another monk asked him, "What is the duty required of a Ch'an monk?"

Tung-shan replied, "When the clouds envelop the top of Mount Ch'u, there will be a heavy rainstorm."

The swimming of the fish and the motion of the lotus leaves have nothing to do with the question concerning the existence of things, and the rainstorm and Mount Ch'u are no reply to the question concerning the monk's duty, yet these are judged by Ch'an masters to be the best answers recorded from Master Tung-shan. They are answers in living words. In Yün-mên's dialogue also we find answers of this sort:

Monk: "What is the fundamental idea of Buddhism?"

Yün-mên: "When spring comes, the grass turns green of itself."

Monk: "What was Niu-t'ou Fa-yung before he saw the Fourth Patriarch?"

Yün-mên: "The Goddess of Mercy is worshipped in every family."

Monk: "What was he after he saw the Fourth Patriarch?"

Yün-mên: "The moth in the flame swallows the tiger."

These answers of Yün-mên's are obviously not logically related to the questions that were put to him. They manifest no rational intention, but the inner light shines forth from them.

In Tung-shan's teaching there is a famous *kung-an* much commented upon by later masters. A monk asked Tung-shan, "What is the Buddha?" Tung-shan replied, "Three *chin* of flax." This reply also brings to mind Yün-mên's reply when he was asked, "What is the teaching beyond the Buddhas and the Patriarchs?" He said, "Pancake!" Apparently Tung-shan and Yün-mên walked the same road, but this type of answer had frequently been employed by earlier Ch'an masters. Long before Yün-mên, Chao-chou was asked, "What is the meaning of Bodhidharma coming from the West?" He replied, "The cypress tree in the courtyard." Some time after Tung-shan had pronounced the famous *kung-an* of the "three *chin* of flax," a monk went to Chih-mên Kuang-tsu and asked what this answer meant. He was told, "Flowers are shining bright, brocade is shining bright." When the monk still did not understand, Chih-mên added, "Bamboos in the south and trees in the north." This famous answer was subsequently recorded in the *Blue Cliff Records*.

All these answers, from Tung-shan, Chih-mên, Yün-mên, Chao-chou, and others, do not carry symbolic implications. They are plain, matter-of-fact utterances, emerging from the innermost consciousness as water flows from a spring or a bud bursts forth in the sun. Yet every one of them contains the immeasurable force of that which lies beyond thought and cuts off all known passageways of the intellect.

In the *Blue Cliff Records* we have Yüan-wu K'ê-ch'in's comments on Tung-shan's *kung-an*, as translated here by Dr. Suzuki:

> There are some people these days who do not truly understand this *koan* [*kung-an*]; this is because there is no crack in it to insert their intellectual teeth. By this I mean that it is altogether too plain and tasteless. Various answers have been given by different masters to the question, "What is the Buddha?" One said, "He sits in the Buddha Hall." Another said, "The one endowed with the thirty-two marks of excellence." Still another: "A bamboo-root whip." None, however, can excel Tung-shan's "Three *chin* of flax," as regards its irrationality which cuts off all passages of speculation. Some comment that Tung-shan was weighing flax at the moment, hence the answer. Others say that it was a trick of equivocation on the part of Tung-shan; and still others think that as the questioner was not conscious of the fact that he was himself the Buddha, Tung-shan answered him in this indirect way.
>
> Such [commentators] are all like corpses, for they are utterly unable to comprehend the living truth. There are still others, however, who take the "three *chin* of flax" as the Buddha [thus giving it a pantheistic interpretation]. What wild and fantastic remarks they make! As long as they are beguiled by words, they can never expect to penetrate into the heart of Tung-shan, even if they live to the time of Maitreya Buddha. Why? Because words are merely a vehicle on which the truth is carried. Not comprehending the meaning of the old master, they endeavor to find it in his words only, but they

"The Swiftness and Steepness"—a Forceful Means to Enlightenment

will find therein nothing to lay their hands on. The truth itself is beyond all description, as is affirmed by an ancient sage, but it is by words that the truth is manifested.[4]

Words of this sort are what Tung-shan called living words, and such will be found in the sermons given by the following masters.

HSÜEH-FÊNG I-TS'UN
(822–908)

"Not To Blind Any Man's Eye"

(*From* The Transmission of the Lamp, *Chüan 16*)

CH'AN Master Hsüeh-fêng I-ts'un of Fu-chou[5] was a native of Nan-an in Ch'üan-chou.[6] His original surname was Tsang. For generations his family had worshipped Buddha. From his earliest days he disliked meat. Even as a baby he was curiously interested when he heard the sound of the temple bells and saw the banners of Buddha. At the age of twelve he went with his father to the Yü-chien Monastery in P'u-t'ien, where he saw the Vinaya master Ch'ing-hsüan. Hsüeh-fêng immediately bowed to him and said, "You are my master." So he lived in the monastery and served as an attendant until he was seventeen, when his head was shaved. He then went to visit Master Chang-chao of the Fu-yung Mountain. This master liked him and thought that he would become a great Buddhist. Later on he went to the Pao-ch'a Monastery in Yu-chou,[7] where he was ordained. Hsüeh-fêng had attended many Ch'an assemblies, but found spiritual affinity and understanding with Master Tê-shan Hsüan-chien.[8]

In the middle of the Hsien-t'ung period [860–873] he returned to Fukien and founded the monastery on the Snow Peak [Hsüeh-fêng] of Hsiang-ku Mountain. Disciples and followers soon joined

"The Swiftness and Steepness"—a Forceful Means to Enlightenment

him. The Emperor I-tsung granted him the title Great Master Chen-chio and gave him an honorary purple robe.

A monk asked, "Is there any difference or any similarity between the teachings of the Patriarch of Ch'an and the teachings of other schools of Buddhism?" To which the Master replied, "The roaring thunder shakes the ground, but nothing is heard inside the chamber." He added, "What is the purpose of your traveling on foot?"[9]

Question: "How is it that my eyes originally focused correctly, but that now, because of the teachings of the Master, my vision has become distorted?"

Master: "In the midst of confusion one sees Bodhidharma."

The questioner continued, "Where is my eye?"

Master: "You won't receive this from your teacher."

Question: "If a man has his head shaved, wears a monk's robe, and takes the shelter Buddha gives, why then should he not be recognized as one who is aware of Buddha?"

Master: "It is not as good to have something as to have nothing."

Once the Master said to an abbot, "The word 'thus' is always used as a division between the texts of the sūtras. What is the main text of the sūtras?" The abbot made no answer.

Question: "Someone asked, 'Among the Threefold Body,[10] which body does not suffer a worldly fate?' The early master says that he always concentrates on this. What did he mean?"

Master: "I have climbed Mount Tung[11] nine times."

The monk wanted to ask more questions, but the Master exclaimed, "Throw this monk out!"

Another monk asked, "What does 'meeting face to face' mean?"

Master: "A thousand miles is not a long way."

Question: "What is a great master like?"

Master: "You have the right to look up to him."

Question: "What did Mañjuśrī and Vimalakīrti discuss?"[12]

Master: "The meaning is lost."

A monk asked, "How is it to be in silence and free from dependence?"

Master: "It is still troubled."

The monk continued, "What is it when it is not troubled?"

Master: "A boatman swiftly leaving Yang-chou."[13]

A monk began, "In ancient times there was a saying . . ." The Master immediately lay down. After a while he stood up and said, "What were you asking?" As the monk started to repeat the question the Master commented, "This fellow wastes his life and will die in vain!"

Another monk asked, "What does it mean when the arrow is about to leave the bow?"

Master: "When the archer is an expert he does not try to hit the target."

Monk: "If the eyes of all the people do not aim at the target, what will happen?"

Master: "Be expert according to your talent."

Question: "An early master said that when one meets a man who understands Tao, one should reply to him neither by words nor by silence. How should one reply?"

Master: "Go and have a cup of tea."

The Master asked a monk where he came from. The answer was, "From the Monastery of Spiritual Light." The Master commented, "In the daytime we have sunlight; in the evening we have lamplight. What is spiritual light?" The monk made no answer. The Master answered for him: "Sunlight, lamplight."

The monk Hsi[14] asked, "The ancients said that he who understands the highest truth maintained by Buddha is qualified to speak. What will he say?" The Master seized him and commanded, "Speak! Speak!" Then the Master knocked him down. When Hsi got up he was perspiring.

The Master asked a monk where he came from. The monk replied that he had recently left central Chekiang. The Master further asked, "Did you come by river or by land?" The monk answered, "Neither route has anything to do with it." The Master pressed him, "How did you get here?" The monk replied, "Was there anything obstructing my way?" The Master immediately struck him.

Question: "What did the ancient Master mean when he said, 'Present yourself to me face to face'?"

The Master said, "Yes!"

"The Swiftness and Steepness"—a Forceful Means to Enlightenment

The questioner continued, "What is it to present oneself to the Master face to face?"

The Master exclaimed, "Good heavens! Good heavens!"

The Master asked a monk, "How old is this water buffalo?" He received no reply and answered himself, saying, "It is seventy-seven." A monk asked him, "Why should you, Master, become a water buffalo?"[15] The Master said, "What is wrong with that?" As the monk left, the Master asked him where he was going. "To visit Ching-shan,"[16] was the reply. The Master said, "If Ching-shan asks you about my teaching of Buddhism, what will you say?" The monk replied, "I'll answer that when he asks me." The Master struck him.

Later the Master asked Tao-fu,[17] "For what mistake did I strike the monk?" Tao-fu answered, "Ask Ching-shan; then it will be completely clear." The Master said, "Ching-shan is in Chekiang. How can I ask him to make this clear?" Tao-fu retorted, "Have you not heard that if you ask those who are far away you will get the answer from those who are near?" The Master remained silent.

One day the Master remarked to Hui-leng,[18] "I have heard that Kuei-shan asked Yang-shan where the early wise men had gone. Yang-shan answered that they may be in heaven or they may be on earth. What do you think Yang-shan meant?" Hui-leng said, "This would not be a correct answer to the question of where the ancient wise men went and where they had come from." The Master said, "You don't entirely agree with Yang-shan? If someone asked you, what would you say?" Hui-leng answered, "I would just say he is mistaken." The Master went on, "Then you are not mistaken?" Hui-leng said, "My answer would not be any different from a mistake."

The Master asked a monk, "Where did you come from?"
Answer: "From Kiangsi."
Master: "How far is Kiangsi from here?"
Answer: "Not far."
The Master held up his *fu-tzu* and said, "Is there any space for this?"
Answer: "If there were space enough for that, then Kiangsi would be far away."

The Master struck the monk.

A monk asked, "I have just come to this monastery. I beg you to show me the way to Truth."

The Master said, "I would rather be crushed to dust. I dare not blind any monk's eye."

A monk asked, "As for what happened after the forty-nine years of Buddha's teaching, I am not going to ask you that. But what happened before those forty-nine years?"

The Master struck his mouth with the *fu-tzu*.

There was a monk who left the Master to visit Ling-yün,[19] whom he asked, "Before Buddha was born, what was he?" Ling-yün lifted his *fu-tzu*. The monk asked, "What was he after he was born?" Ling-yün again lifted his *fu-tzu*. The monk, failing to understand this, returned to the Master. The Master asked him, "You just left and now you have come back. Is this not too soon?" The monk replied, "When I asked Ling-yün about Buddhism, his answers did not satisfy me, so I have returned here." The Master demanded, "What did you ask?" The monk then recounted his experience with Ling-yün. Whereupon the Master said, "Please put the same question to me and I will answer you." The monk then asked, "Before Buddha was born, what was he?" The Master lifted his *fu-tzu*. The monk asked, "What was he after he was born?" The Master put down his *fu-tzu*. The monk made a deep bow and the Master struck him.

The Master mentioned a saying of the Sixth Patriarch: "It is neither the wind nor the banner that moves. It is your mind that moves." He commented, "Such a great patriarch! He has 'a dragon's head but a snake's tail.'[20] I will give him twenty blows." The monk Fu[21] of T'ai-yüan, who was standing beside the Master, gnashed his teeth when he heard this. The Master confessed, "After what I said a moment ago, I also should be given twenty blows."

The Master asked Hui-ch'üan, "How did you enter Ch'an?" Hui-ch'üan answered, "I have discussed this with you, Master!" The Master said, "When did we discuss it?" Hui-ch'üan replied, "How could you have forgotten?" The Master said, "How did you enter Ch'an?" Hui-ch'üan did not answer and was struck by the Master.

Ch'uan-t'an asked, "In the short grass of a level clearing there

"The Swiftness and Steepness"—a Forceful Means to Enlightenment

is a herd of deer. How can you shoot the leader of the herd?" The Master called Ch'uan-t'an's name, to which Ch'uan-t'an responded. The Master said to him, "Go there and have a cup of tea!"

The Master asked a monk, "Where have you just come from?" The monk replied, "I left Kuei-shan after having asked him to explain the idea of Bodhidharma coming from the West. He answered merely by sitting silently in his seat." The Master questioned him, "Do you agree with that?" "I do not," he replied. The Master went on: "Kuei-shan is an old Buddha. You should rush back and bow to him and confess your mistake." When Hsüan-sha Shih-pei[22] heard of this, he said, "The old fellow on top of the mountain [Hsüeh-fêng] missed the point of Kuei-shan's lesson."

A monk pleaded, "Master! Please express what I cannot express myself." The Master answered, "For the Dharma's sake I have to save you!" Thereupon he lifted his *fu-tzu* and flourished it before the monk. The monk departed immediately.

The Master asked Hui-leng, "What did the ancient master mean when he said, 'In front, three and three; behind, three and three'?"[23] Hui-leng immediately went away.

The Master asked a monk, "Where did you come from?" The monk answered, "From Lan-t'ien [Blue Field]." The Master asked, "Why don't you go burrow in the grass?"

A monk asked, "What is the greatest endeavor?" The Master took the monk's hand and said, "Of whom do you ask this?"

A monk bowed to the Master, for which the Master gave him five blows. The monk complained, "What did I do wrong?" The Master struck him again five times and shouted at him to go away.

The Master asked a monk, "Where did you come from?"
Answer: "From across the mountain range."[24]
The Master: "Have you met Bodhidharma?"
Answer: "Blue sky, bright sun."
The Master: "How about yourself?"
Answer: "What more do you want?"
The Master struck him.

Later Master Hsüeh-fêng saw this monk off. When he had gone

several steps, the Master called to him. As the monk turned his head to look back, the Master said, "Do your best while you are traveling."

A monk asked, "What do you think of the idea that picking up a hammer or lifting up a *fu-tzu* is not teaching Ch'an?" The Master lifted up his *fu-tzu*. The monk who had raised the question lowered his head and departed while Hsüeh-fêng ignored him.

A monk asked, "Are the teachings in the Three Vehicles and the Twelve Divisions[25] expounded for the ordinary man, or not?" The Master replied, "It is no use singing the song of the willow branches."[26]

The Master told Ching-ch'ing, "Long ago an old master took an officer with him to see the assembly hall and told him, 'All these men are monks pursuing their study of Buddhism.' The officer commented, 'How is it that although gold is precious, it causes cataracts if its fragments get into the eyes?'[27] The old master made no answer." Ching-ch'ing gave the answer: "Recently I gave away a piece of brick and got in exchange a piece of jade."[28]

The Master came to the assembly, lifted his *fu-tzu*, and said, "This is for those who are inferior." A monk asked, "What would you do for those who are superior?" The Master lifted his *fu-tzu*. The monk retorted, "That was for those who are inferior." The Master struck him.

A monk asked, "What did it mean when the National Teacher Nan-yang Hui-chung called his attendant three times?" The Master immediately stood up and went to his chamber.

The Master asked a monk, "Where were you this summer?" The monk replied, "At Yung-ch'üan [bubbling spring]." The Master continued, "Does the spring bubble all the time or only occasionally?" The monk answered, "That is something which you cannot ask." The Master retorted, "It is something that I cannot ask?" The monk said, "Yes." The Master struck him.

The Master and his disciples were going to the village to work together; on their way they met a band of monkeys in the road. The Master said, "Every one of these animals carries an ancient mirror,[29] but they come to break off the tops of my rice plants." A

"The Swiftness and Steepness"—a Forceful Means to Enlightenment

monk argued, "From the infinite past, it has been nameless. Why do you call it an ancient mirror?" The Master said, "Now it has a flaw." The monk went on, "Why should you be so impatient? You did not grasp what we were talking about." The Master replied, "I am guilty."

The General of Fukien donated a silver chair to the Master. A monk asked the Master, "You have received a fine gift from the General. What are you going to give him in return?" The Master laid both hands upon the ground and said, "Please strike me lightly."

Question: "What does it mean when one absorbs *vairocana*?"
Master: "Has Fu-t'ang been all right since he came back?"

The Master spoke to the assembly: "If I talk about this and that, you will search for a meaning in my words. If I should be free from any trace and leave no tracks like a goat hanging by its horns from a tree, how would you find me?"

The Master stayed in Fukien for more than forty years. Every winter and every summer no fewer than one thousand five hundred people came to learn from him. In the third month of the second year of K'ai-p'ing [908] in the Liang Dynasty, the Master announced his illness. The General of Fukien sent a physician to examine him. The Master said, "My illness is not an illness." He declined to take the medicine prescribed for him, but devoted himself to composing a *gāthā* for the transmitting of the Dharma.

On the second day of the fifth month he visited Lan-t'ien in the morning. When he returned in the evening he bathed and, in the middle of the night, entered *nirvāna*. He was then eighty-seven, and it had been fifty-nine years since he was ordained.

YÜN-MÊN WÊN-YEN
(?–949)

"The Mountain Is Steep; the Clouds Are Low"

(*From* The Transmission of the Lamp, *Chüan* 19)

CH'AN Master Wên-yen of the Yün-mên Mountain in Shao-chou[30] was a native of Chia-hsing in Su-chou.[31] His original surname was Chang. He studied first under Chên Tsun-su of Mu-chou.[32] After he had some understanding of Ch'an he went to study with Master Hsüeh-fêng, penetrating further into Ch'an and grasping its essence. In trying to conceal his capacity, he made no distinctions between himself and others. However, he soon took the first seat among the monks in the Monastery of Ling-shu in Shao-chou, where Ch'an Master Jü-min[33] presided, and when this master was about to pass away, he recommended Wên-yen to the Prince of Kwang-chou to succeed him as abbot of the monastery. Wên-yen did not forget his previous teacher, Hsüeh-fêng, and still esteemed him as his master.

When he addressed the assembly for the first time, the Prince of Kwang-chou was present and asked him for advice. Master Wên-yen replied, "No divergent ways lie in front of you."[34]

Master Wên-yen said to the assembly:

"Please do not think that I am trying to deceive you with words today. I can hardly help talking, that is, making a mess of it. If a

"The Swiftness and Steepness"—a Forceful Means to Enlightenment

clear-sighted man saw me doing this, I would be an object of ridicule. How can I avoid his ridicule now? Let me ask you all, What do you lack at the very beginning? Even though I tell you that there is nothing lacking within you, this too is deceit. Unless your understanding has reached this stage, you are not yet on the right path. Do not ask questions carelessly and hurriedly when your mind is completely dark. Tomorrow and the days thereafter, you will have the most important work to do in order to achieve enlightenment. Those whose grasp is poor and fumbling should go to the well-established schools of the great ancients and search on every side for Truth. Should you gain some inner awareness, all this is due to what is within yourself. When you are drifting in the endless kalpa, your mind is full of illusion. The moment you hear others talk about Tao, you will immediately want to know about it and start asking what the Buddha and the Patriarchs are. Thus you will seek high and low for understanding, but in doing so you will get even further away from Ch'an, because the searching mind is a deviation and talking about it is even worse. Is it not then true that not searching for it is the correct way? Well, what other alternatives are there, besides these two? Take good care of your own lives!"

The Master came to the assembly again and said:

"My work here is something that I cannot help. When I tell you to penetrate directly into all things and to be non-attached to them, I have already concealed what is within you. Yet you all continue looking for Ch'an among my words, so that you may achieve enlightenment. With myriad deviations and artificialities, you raise endless questions and arguments. Thus, you merely gain temporary satisfactions from verbal contests, repeatedly quarrel with words, and deviate even further from Ch'an. When will you obtain it, and rest?

"If the Truth could be expressed in words, the traditional teachings of the Three Vehicles and the Twelve Divisions would not be found lacking. Why should we seek the secret transmission handed down outside the traditional teachings? To pursue Truth through intellectual explanations and traditional wisdom, as in the doctrines given by the saints of *daśabhūmi*,[35] though they are forceful as the downpouring rain of the thunderclouds, is not approved by Buddha, because there is a barrier, as ethereal as a gossamer garment, which prevents one's true nature from being revealed. Hence we know that in all intentional thinking there is a separation from Ch'an as great as between heaven and earth. However, when a man who has obtained Ch'an speaks, it is as if he stood unharmed in the midst of flames. He may speak all day but not carry a word in his mouth. He eats and dresses every day, yet it is as if he had neither tasted a grain of rice nor covered himself with so much as a thread. Nevertheless his verbal expressions are still those of the Ch'an schools. What we really should have is the actual experience of Ch'an. If we, the Ch'an monks, try to reveal the process of mind-awakening through play with words, it is simply useless intellectual reasoning. In fact, even though one obtains something directly through one word, one is still slumbering."

The Master continued: "The teachings of the Three Vehicles, and of the Twelve Divisions of the Canon, expound Buddhism in this way and that. The old masters of the present-day world give talks on Ch'an everywhere. Compared with my approach, which concentrates on the needle point, their methods are like the medicine given by clumsy animal doctors, who often kill the animals. However, there are a few who can attain to Ch'an by such methods. How can you expect there to be roaring thunder in speech and the sharpness of swords in words? In the twinkling of an eye a thousand changes can take place. When the wind ceases, the waves become calm. I beg you to accept my offer! Be careful!"

Another time the Master came to the assembly, saying, "Brothers! You have visited many masters in various places, trying to solve the problems of life and death. Everywhere you go you hear the sayings of the famous old masters, which may lead you to enlightenment. Do you have any difficulty in understanding them? If so, please let me know. Let me discuss them with you." At that moment a monk came forward and made a bow. When he was about to speak, the Master stopped him and cried out, "Go, Go! The Western Heaven is ten thousand miles away from you!"

A question was asked: "What do these devotees gathered here

"The Swiftness and Steepness"—a Forceful Means to Enlightenment

discuss?" The Master answered, "All of you stand here too long."

The Master said, "If I should give you a statement that would teach you how to achieve Ch'an immediately, dirt would already be spread on top of your head. Even plucking out a single hair would make you understand everything in the world in a second, but it would still be like cutting one's flesh to patch up a boil. To grasp Ch'an, you must experience it. If you have not experienced it, do not pretend to know. You should withdraw inwardly and search for the ground upon which you stand; thereby you will find out what Truth is. Outwardly not even the slightest explanation can be used to reveal your inner awareness. Every one of you should devote himself to the task of self-realization. When the Great Function takes place, no effort will be required of you. You will immediately be no different from the Patriarchs and the Buddha.

"Because the root of your faith is so shallow and your evil karma[36] so heavy, there suddenly emerges in your thought a strong will, which makes you take up your bowl-bag[37] and set out to wander to a thousand distant places. Let me ask you all: What are you lacking? All men have their own Buddha-nature. Yet even if it were before your very eyes, you would miss it.

"Do not let others deceive you and manage you. As soon as the old master begins to talk, you swallow what he says—like flies struggling to gobble up manure. You gather together in threes and fives, and engage in endless discussions. What a pity, brothers! Our ancient masters could not help leaving some words to help you gain insight into Ch'an. Such words should be put aside. You should be independent of them and straighten out your own backbones. Is this not the way to the Truth? Hurry! Hurry! Time does not wait for you. When you exhale there is no guarantee that you will inhale again. How can you waste yourselves on useless things? You must watch and beware! Take good care of yourselves!"

The Master [came to the assembly and] said:

"Let me put the entire heaven and earth at once upon the very tips of your eyelashes. When you hear this, do not become impatient, but slowly and carefully find out if there is any truth in what I say, and what this truth is. Even though you may have gained some insight from this statement, when you go to the Ch'an master's door he will still break your leg.* If you are one of those who believe that a great master will come to the world to teach you, you may spit in my face. As long as you are a man who is not master of himself, you may think that you obtain something from what you hear, but it will be secondhand, and not your own.

"Take a look at Master Tê-shan. The minute he sees a monk coming to him, he chases him away with his staff. When Master Mu-chou sees a monk coming to the door he immediately says to him, 'According to the established *kung-an*, I will release you from thirty blows!' Look at these examples! What can other masters do? If they simply pretend to know and repeat what others have said, it is just like piling up rubbish. Everywhere they go they talk a great deal, and they are proud of their skill in asking subtle questions; their discussions last from morning to night. What do they expect to achieve? And what will their contribution to Ch'an be? When such persons are treated to meals, they claim that they have earned their support. But what is the value of their teachings? When death comes and they face the King of Hell, he will not accept what they say. My brothers, those who really have it live like ordinary men. Those who do not have it should not let time pass by so easily. Be very careful!

"Among the old masters there were quite a few who transmitted to us their teachings, which are helpful. For example, Master Hsüeh-fêng said, 'The entire great earth is nothing but yourself.' Master Chia-shan said, 'Find me on top of a hundred blades of grass and recognize the king in the noisy market place.' Master Lo-p'u said, 'When you hold a grain of dust, you are holding the great earth in your hand. A hairy lion, all of it, is you.' Take these teachings and reflect on them again and again. After days, years, you will find your entrance. However, no one can do it for you but you yourself. Every one of you should work toward self-realization. The old master, though he has come to be known widely, can only bear you testimony. If you have gained something within, he cannot conceal

---

* This had actually happened to Yün-mên; see page 269 above.

"The Swiftness and Steepness"—a Forceful Means to Enlightenment

it from you; if you have not gained anything within, he cannot find it for you.

"My brothers, when you travel on foot, leaving your parents and teachers, the fundamental thing for you to do is to obtain the essence of Ch'an. Then your travels will not have been in vain. If you find a way to guide your understanding under a severe master, you must not care even for your life, but struggle with him through all kinds of hardships. If there is a chance for enlightenment, wake up, hang up your bowl-bag, and break your staff. Spend ten or twenty years of study under him until you are thoroughly enlightened. Do not worry that you may not accomplish it. Even if you are not completely enlightened in this life, you will be a man again in the next life to continue your efforts. Thus you will have spent your life well and your endeavors will not have been in vain. You will not have failed your masters, parents, or patrons.

"You must be cautious! Do not waste your time wandering thousands of *li*, through this town and that, with your staff on your shoulder, wintering in one place and spending the summer in another. Do not seek out beautiful mountains and rivers to contemplate, nor spend your time calculating, when sacrifice might be better. What a pity when one craves for trifles and loses the important things! Such a search for Ch'an is useless! You do not deserve the offerings of your patrons. Time does not wait for you. If you should suddenly fall fatally ill, what would you do? Would you not be like a crab that has fallen into hot water, its legs flailing in confusion? At that time you would not be able to pretend; you would have nothing to boast of. Do not be idle and waste your time. Do not miss what this life has to offer, for you will never have another chance. This is no small matter. Do not take whatever you happen to see as being real. Even a worldly man said, 'To learn Tao in the morning and die at night—therein is my satisfaction.' What efforts we Buddhists must put into this! We must work hard. Be careful!"

The Master said to the assembly:

"You must not ask, 'What is beyond the sayings of Buddha and the Patriarchs?' when you hear people talk about their teachings.

Do you know who the Buddha is, and who the Patriarchs are? Tell me, what makes them talk as they do? When you ask, 'How can one be free from the Triple World?' you must first find out what the Triple World is. Do any of your senses obstruct your way? Your hearing, your seeing? Where is the real world of differentiation and discrimination? The ancient sages could not bear your sufferings and threw their whole beings in front of you, crying, 'The entire being is the Truth, and every objective pursuit of it fails.' Let me tell you that anything you can directly point at will not lead you to the right trail. Really, you have not found, as yet, your entrance to Ch'an. You would do better to study and find out for yourself. Besides dressing, eating, moving bowels, releasing water, what else is there to do? There is no reason for you to create so many illusions. What is the use of it?

"Furthermore, some monks, idle and not serious in their studies, gather together trying to learn the sayings of the ancients, and attempt to reveal their own nature through memorizing, imagining, and prophesying. These people often claim that they understand what Dharma is. What they actually do is simply talk themselves into endless entanglements and use meditation to pass the time. After a time, they are dissatisfied with themselves, so they leave their parents, teachers, fellow monks, and travel on foot from place to place ten thousand *li*. To travel in such a way is not different from beating an old stump. What is the good of being in such a hurry to start traveling on foot?"

The Master came to the assembly and said:

"We all know that contemporary life is demoralized since we have approached the period of decline in Buddha's teaching. Nowadays masters and monks go north to visit Mañjuśrī and south to Mount Heng. Such foot travelers who hear only the name of Bhiksu are simply wasting the offerings of the faithful. What a pity! What a pity! When they raise questions their minds are as black as pitch. They practice meditation to pass time. There are some of these who pursue useless studies, memorize the old sayings, and wander about looking for the approval of various masters; they have neglected the true upward approach to *nirvāna* and created evil karma.

"The Swiftness and Steepness"—a Forceful Means to Enlightenment

Someday when the King of Hell judges them for their deeds, they will not be able to complain that no one warned them! As for beginning students, they must keep up their spirits and not waste time memorizing the sayings of others. Many empty words are not as good as having a direct grasp of reality, because later on you will achieve nothing but self-deceit."

Entering the assembly hall when all his followers were gathered together, Master Yün-mên held up his staff, pointed it ahead, and said:

"All Buddhas in the world, as numberless as grains of sand, are here on the point of my staff. They are disputing the teachings of Buddhism, and each of them tries to win the argument. Is there anyone who is going to testify? If no one is going to testify, I will give testimony myself." At that moment a monk came out of the group and said, "Please do so immediately." The Master remarked, "You fox!"

The Master said to the assembly:

"All of you travel on foot, some south of the river, some north of the seas. Anywhere you go, you each can find your own native place, according to your karma. Are you aware of this? Come forward, then, and tell me. I will be your witness. If you have it, speak out! If you do not understand, you will be deceived by me. Do you wish to know? If your native place is in the north, Master Chao-chou, and Mañjuśrī in Mount Wu-t'ai, are there. All abide in Suchness. If your native place is in the south, Hsüeh-fêng, An-lung, Hsi-t'ang, and Ku-shan are there. All abide in Suchness. If you do not see the point, don't pretend! Can you see the point? Can you see the point? Watch me ride out of the Buddha Hall. Be careful!"

The Master came to the assembly and said:

"Bodhisattva Vasubandhu[38] is unwittingly transformed into a chestnut-wood staff." The Master took his staff, marked on the ground once, and continued, "All Buddhas, numberless as grains of sand, are here engaged in endless dispute." After these remarks he left the assembly.

Once the Master said, "I see that you people cannot be awakened even when you have been given two or three opportunities.

Why should you wear the monk's robe? Do you understand? Let me explain to you clearly. Later on, when you go to various places and meet an old master who lifts a finger, or holds up a *fu-tzu*, and calls it Ch'an, or Tao, you should give him a blow on the head with your staff and then take your leave. If you do not follow these instructions, you all are related to *deva māra*[39] and you destroy my teachings of Ch'an. If you fail to understand me, watch those who are vainly engaged in endless discussion. I often have mentioned that the numberless Buddhas, past, present, and future, the twenty-eight Patriarchs in India, and the six Patriarchs in China all are disputing at the tip of my staff. Their spirit is manifested in all forms and their inimitable voices echo from all directions, moving free and unobstructed. Do you understand this? If not, please do not pretend to. And even if you do understand it, is your understanding correct? Even if you reach this stage, you shall not yet have dreamed of what a Ch'an monk really is. Looking for such a true Ch'an monk is like going to a deserted village with few houses and meeting no one there." Thereupon the Master suddenly rose, and taking his staff, drew a line on the ground, saying, "All is here." Then he repeated the gesture and said, "All is gone out of here. Take good care of yourselves!"

The Master came to the assembly and said, "My fellow monks! To be a Ch'an Buddhist one must immediately obtain a Ch'an Buddhist nose. Let me ask you, what is a Ch'an Buddhist nose?" No one answered. The Master said, "*Mahāprajñāpāramitā*.[40] Today we all work together. The meeting is adjourned."

The Master came to the assembly and said:

"All of you, no matter what you say or what you have obtained, are simply building another head on top of your own head, or piling frost on snow. You make a dead man in his coffin stare, or burn moxa on top of a burn scar. The resultant mess is no trivial thing. What should you really do? Each of you must find firm ground to stand on. Do not travel meaninglessly, dealing in idle words, waiting for the Ch'an masters to open their mouths so that you can ask about Ch'an and Tao and this and that, copying down their remarks to memorize and deliberate upon. And then, whenever three or five of you gather around the fireside, discuss these remarks and argue which is the best and most unbiased, which is expressed through reasoning, which describes only the event, and which reveals reality through reality. Oh, you mothers and fathers! You just get yourselves well fed and talk in your dreams, and you claim that you understand Buddhism! Do you know that no matter how many years you search for Ch'an through traveling, you will never reach it? Furthermore, there are some Buddhists who, as soon as they hear someone talk about enlightenment, would commit themselves to sitting in hell with their eyes shut, to living in a rathole, to abiding under a dark mountain, or to enjoying the company of ghosts—and yet they claim they have found the entrance to enlightenment! Are they dreaming? Even if we punished ten thousand such people, we would not be committing a crime. Those we would punish are not Buddhists, but liars!

"When you have really achieved something, please show it to me. I will discuss it with you. Do not ignore good advice and do not gather together in groups, to engage in vain and endless discussions. Be careful lest I should find you out and catch you and break your leg. Don't say I didn't tell you that you still have blood flowing in your veins and that you will suffer wherever you go. What sort of creatures are you? You are all a pack of foxes! What are you here for?" When the Master had finished his talk, he threw down his staff.

There was a question put to him: "What is the fundamental idea of Buddhism?" The Master answered, "When spring comes, the grass turns green of itself."

The Master asked the monk from Sila, "What do you use to cross the sea?" The monk answered, "The pirate is beaten." Then the Master grabbed his hand and said, "Why should you be in my hand?" The answer was, "It is exactly what it is." The Master remarked, "Another useless jump!"

A question was raised: "What was Niu-t'ou Fa-yung before he saw the Fourth Patriarch?"

"The Goddess of Mercy is worshipped in every family," was the answer.

"What was he after he saw the Fourth Patriarch?"
"The moth in the flame swallows the tiger."
There was a question: "What is the song of Yün-mên?"
The Master answered, "The twenty-fifth day of the twelfth month."

The monk: "What is the roar of the earthen ox on top of the snow ridge?"
The Master: "Heaven and earth darkened red."
The monk: "What is the neighing of the wooden horse of Yün-mên?"
The Master: "Mountains and rivers are running."
The monk: "Please give us a basic principle for our pursuit of the ultimate."
The Master: "Look to the southeast in the morning and to the northwest in the evening."
The monk: "What would it be like if one reached an understanding in accordance with your remarks?"
The Master: "Light the lamp in the eastern house and sit in the darkness of the western house."
The monk: "How can one pass the twelve periods of the day without wasting time?"
The Master: "Where is your question directed?"
The monk: "I do not understand; please explain!"
The Master asked for brush and inkstand and the monk brought them to him. Thereupon the Master composed a *gāthā*:

> I try to awaken you, but you fail to reflect.
> What discordance this is!
> If you begin to reason about it,
> When will you ever achieve enlightenment?

The monk: "What is my real self?"
The Master: "Roaming over mountains and rivers."
The monk: "What is your real self, Master?"
The Master: "Fortunately my attendant isn't here."
The monk: "What is it like to swallow it in one gulp?"
The Master: "I shall be inside your stomach."

"The Swiftness and Steepness"—a Forceful Means to Enlightenment

The monk: "Why should you, Master, be in my stomach?"
The Master: "Give me back my words!"
The monk: "What is Tao?"
The Master: "Go away!"
The monk: "I do not understand. Please tell me!"
The Master: "Your judgment is very clear. Why should I make another judgment?"
The monk: "How can you be free from distress when birth and death occur?"
The Master opened his hands and unfolded his arms and said, "Give me back death and birth."
The monk: "Why is it that one cannot become a monk if one's parents do not allow it?"
The Master: "Shallow."
The monk: "I do not understand."
The Master: "Deep."
The monk: "What is my real self?"
The Master: "You are afraid that I do not know?"
The monk: "What is it when all possibilities are gone?"
The Master: "Pick up the Buddha Hall for me, and then I will discuss it with you."
The monk: "What has this to do with the Buddha Hall?"
The Master cried out, "You liar!"
The monk: "What is the transmission of Buddha outside of tradition?"
The Master: "Put the question before the assembly!"
The monk: "If I ask them, what would they answer?"
The Master: "On what grounds is illumination established?"
The monk: "What is the spirit of your school?"
The Master: "In front of the door there are scholars."
The monk: "What word penetrates the essence of being?"
The Master: "Hide your body in the Big Dipper."
The monk: "What is the meaning of Bodhidharma coming from the West?"
The Master: "It has been raining for so long without clearing." Then he added, "The steam vapor of the rice gruel."

The monk: "The ancients tried to explain it this way and that way, but never understood the secret of making the further leap to the Ultimate. What is this secret?"

The Master: "The eastern ridge of the western mountain is green."

Again the question: "What is the meaning of Bodhidharma coming from the West?"

The Master said, "Search for the coin in the river where you lost it."

Once the Master sat silently for a long time. A monk asked him how he compared his own silence with that of Buddha. The Master said, "You have all stood here too long. Hurry, make three bows!"

The Master once made the following *gāthā*:

> How steep is Yün-mên's mountain!
> How low the white clouds hang!
> The mountain stream rushes so swiftly
> That fish cannot venture to stay.
> One's coming is well understood
> From the moment one steps in the door.
> Why should I speak of the dust
> On the track that is worn by the wheel?

TUNG-SHAN SHOU-CH'U
(?–990)

"Living Words and Dead Words"

(*From* The Transmission of the Lamp, *Chüan 23*)

CH'AN Master Shou-ch'u Tsung-hui of Tung-shan in Hsiang-chou[41] visited Yün-mên, who asked him:
"Where have you come from recently?"
"From Ch'a-tu."
"Where were you during the summer?"
"I was in the Pao-tzu Monastery in Hunan."
"When did you leave there?"
"In the eighth month of last year."
"I absolve you from thirty blows!"

The next day Tung-shan went to question Master Yün-mên, saying, "Yesterday you were pleased to release me from thirty blows, but I do not know what my fault was."

"Oh, you rice-bag! This is the way you wander from the west of the River to the south of the Lake!"[42]

When Tung-shan heard this, he was suddenly enlightened.

When Tung-shan had become an abbot himself, a monk asked him, "What is that path which is very remote?" He replied:

"One does not want to go out on a fine day, but postpones it until the rain is falling heavily on one's head."

Monk: "Who are all the wise men?"
Master: "Those who get into mud and water."
Monk: "Before mind exists, where are things?"
Master: "The lotus leaves move without a breeze, so there must be fish swimming by."
Monk: "Master! When you ascend to your lion-seat,[43] please sing a song of Tao!"
Master: "During the dry season the irrigation ditches are dredged. There is no need of a waterworks office, as there is no flood."
Monk: "Such being the case, may I thank you for your instruction?"
Master: "The old woman who sells shoes walks fast."
Monk: "What are the Three Precious Ones?"[44]
Master: "It is beyond discussion."
Monk: "What is the seamless pagoda?"
Master: "The stone lion at the crossroads."
Monk: "What is the Dharma that is free from life and death?"
Master: "It is what you look at but do not take, though you have longed for it for three years."
Monk: "Free yourself from mental activity and perception and then say a word!"
Master: "The Taoist priest wearing a yellow robe sitting in an earthen jar."
Monk: "I just happen to have come back to visit you. Please say a word!"
Master: "How can one say anything when one has arrived there?"
Monk: "Please say what is revealed in meditation."
Master: "I will absolve you from thirty blows."
Monk: "Where is it that I am at fault?"
Master: "A crime may not be punished twice."
Monk: "What is the lotus blossom before it comes out of the water?"
Master: "The top of Mount Ch'u[45] when it is turned upside down."

"The Swiftness and Steepness"—a Forceful Means to Enlightenment

Monk: "What is it after it comes out of the water?"

Master: "The River Han[46] follows its course and flows eastward."

Monk: "What is the sharpest sword, which cuts a hair blown against its edge?"

Master: "The visitor from Chin-chou."[47]

A nun asked, "How is it when the cart stops but the cow does not?"

Master: "What is the use of a driver?"

Monk: "What is the duty required of a Ch'an monk?"

Master: "When the clouds envelop the top of Mount Ch'u, there will be a heavy rainstorm."

Monk: "How will it be when all the water in the sea is gone, and all the men in the world have passed away?"

Master: "It is very hard to be like that."

Monk: "How is it to be just that way?"

Master: "The clouds are in the sky, and water is in the vase."[48]

Monk: "What is it when being and non-being both disappear and both temporal and real are forgotten?"

Master: "The top of Mount Ch'u when it is turned upside down."

Monk: "Is it possible for me to understand this?"

Master: "There is a way."

Monk: "Please tell me the way."

Master: "It is one thousand miles and ten thousand miles."

Monk: "How about Niu-t'ou before he saw the Fourth Patriarch?"[49]

Master: "A staff of chestnut wood."

Monk: "What was he after his interview?"

Master: "Tou-pa's[50] cotton garment."

Monk: "What is Buddha?"

Master: "Obviously, correct."

Monk: "What is the state in which all causation has completely ceased?"

Master: "The stone man inside the earthen jar sells date candies."

Monk: "What is the sword of Tung-shan?"
Master: "Why?"
The monk persisted, "I want to know."
Master: "Blasphemy!"
Monk: "To give no attention to heaven and earth and to have no concern for the universe—this is my attitude. How about you?"
Master: "Around the pavilion on Hsien-shan[51] the mist is rising; the foreshore is steep and the boat cannot linger."
Monk: "Now the audience is all gathered together here. Please point out the essence of Ch'an, and tell us its general principles."
Master: "Bubbles on the surface of the water reflect all kinds of color; frogs from the depth of the pond croak under the bright moonlight."
Monk: "At this very moment, where are Mañjuśrī and Samantabhadra?"
Master: "The elder's age is eighty-one. Such a tree does not grow mushrooms."
Monk: "What is the meaning of this?"
Master: "In the first place, it is not possible; in the second place, it is not of the right kind."
[In the seventh month of the first year of Shun-Hua (990) the Master, without illness, seated himself with his legs crossed, and passed away.[52]]

NOTES

1. Foot travel was one traditional way of learning Ch'an. Usually a monk who was making no progress toward enlightenment in his own monastery would leave his master, hoping to find in his journeying another master or some accidental happening that would lead to his awakening.

2. Hui-nêng was a rice pounder in the temple of Hung-jên, the Fifth Patriarch, on Yellow Plum Mountain. Hung-jên discovered a *gāthā* composed by Hui-nêng and gave him the robe and bowl which signified that Hui-nêng would become the Sixth Patriarch. Hui-nêng then fled from the monastery and led a secluded life for the next sixteen years, until the incident described took place and he was recognized.

"The Swiftness and Steepness"—a Forceful Means to Enlightenment

3. *Kan-shih chüeh*. This may be translated in either of two ways: a piece of dried excrement, or a bamboo stick used for cleaning as toilet tissue is today.
4. Suzuki, *Essays in Zen Buddhism*, Series II, pp. 89–90.
5. Foochow, now the capital of Fukien Province.
6. Now Chin-chiang (Tsinkiang), in southeastern Fukien Province on the Formosa Strait.
7. Now Cho-hsien, southwest of Peking in Hopeh Province.
8. 780–865. See *The Lamp*, Chüan 15.
9. See note 1 above.
10. The Threefold Body is *dharmakāya*, *sambhogakāya*, and *nirmānakāya*, which may be rendered as absolute reality, wisdom, and liberation.
11. On Mount Tung is the monastery where Master Tung-shan Liang-chieh taught. It is said that Hsüeh-fêng I-ts'un went there nine times to study under his guidance.
12. Mañjuśrī is a Bodhisattva who is often placed on Śākyamuni's left as guardian of wisdom. Vimalakīrti was a contemporary of Śākyamuni.
13. Yangchow, north of the Yangtze River in Kiangsu Province. The main waterways meet here, making it a center of transportation.
14. Hsi was in charge of the food supplies for the monastery.
15. The Master was seventy-seven at the time, hence the monk's response.
16. Ching-shan Hung-yin (d. 901). See *The Lamp*, Chüan 11.
17. Ching-ch'ing Shun-tê (864–937). See *The Lamp*, Chüan 18.
18. Ch'ang-ch'ing Hui-leng (854–932). See *The Lamp*, Chüan 18.
19. Ling-yün Chih-ch'in. See *The Lamp*, Chüan 11.
20. A common expression which means dwindling away to nothing after an initial display of greatness.
21. See *The Lamp*, Chüan 19.
22. 835–908. See *The Lamp*, Chüan 18.
23. This was in reply to the question, "How many monks are in your monastery?"
24. A range of mountains lies between Fukien and the northern provinces. The monk probably came from Kiangsi or Chekiang.
25. The Three Vehicles are the three divisions of the teachings of the Buddha. In Mahāyāna Buddhism, they include Śrāvakayāna, Pratyekabuddhayāna, and Bodhisattvayāna. (For a detailed explanation, see page 38, note 55.)

The Twelve Divisions are the twelve types of Mahāyāna scriptures: (1) *sūtra*, prose discourses of the Buddha; (2) *geya*, verses which repeat the substance of the sūtras; (3) *gāthā*, verses containing ideas not included in the sūtras; (4) *nidana*, historical narratives; (5) *itivrittaka*, past lives of disciples of the Buddha; (6) *jātaka*, past lives of the Buddha; (7) *adbhutadharma*, tales of miracles performed by the Buddha; (8) *avadana*, allegories; (9) *upadeśa*, discussions of doctrine, often in the form of questions and answers; (10) *udana*, statements by the Buddha *not* in reply to questions by his disciples; (11) *vaipulya*, sūtras which deal with broad topics; and (12) *vyakarana*, prophecies of the Buddha regarding the enlightenment of his disciples.

26. This was a popular song about the separation of friends.

NOTES

27. This refers to a common Buddhist expression implying that studying Buddhism improperly is like having fragments of gold in the eyes.
28. Another common expression, implying, of course, that what one received is more valuable than what one gave away.
29. The "ancient mirror" symbolizes the mind free of time and space, or Original Mind.
30. Now Ch'ü-chiang (Kükong), a town in northern Kwangtung Province; until 1912 it was called Shao-chou. The Yün-mên Mountain is west of Ch'ü-chiang and north of Yüyüan; the famous Yün-mên Monastery is at its top.
31. Soochow, now Wuhsien, a town in southern Kiangsu Province, west of Shanghai, on the Grand Canal.
32. Now Chien-te (Kienteh), in western Chekiang Province, south of Hangchow and west of Shun-an.
33. Ling-shu Jü-min. See *The Lamp*, Chüan 11.
34. At that moment the Prince of Kwang-chou was attempting to start a rebellion against the central government. The Master's ambiguous answer was simply advice to abandon his intentions.
35. Daśabhūmi is the tenth stage in the fifty-two steps in the development of a Bodhisattva into Buddha.
36. The evil karma signifies the burden of evil thoughts, words, and deeds.
37. The bowl-bag was used by the traveling monk for begging food.
38. Vasubandhu was a younger brother of Asaṅga of the Yogācāra School. He would have cut out his tongue for his heresy against Hīnayāna, but followed his brother's advice to use his tongue instead to correct his errors. He wrote many important works on Mahāyāna Buddhism.
39. One of the four *māras*, who dwells in the sixth heaven and constantly obstructs the Buddha-truth.
40. Mahāprajñāpāramitā is the acme of wisdom, which enables one to reach the other shore.
41. Now Hsiang-yang, a town on the Han River in northwestern Hupeh Province.
42. The Yangtze River and the Pan-yang Lake.
43. Tradition holds Buddha the lion among men. The place where he sits is called the *siṁhasana*, or lion-seat.
44. The Triratna: Buddha, Dharma, Saṅgha (monk).
45. A mountain in northern Hupeh Province.
46. The Han River has its source in southern Shensi Province, then flows southeastward and enters the Yangtze in Hupeh Province.
47. Now An-k'ang, a town on the Han River in southern Shensi Province.
48. This was the statement made by Yo-shan Wei-yen (751–834) when he interviewed Li Ao, a great neo-Confucianist and also Governor of Langchou.
49. Tao-hsin (580–651).
50. "Tou-pa" is a name for rural folk.
51. Mount Hsien, south of Hsiang-yang, Hupeh Province.
52. *Records of Pointing at the Moon*, Chüan 21.

Final Remarks

After we have gone through this work, with all its radical variations —from metaphysical profundity to the most bizarre irrationalities, from complex logic to the purely illogical, from contemplation and cessation to shocking physical treatment—we may feel that Ch'an, with all these attributes, intends to teach us something new. This is not so. The efforts of all these great Ch'an masters are directed toward uncovering that which was within us in the beginning and is still there, even at this very moment. Ch'an is never grasped by the intellect, or by an ideational representation. It is not a process of learning, but of unlearning, a return to the original source of all being. This is referred to as Suchness, or *tathatā*. The wisdom contained in the foregoing nineteen fascicles, once it is totally understood, is not, after all, anything mystical or esoteric. Su T'ung-p'o of the twelfth century composed the following lines:

> The mists of the Mountain Lü, the surf of the River Chê
> Cause a thousand yearnings when you have not been there;
> But once seen, they are just what they are:
> The mists of Mountain Lü, the surf of River Chê.

Ch'an does not attempt to transform us into something different from what we are, but lets us be just what we are, like "the mists of the Mountain Lü, the surf of the River Chê." In the

September 1965 issue of the *Eastern Buddhist Journal*, Dr. Suzuki said: "Let it suffice here to say that Zen has nothing mystical about it or in it. It is most plain, clear as daylight, all out in the open with nothing hidden, dark, obscure, secret, or mystifying in it."

Once Chang Shang-ying, a twelfth-century lay Buddhist and statesman (d. 1122), asked Ch'an Master P'ao-an of Ta-hung Shan, "What is the correct way to reach the truth?" P'ao-an replied that the incorrect ways are many, but may be summarized as four: affirmation, negation, both affirmation and negation, and neither affirmation nor negation. These paths do not immediately identify the mind with the truth. In other words, we deviate from the truth through our intellection. When the mind is not identified with the truth, and the truth changes according to objective situations, this is the incorrect way. When affirmation is maintained, it is naturally followed by negation. When negation is maintained, it is naturally followed by affirmation. This unceasing continuum holds true for both affirmation and negation and neither affirmation nor negation. The outcome is that one cannot be free from all these conditions, and therefore one's original mind cannot be revealed. When Original Mind cannot be revealed, inner awareness of Ch'an cannot take place. Thus, the truths expounded by words are merely false differentiations of lesser intellection. How can one be aware of Ch'an through this?

The essence of Ch'an can never be expressed in words. Nevertheless, we have had many words! This recalls a story about Yang-shan. For every word that his master had to say, Yang-shan was said to have ten. Finally his master said to him, "Someday you will meet someone who will fix you!" Years later Yang-shan went to study under Master Kuei-shan, who said to him, "I have heard that when you studied under your first master, you spoke ten words to his one. Is that true?" Yang-shan replied, "That is what people say." Kuei-shan asked him, "What do you have to say about the real meaning of Buddhism?" As Yang-shan took a deep breath to answer, Kuei-shan shouted a silencing "Ho!" Three times Kuei-shan put the question, three times Yang-shan attempted to reply, and three

Final Remarks

times he was silenced with a peremptory "Ho!" Finally, with tears in his eyes, Yang-shan hung his head: "My late master foretold that I would learn better with someone else, and today I have met him!"

In this work I have used many words. If Kuei-shan were present now, he would give me a silencing "Ho!"

*The following pages
of charts show
The Eminent Ch'an Masters
(594-990)*

Selected from *The Transmission of the Lamp*
and represented in the present volume

Name of Master (Chinese and Japanese) and Dates	Native Place (may indicate dialogue spoken)	Chief work or compilation by followers	Appears in The Transmission of the Lamp [compiled 1004]	Appears in Amalgamation of the Essentials of the Lamps [compiled 1183]	Appears in Records of Pointing at the Moon [compiled 1602]	Appears in Biographies of the Eminent Buddhist Monks, Sung, Ming,
Niu-t'ou Fa-yung (Cozu Hoyū) [594–657]	Jun-chou	*Mind Inscription*	Chüan 4	Chüan 2	Chüan 6	Supp. Comp. Chüan
Yung-chia Hsüan-chio (Yōka Gerkaku) [665–713]	Wên-chou	*Collected Works of Ch'an Master Yung-chia Hsüan-chio*	Chüan 5		Chüan 6	Sung Comp. Chüan
Tung-shan Liang-chieh (Dozan Ryōkai) [807–869]	Kuai-chi	*Recorded Dialogues of Ch'an Master Tung-shan Liang-chieh* *Records of Two Masters: Ts'ao and Tung* *The Way to Understand Zen: Tung-shan & Shen-tsan*, written by H. Yamada	Chüan 15	Chüan 20	Chüan 16	Sung Comp. Chüan
Ts'ao-shan Pên-chi (Sōzan Honjaku) [840–901]	Ch'üan-chou	*Recorded Dialogues of Master Ts'ao-shan Pên-chi of Fu-chou*	Chüan 17	Chüan 22	Chüan 18	Sung Comp., Chüan
Huang-po Hsi-yün (Yakusan Igen) [d. 849]	Fu-chou	*Doctrine of Universal Mind*, trans. by Chu-ch'an (John Blofeld)	Chüan 9	Chüan 7	Chüan 10	Sung Comp., Chüan
Mu-chou Tao-tsung Chên Tsun-su) (Bokuju Chinson-shuku)	Mu-chou		Chüan 12	Chüan 8	Chüan 13	

CONTINUED ON THI

Appears in Records of Buddhas and Patriarchs in Various Dynasties [published 1344]	Mentioned in General Records of Buddhas and Patriarchs [compiled 1269]	Appears in Recorded Sayings of Ancient Worthies (limited to only a few branches) [compiled 1271]	A Collection from the Halls of the Patriarchs [published 1245 in Korea]	Appears in Records of the Regular Transmission of the Dharma [published 1062]	Appears in Amalgamation of the Sources of the Five Lamps [compiled 1253]	Remarks
Chüan 12	Chüan 39		Chüan 3	Chüan 9	Chüan 2	Founder of Niu-t'ou School. A great disciple of Fourth Patriarch, Tao-hsin, whose approach represented the teaching of Ch'an before Sixth Patriarch. Also famous for philosophical approach of Prajñāpāramitā in Ch'an.
Chüan 13	Chüan 10		Chüan 3	Chüan 7	Chüan 2	Known as Master of "Enlightenment from One Night's Lodging"; combined T'ien-t'ai philosophy with Ch'an; noted for applying Mādhyamika dialectic to Ch'an.
Chüan 17	Chüan 42	Chüan 34	Chüan 6	Chüan 7	Chüan 13	Founder of Ts'ao-tung School; applied Hua-yen philosophy to teaching of Ch'an.
	Chüan 42	Chüan 46 Supplement, Chüan 1	Chüan 8	Chüan 7	Chüan 13	Co-founder of Ts'ao-tung School.
Chüan 16	Chüan 42	Chüan 3	Chüan 16	Chüan 7	Chüan 4	Formerly a student of T'ien-t'ai philosophy; famous for enlightening Lin-chi I-hsüan.
		Chüan 6	Chüan 19	Chüan 7	Chüan 4	Teacher of Great Master Yün-mên Wên-yen; first man to recognize great capacity of Lin-chi I-hsüan. Appears in *Blue Cliff Records*, Section 10.

FOLLOWING PAGES

Name of Master (Chinese and Japanese) and Dates	Native Place (may indicate dialogue spoken)	Chief work or compilation by followers	Appears in The Transmission of the Lamp [compiled 1004]	Appears in Amalgamation of the Essentials of the Lamps [compiled 1183]	Appears in Records of Pointing at the Moon [compiled 1602]	Appears in Biographies of the Eminent Buddhist Monks, Sung, Ming, or Supplement Compilation
Lin-chi I-hsüan (Rinzai Gigen) [d. 867]	Ts'ao-chou	Recorded Dialogues of Ch'an Master Lin-chi	Chüan 12	Chüan 9	Chüan 14	Sung Comp., Chüan 12
Kiangsi Tao-i (Ma-tsu) (Baso Dōitsu) [709–788*]	Han-chou (in Szechwan Province)	Recorded Dialogues of Ch'an Master Kiangsi Tao-i	Chüan 6	Chüan 4	Chüan 5	Sung Comp., Chüan 10
Nan-ch'üan P'u-yüan (Nansen Fugan) [748–834]	Ch'eng-chou (in Honan Province)	Extensive Records of Ch'an Master Nan-ch'üan P'u-yüan	Chüan 8	Chüan 4	Chüan 8	Sung Comp., Chüan 11
Chao-chou Ts'ung-shen (Joshu Jushin) [788–897]	Ts'ao-chou (in Shantung Province)	Recorded Dialogues of Ch'an Master Chao-chou	Chüan 10	Chüan 6	Chüan 11	Sung Comp., Chüan 11
P'ang Yün (Ho on) [d. 811†]	Heng-Yang (in Hunan Province)	Collection of Three Hundred Poems and Gāthās	Chüan 8	Chüan 6	Chüan 9	
Kuei-shan Ling-yu (Isan Reiyū) [771–853]	Fu-chou (in Fukien Province)	Recorded Dialogues of Ch'an Master Kuei-shan Ling-yu of T'an-chou	Chüan 9	Chüan 7	Chüan 12	Sung Comp., Chüan 11
Yang-shan Hui-chi (Kyozan Ejaku) [814–890‡]	Shao-chou (in Kwangtung Province)	Recorded Dialogues of Ch'an Master Yang-shan Hui-chi of Yuan-chou	Chüan 11	Chüan 8	Chüan 13	Sung Comp., Chüan 1

* See *Biographies of the Eminent Buddhist Monks*. Sung compilation, Chüan 10 (*chüan* means volume in Chinese).
† See *Records of Buddhas and Patriarchs in Various Dynasties*, Chüan 15.

CONTINUED ON THE

Appears in Records of Buddhas and Patriarchs in Various Dynasties [published 1344]	Mentioned in General Records of Buddhas and Patriarchs [compiled 1269]	Appears in Recorded Sayings of Ancient Worthies (limited to only a few branches) [compiled 1271]	A Collection from the Halls of the Patriarchs [published 1245 in Korea]	Appears in Records of the Regular Transmission of the Dharma [published 1062]	Appears in Amalgamation of the Sources of the Five Lamps [compiled 1253]	Remarks
hüan 17	Chüan 42	Chüan 4, 5 Supplement, Chüan 1	Chüan 19	Chüan 7	Chüan 11	Founder of Lin-chi School. Well versed in Vinaya sūtra before being converted to Ch'an.
hüan 14	Chüan 41	Chüan 1	Chüan 14	Chüan 7	Chüan 3	Known as Patriarch Ma; father of the unconventional teaching of Ch'an.
hüan 16	Chüan 42	Chüan 12	Chüan 16	Chüan 7	Chüan 3	Formerly a scholar of Middle Way and Hua-yen Schools.
hüan 17	Chüan 42	Chüan 13, 14	Chüan 18	Chüan 7	Chüan 4	Famous for use of everyday conversation rather than unconventional gestures in teaching of Ch'an. Lived to be 120 years old.
hüan 15	Chüan 41	Chüan 1, 46	Chüan 5		Chüan 3	The most noted lay Buddhist; formerly a Confucianist.
hüan 16	Chüan 42	Chüan 19	Chüan 16	Chüan 7	Chüan 9	Founder of Kuei-yang School.
hüan 17	Chüan 42	Chüan 20, 46	Chüan 18	Chüan 7	Chüan 9	Co-founder of Kuei-yang School.

‡ According to *Records of Buddhas and Patriarchs in Various Dynasties*, Chüan 17, Yang-shan died in the first year of Ta-shun (Keng-hsu), 890, but according to *General Records of Buddhas and Patriarchs*, he died in the second year of Ta-shun, 891.

FOLLOWING PAGES

Name of Master (Chinese and Japanese) and Dates	Native Place (may indicate dialogue spoken)	Chief work or compilation by followers	Appears in The Transmission of the Lamp [compiled 1004]	Appears in Amalgamation of the Essentials of the Lamps [compiled 1183]	Appears in Records of Pointing at the Moon [compiled 1602]	Appears in Biographies of the Eminent Buddhist Monks, Sung, Ming, or Supplement Compilation
Hsiang-yen Chih-hsien (Kyogen Chikan)	Tsing-chou (in Shantung Province)	"Hymn of Exhortation to Enlightenment" "Hymn of Returning to the Void"	Chüan 11	Chüan 8	Chüan 13	Sung Comp., Chüan
Fa-yen Wên-i (Hōgen Buneki) [885–958]	Yü-hang	Recorded Dialogues of Ch'an Master Wên-i Gāthās of Wên-i Commentary on Buddhist Sūtra	Chüan 24	Chüan 26	Chüan 22	Sung Comp., Chüan
Yung-ming Yen-shou (Yōmyō Enju) [904–975]	Yü-hang	Records of the Source Mirror	Chüan 26	Chüan 28	Chüan 24	Sung Comp., Chüan
Hsüeh-fêng I-ts'un (Seppo Gizon) [822–908]	Ch'üan-chou	Recorded Dialogues of Master Hsüeh-fêng	Chüan 16	Chüan 21	Chüan 17	Sung Comp., Chüan
Yün-mên Wên-yen (Unmon Bunen) [d. 949]	Chia-hsing	Records of Master Yün-mên	Chüan 19	Chüan 24	Chüan 20	
Tung-shan Shou-ch'u (Tōsan Shusho) [d. 990§]	Hsiang-chou	Recorded Dialogues of Ch'an Master Tung-shan Shou-ch'u	Chüan 23		Chüan 21	

§ See *Records of Pointing at the Moon*, Chüan 21.

Patriarchs in Various Dynasties [published 1344]	Mentioned in General Records of Buddhas and Patriarchs [compiled 1269]	Appears in Recorded Sayings of Ancient Worthies (limited to only a few branches) [compiled 1271]	A Collection from the Halls of the Patriarchs [published 1245 in Korea]	Appears in Records of the Regular Transmission of the Dharma [published 1062]	Appears in Amalgamation of the Sources of the Five Lamps [compiled 1253]	Remarks
	Chüan 42		Chüan 19	Chüan 7	Chüan 9	Noted for unusual occurrence which led to his enlightenment. Master of Emperor Hsuan-tsung of T'ang Dynasty when Hsuan-tsung was a prince.
an 17	Chüan 42	Supplement, Chüan 2		Chüan 8	Chüan 10	Founder of Fa-yen School.
an 18	Chüan 43			Chüan 8	Chüan 10	A great scholar of Buddhist philosophy; advocated combining Pure Land teaching with Ch'an.
an 17	Chüan 42	Chüan 46	Chüan 7	Chüan 7	Chüan 7	Noted for diligent devotion to Ch'an; visited Tung-shan Liang-chieh in Mountain Tung nine times and T'ou-chih Ta-t'ung in Mountain T'ou-chih three times.
an 17	Chüan 42	Chüan 15, 16, 17, 18	Chüan 11	Chüan 8	Chüan 15	Founder of Yün-mên School.
		Chüan 38		Chüan 8	Chüan 15	Famous for *koan* "Three *chin* of flax."

Bibliography

The following bibliography includes only works referred to in the text.

Amalgamation of the Essentials of the Lamps (*Lien-têng Hui-yao*), 30 *chüan*, compiled by Wu-ming, first published 1183. In *Dainihon zokuzōkyō*, Part 2, Section 2, Case 9.

Amalgamation of the Sources of the Five Lamps (*Wu-têng Hui-yüan*), 20 *chüan*, compiled by Hui-ming, first published 1253. Recent scripts reprinted 1906 by Liu-shih Hêng.

Aryadeva, *Sata Sāstra* (*Po Lun, or Treatise of the Hundred Verses*), translated into Chinese by Kumārajīva, introduction by Sêng-chao. In *Taishō shinshū daizōkyō*, No. 1569, Vol. 30.

Avataṁsaka Sūtra (*Hua-yen Ching*), translated into Chinese by:
(1) Buddhabhadra in A.D. 418–420; called the Chin script (*Chin Ching*).
(2) Śikṣānanda in 695–699; called *T'ang Ching*.
(3) Prajñā in 796–797.

Biographies of the Eminent Buddhist Monks, Sung Compilation (*Sung Kao Sêng Ch'uan*), compiled 1495 by Tsan-ning. In *Taishō shinshū daizōkyō*, No. 2061, Vol. 50.

Chao-chou Ts'ung-shen, *Dialogues and Biography of Ch'an Master Chao-chou Chên-chi* (*Chao-chou Chên-chi Ch'an-shih Yü-lu Hsing-chuang*). In *Recorded Sayings of Ancient Worthies*, Chüan 13, 14 (*Dainihon zokuzōkyō*, Part 2, Case 23).

Ch'êng-kuan, *The Mysterious Mirror of the Avataṁsaka Dharma-dhātu* (*Hua-yen Fa-chieh Hsüan-ching*). In *Taishō shinshū daizōkyō*, No. 1883, Vol. 45.

The Chia-t'ai Comprehensive Record of the Transmission of the Lamp (*Chia-t'ai P'u-têng Lu*), 30 *chüan* (with three additional introductory *chüan*), compiled by Lêi-an Chêng-shou (1146–1208), in fourth year of the Chia-t'ai period (1204).

Chinese Buddhist Canon (*Chung-hua Ta-ts'ang Ching*). Published by the Society for the Compilation of the Buddhist Canon, Taipei. First Collection, 40 vols., published 1962–1966; Second Collection, 12 vols., published 1968.

Bibliography

Chinese Dictionary of Buddhism (*Fu Hsüeh Tzu Tien*). Taipei, Chung-hua Book Company, 1950.

Ching-tê Record of the Transmission of the Lamp (*Ching-tê Ch'uan-têng Lu*), 30 chüan, compiled by Tao-yüan in 1004, edited by Yang-i (968–1024).
Five editions collected by the author:
(1) Script reprinted in *Collected Works of Four Categories: Classics, History, Philosophy, and Literature* (*Szu-pu Chung-k'an*), Part 3, Section 1, by the Commercial Press, Shanghai, 1935; based on the Sung edition of the Hsu family collection in Ch'ang-shu, Kiangsu. Has many copy mistakes and alterations.
(2) Script reprinted in Japan in *Taishō shinshū daizōkyō*, No. 2076, Vol. 51; based on the Yüan edition (reprinted 1317), which is based on the Sung edition collected by Wên-an of Lu-shan, Kiangsi. According to Liu-fei's introduction, this edition was reprinted previously in 1134 by the monk Szu-chien. Also has many copy mistakes and alterations.
(3) Script recently reprinted by Ki-chu Do in Kyoto; based on the 1348 edition printed by the Japanese monk Kampo Shidon (1285–1361), which is based on the 1317 Yüan edition. Recommended by Suzuki.
(4) Script reprinted 1919 by the T'ien-ning Temple in Ch'ang-chou, Kiangsu. This script is identical to the Ki-chu Do edition above.
(5) Script collected in the *Chinese Buddhist Canon*, First Collection, Section 9, Vol. 33, published 1965. Identical to the T'ien-ning and Ki-chu Do editions.

Ch'i-sung, *Records of the Regular Transmission of the Dharma* (*Ch'üan-fa Chêng-tsung Chi*), 2 chüan. In *Taishō shinshū daizōkyō*, No. 2080, Vol. 51.

Chi-tsang, *Commentary on the Mādhyamika Śāstra* (*Chung-kuan Lun*). In *Taishō shinshū daizōkyō*, No. 1824, Vol. 42.

———, *Commentary on the Śata Śāstra* (*Pai-lun Su*). In *Taishō shinshū daizōkyō*, No. 1854, Vol. 45.

———, *Essay on the Double Truth* (*Erh-ti Ch'ang*). In *Taishō shinshū daizōkyō*, No. 1827, Vol. 42.

Collected Commentaries on the Nirvāna Sūtra (*Nieh-pan Ching Chi-chieh*), compiled by Pao-liang. In *Dainihon zokuzōkyō*, Part 1, Section 1, Case 94, Vols. 2–4.

Collected Essentials of the Ch'an Schools (*Tsung-mên T'ung-yao*), 22 chüan, compiled by Tsung-yung in third year of the Shao-hsing period (1133). In the *Chinese Buddhist Canon*, Second Collection, Vol. 2.

Collection and Classification of Ch'an Materials (*Ch'an-lin Lei-*

chu), compiled 1307 by Tao-t'ai. In *Dainihon Zokuzōkyō*, Part 2, Case 22, Vol. 1.

A Collection from the Halls of the Patriarchs (*Chodang Chip*), 20 *chüan*, compiled in 952 by the monks Ching and Yün, published in Korea 1245.

Dainihon zokuzōkyō (*Supplement to the Japanese Edition of the Buddhist Canon*). Kyoto, Zōkyō shoin, 1905–1912. 150 cases, 750 fascicles.

Fa-tsang, *Treatise on the Golden Lion* (*Chin Shih-tzŭ Ch'ang*). In *Taishō shinshū daizōkyō*, No. 1880, Vol. 45.

———, *The Hundred Theories in the Sea of Ideas of the Avataṁsaka Sūtra* (*Hua-yen Ching Yi-hai P'o-mên*). In *Taishō shinshū daizōkyō*, No. 1875, Vol. 45.

Fa-yen Wên-i, *Recorded Dialogues of Ch'an Master Wên-i of the Ch'ing-liang Monastery in Chin-ling* (*Chin-ling Ch'ing-liang Wên-i Ch'an-shih Yü-lu*), compiled by Yüan-hsin (1571–1646), and Kuo Ning-chih (known between 1621–1627), in *Taishō shinshū daizōkyō*, No. 1991, Vol. 47.

Fang-kuang (abbreviated Chinese title of *Pañcaviṁsatisāhasrikā Prajñāparamitā Sūtra*), translated by Hsüan-tsang. In *Taishō shinshū daizōkyō*, No. 221, Vol. 8.

Four-Division Vinaya (*The Old Text of Hsiang-pu*), version of Dharmagupta; translated into Chinese by Buddhayasas, commentary by Fa-li (589–635), of Jih-k'ung Monastery in Hsiang-chou.

General Records of Buddhas and Patriarchs (*Fu-tsu Tung-chi*), 54 *chüan*, compiled by Chih-pan, published 1269. In *Taishō shinshū daizōkyō*, No. 2035, Vol. 49.

Huang-po Hsi-yün, *Dialogues of Ch'an Master Huang-po Tuan-chi of Yün-chou* (*Yün-chou Huang-po Tuan-chi Ch'an-shih Yü-lu*). In *Recorded Sayings of Ancient Worthies*, Chüan 2, (*Dainihon zokuzōkyō*, Part 2, Case 23).

Huang-po Hsi-yün, *Essentials of the Transmission of the Mind* (*Ch'üan-hsin Fa-yao*), recorded by Pei Hsiu (797–870). Reprinted 1884 by the Printing House of Buddhist Canons in Nanking; also in *Taishō shinshū daizōkyō*, No. 2012A, Vol. 48.

———, *Wan-ling Records of Ch'an Master Huang-po* (*Huang-po Tuan-chi Ch'an-shih Wan-ling Lu*), recorded by Pei Hsiu. In *Taishō shinshū daizōkyō*, No. 2012B, Vol. 48.

―――, *The Zen Teaching of Huang-po on the Transmission of the Mind*, English translation by John Blofeld. New York, Grove Press, 1959.

Hui-k'ai, *The Gate of Gatelessness* (*Wu-mên-kuan*), written in 1228. In *Taishō shinshū daizōkyō*, No. 2005, Vol. 48.

Hui-nêng, *Platform Sūtra of the Sixth Patriarch with Annotations* (*Liu-tsu T'an-ching Chien-chu*), edited by Ting Fu-pao, originally compiled by Fa-hai. Reprinted by the Ku-lin Temple, Shanghai, 1933.

Hung-chih Cheng-chio, *Extensive Records of Ch'an Master Hung-chih* (*Hung-chih Ch'an-shih K'uang-lu*), compiled by Chi-ch'êng in 1132. In *Taishō shinshū daizōkyō*, No. 2001, Vol. 48; also in *Collected Essentials of the Ch'an Schools*, Chüan 22 (*Chinese Buddhist Canon*, Second Collection, Vol. 2).

The I Ching, or Book of Changes, the Richard Wilhelm translation rendered into English by Cary F. Baynes, Foreword by C. G. Jung, Bollingen Series XIX; New York, Pantheon Books, 1950, 2 vols.

Kang-hsi Dictionary, edited by Chang Yu-shu and others, published in the Kang-hsi period (1662–1722). 42 vols.

Kiangsi Tao-i, *Recorded Dialogues of Ch'an Master Kiangsi Tao-i* (*Kiangsi Tao-i Ch'an-shih Yü-lu*), in *Records of Four Great Masters* (*Szu-chia Lu*), compiled by Chêng-ch'üan, first published 1085, reprinted 1607.

Kuei-fêng Tsung-mi, *Preface to the Complete Explanation of the Source of Ch'an* (*Ch'an-yüan Chu-ch'uan Chi-hsü*), introduction by Pei Hsiu. In *Taishō shinshū daizōkyō*, No. 2015, Vol. 48.

Kuei-shan Ling-yu, *Recorded Dialogues of Ch'an Master Kuei-shan Ling-yu of T'an-chou* (*T'an-chou Kuei-shan Ling-yu Ch'an-shih Yü-lu*), compiled by Yüan-hsin and Kuo Ning-chih. In *Taishō shinshū daizōkyō*, No. 1989, Vol. 47.

Laṅkāvatāra Sūtra (*Lêng-chia Ching*): literally "entering Laṅkā" to teach; Chinese translation by (1) Dommusen (385–433), (2) Günabharda (arrived in China 435), (3) Bodhiruchu (arrived in China 508), and (4) Śikṣānanda (652–710); translated into English by Daisetz T. Suzuki (London, Routledge & Kegan Paul, 1956).

Liang-su, *General Rules for Cessation and Contemplation* (*Chih-kuan T'ung-li*). In *Taishō shinshū daizōkyō*, No. 1915, Vol. 46.

Lin-chi I-hsüan, *Recorded Dialogues of Ch'an Master Lin-chi Hui-chao of Chên-chou* (*Chên-chou Lin-chi Hui-chao Ch'an-shih Yü-lu*). In *Recorded Sayings of Ancient Worthies*, Chüan 4, 5 (*Dainihon zohu-zōkyō*, Part 2, Case 23); also in *Taishō shinshū daizōkyō*, No. 1985, Vol. 47, compiled by San-shêng Hui-jan.

The Lotus of the Wonderful Law (*Miao-fa Lien-hua Ching*). The

BIBLIOGRAPHY

Lotus Sūtra, translated by W. E. Soothill. Oxford, Clarendon Press, 1930.

Mahāyāna Method of Cessation and Contemplation (Ta-ch'êng Chih-kuan Fa-mên), attributed to Hui-ssu (514–577). In *Taishō shinshū daizōkyō*, No. 1924, Vol. 46.

Matthews, Robert Henry, *Chinese-English Dictionary*, rev. ed. Cambridge, Mass., Harvard University Press, 1963.

Mu-chou Tao-tsung(*Dialogues of Monk Mu-chou (Mu-chou Ho-shang Yü-lu)*. In *Recorded Sayings of Ancient Worthies*, Chüan 6 (*Dainihon zokuzōkyō*, Part 2, Case 23).

Murti, T. R. V., *The Central Philosophy of Buddhism: A Study of the Mādhyamika System*. New York, The Macmillan Company, 1955.

Nāgārjuna (Lung-shu), *Mādhyamika Śāstra (Chung Lun)*, translated into Chinese by Kumārajīva, introduction by Sêng-jui. In *Taishō shinshū daizōkyō*, No. 1564, Vol. 30.

———, *Dvadāsanikaya Śāstra (Shih-erh-mên Lun, or Treatise of the Twelve Gates)*, translated into Chinese by Kumārajīva, introduction by Sêng-jui. In *Taishō shinshū daizōkyō*, No. 1568, Vol. 30.

———, *Mahāprajñāpāramitopadeśa (Ta-chih-tu Lun, or Treatise on the Great Wisdom)* translated into Chinese by Kumārajīva. In *Chinese Buddhist Canon*, First Collection, Vol. 14.

Nan-ch'üan P'u-yüan, *Extensive Records of Ch'an Master Nan-ch'üan P'u-yüan of Ch'ih-chou (Ch'ih-chou Nan-ch'üan Pu-yüan Ch'an-shih Kuang-lu)*. In *Recorded Sayings of Ancient Worthies*, Chüan 12 (*Dainihon zokuzōkyō*, Part 2, Case 23).

Nishida, Kitarō, *A Study of Good*, translated by V. H. Viglielmo. Tokyo, Japanese Government Printing Office, 1960.

Recorded Sayings of Ancient Worthies (Ku-tsun-hsü Yü-lu), 48 chüan. In *Dainihon zokuzōkyō*, Part 2, Case 23.

Records of Buddhas and Patriarchs in Various Dynasties (Li-tai Fu-tsu T'ung-tsai), 22 chüan, compiled by Nien-ch'ang, published 1344. In *Taishō shinshū daizōkyō*, No. 2036, Vol. 49.

Records of the Mind Lamp (Hsin-têng Lu), compiled 1715 by Chang-yü Lao-jen. Reprinted 1967 by the East Asia Printing House, Taipei.

Records of Pointing at the Moon (Chih-yüeh Lu), 32 chüan, compiled by Hsu Jü-chi in 1602. Reprinted 1959 in Taipei.

Records of Serenity (Ts'ung-yung Lu), 6 chüan, compiled by Hung-chih Cheng-chio, commentary by Wan-sung Hsing-hsiu, published 1224. In *Taishō shinshū daizōkyō*, No. 2004, Vol. 48 (entitled *Wan-*

Bibliography

sung Lao-jen P'ing-ch'ang T'ien-tung Chio Ho-shang Sung-ku Ts'ung-yung-an).

Records of the Source Mirror (Ts'ung-ching Lu), 100 chüan, compiled by Yung-ming Yen-shou (904–975). In Taishō shinshū daizōkyō, No. 2016, Vol. 48.

Sayings of Ch'an Masters Selected by the Emperor (Yu-hsüan Yü-lu), 19 chüan, compiled by Emperor Yung-chêng of the Ts'ing Dynasty, in 1733. Reprinted 1878 by the Printing House of Buddhist Canons, Nanking.

Sêng-chao, The Treatises of Sêng-chao (Chao Lun), translated into English by Walter Liebenthal. Hong Kong, University Press, 1968.

Sêng-ts'an, Inscription on the Believing Mind (Hsin-hsin Ming). In Taishō shinshū daizōkyō, No. 2010, Vol. 48.

Supplement to the Transmission of the Lamp (Hsü Ch'üan-têng Lu), 36 chüan, compiled by Yüan-chi Chü-ting (d. 1404). In Taishō shinshū daizōkyō, No. 2077, Vol. 51.

Suzuki, Daisetz T., An Introduction to Zen Buddhism. New York Harper & Row, 1949.

———, Essays in Zen Buddhism. First Series: New York, Harper & Row, 1949; Second Series: Boston, Beacon Press, 1952.

———, Zen Buddhism, ed. William Barrett. Garden City, N.Y., Doubleday & Company, 1956.

Ta-hui Tsung-kao, Recorded Dialogues of Ch'an Master Ta-hui P'u-chio (Ta-hui P'u-chio Ch'an-shih Yü-lu), compiled by Yün-wên in 1171. In Taishō shinshū daizōkyō, No. 1998A, Vol. 47.

Taishō shinshū daizōkyō (Buddhist Canon Published in the Taishō Era). Tokyo, Taishō issaikyō kankōkai, 1924–1934. 100 vols.

The T'ien-shêng Extensive Record of the Lamp (T'ien-shêng Kuang-têng Lu), 30 chüan, compiled by Li Tsun-hsü (d. 1038), published 1036.

Ts'ao-shan Pên-chi, Recorded Dialogues of Ch'an Master Ts'ao-shan Pên-chi of Fu-chou (Fu-chou Ts'ao-shan Pên-chi Ch'an-shih Yü-lu), compiled by Kuo Ning-chih. In Taishō shinshū daizōkyō, No. 1987B, Vol. 47.

———, Recorded Dialogues of Ch'an Master Ts'ao-shan Yüan-chêng of Fu-chou (Fu-chou Ts'ao-shan Yüan-chêng Ch'an-shih Yü-lu), compiled by the Japanese monk Hui-ying. In Taishō shinshū daizōkyō, No. 1987A, Vol. 47.

Tung-shan Liang-chieh, Recorded Dialogues of Ch'an Master Tung-shan Liang-chieh of Shui-chou (Shui-chou Tung-shan Liang-chieh

BIBLIOGRAPHY

Ch'an-shih Yü-lu), compiled by Yüan-hsin (1571–1646) and others. In *Taishō shinshū daizōkyō*, No. 1986B, Vol. 47.

―――――, *Recorded Dialogues of Ch'an Master Tung-shan Wu-pên of Yün-chou* (*Yün-chou Tung-shan Wu-pên Ch'an-shih Yü-lu*), compiled by Hui-ying. In *Taishō shinshū daizōkyō*, No. 1986A, Vol. 47.

Tung Tso-pin, *Chronological Tables of Chinese History* (*Chung-kuo Nien-li Tsung-p'u*), Hong Kong, Hong Kong University Press, 1960. 2 vols.

Tzu-ssu, *Doctrine of the Mean* (*Chung-yung*), translated into English by James Legge in *The Four Books*, distributed by Ione Perkins, California.

Vimalakīrti Sūtra (*Wu-mo-chieh So-shuo Ching*, or *Sūtra of the Discourse of Vimalakīrti*), 3 chüan, translated into Chinese by Kumārajīva, commentary by Sêng-chao. In *Taishō shinshū daizōkyō*, No. 537, Vol. 14; also recently reprinted by the Buddhist Association of the United States, New York, 1965.

Yang-shan Hui-chi, *Recorded Dialogues of Ch'an Master Yang-shan Hui-chi of Yüan-chou* (*Yüan-chou Yang-shan Hui-chi Ch'an-shih Yü-lu*), compiled by Yüan-hsin and Kuo Ning-chih. In *Taishō shinshū daizōkyō*, No. 1990, Vol. 47.

Yüan-wu Fu-kuo, *Blue Cliff Records* (*Fu-kuo Yüan-wu Ch'an-shih Pi-yen Lu*), 10 chüan, 100 kung-an, compiled by Yüan-wu K'ê-ch'in, commentary by Hsüeh-t'ou Ch'ung-hsien, published 1128. In *Taishō shinshū daizōkyō*, No. 2003, Vol. 48.

―――――, *Recorded Dialogues of Ch'an Master Yüan-wu Fu-kuo* (*Yüan-wu Fu-kuo Ch'an-shih Yü-lu*), compiled by Shao-lung and others in 1134. In *Taishō shinshū daizōkyō*, No. 1997, Vol. 47; also in *Dainihon zokuzōkyō*, Part 2, Case 24.

Yün-mên Wên-yen, *Essential Sayings of Ch'an Master K'uang-chên of Yün-mên* (*Yün-mên K'uang-chên Ch'an-shih Kuang-lu*). In *Recorded Sayings of Ancient Worthies*, Chüan 15, 16, 17, (*Dainihon zokuzōkyō*, Part 2, Case 23); also in *Taishō shinshū daizōkyō*, No. 1988, Vol. 47, compiled by Shou-chien.

Yung-chia Hsüan-chio, *Collected Works of Ch'an Master Yung-chia Hsüan-chio*. In *Taishō shinshū daizōkyō*, No. 2013, Vol. 48; also in *Collected Essentials of the Ch'an Schools*, Chüan 3 (*Chinese Buddhist Canon*, Second Collection, Vol. 2).

―――――, *Odes on Enlightenment* (*Chêng-tao Ko*). In *Taishō shinshū daizōkyō*, No. 2014, Vol. 48.

Index

An asterisk precedes the name of each Ch'an master whose fascicle is translated in the present volume, at the pages given in bold type. The chart on pages 306–11 contains classified data on each of these masters.

Absolute Void, see *śūnyatā*; Void
Admonition on Sitting in Meditation (by Hung-chih Cheng-chio), 54–5
ālayavijñāna (all-conserving consciousness), 34[1]
Amalgamation of the Essentials of the Lamps (Lien-têng Hui-yao), 196–7
Amalgamation of the Sources of the Five Lamps (Wu-têng Hui-yüan), 115, 224[4]
arhat, 225[14]
arūpadhātu (realm of pure spirit), 36[28]
Aryadeva, 35[3]
Asaṅga, 125[54], 301[38]
asañjñisattvah (fourth *dhyāna*), 254[14]
Astasāhasrikā, 35[2]
Aśvaghosa, 188
Avalokiteśvara, 5
Avataṁsaka Sūtra (Hua-yen Ching), 36[36], 42–3, 153, 178[20]
awakening, see enlightenment
Awakening of Faith, The (by Aśvaghosa), 188, 193

bala-abhijñā (shen-t'ung), 36[25]
Barrett, William, viii, ix
begging, 36[31], 226[35]
Bergson, Henri, ix
bhūtalathatā (reality), 31
Biographies of the Eminent Buddhist Monks, 178[19]

Blake, William, 47
Blofeld, John, 123[5]
blows, see striking
Blue Cliff Records (Fu-kuo Yüan-wu Ch'an-shih Pi-yen Lu), 125[56], 135–6, 267, 273–4
bodhi (wisdom), 5–6, 19, 36[26], 125[40], 149, 225[26]
Bodhidharma, First Patriarch, 3, 63, 85, 86, 105, 110, 116, 125[46], 149, 191–2
Bodhisattvayāna, 38[55], 241
Book of Changes (I Ching), 216, 225[29]
Buddha, the, ix, 25, 42, 80[17], 159, 179[38], 159, 205, 301[43], & *passim*; see also Śākyamuni
Buddha-eye, 12, 31, 38[58]

cangue, 108, 123[15]
Chang (valet), 144
Ch'ang-ch'ing Hui-leng, 238, 254[8], 259, 260, 278, 300[18]
Ch'ang-sha Ching-ch'ên, 135
Chang Shang-ying, 303
Ch'an-lin Lei-chu, see Collection and Classification of Ch'an Materials
*Chao-chou Ts'ung-shên, 164–73; 15, 16, 48, 49, 135, 147; life, 139, 164, 173; as Nan-ch'üan's disciple, 139–44, 154, 158, 159, 261; teachings, 139, 144, 165–73, 264
Chê-chuan, 146

323

Index

Chên, see Mu-chou Tao-tsung
cheng, see Void
cheng chung lai (enlightenment from universality), 46, 48–9, 52
cheng chung p'ien (particularity in universality), 46, 47
Ch'êng-kuan, 41
Cheng Yü, Prime Minister, 214
chen-k'ung miao-yu (real void and subtle reality), 13
Chen Tsao, Minister, 111, 124²⁴
Chên Tsun-su, see Mu-chou Tao-tsung
Chia-shan Shan-hui, 51, 125⁴⁸, 166, 180⁵⁴, 287
Chiang-nan Kuo-chu, King, 229
Ch'iang-tê (monk), 75
chien chung tao (enlightenment between universality and particularity), 46, 50, 79²
chien-hsin (seeing one's true nature), 129
Chih-i, 14, 63, 80¹⁸
Chih-mên Kuang-tsu, 266
Chin Ching (script/trans. of Avataṁsaka Sūtra), 42, 178²⁰
Chinese Buddhist Canon (Chung-hua Ta-ts'ang Ching), xiii
ching (mental attitude), 36²⁹
Ch'ing-ch'i Hung-chin, 239
Ching-ch'ing Shun-tê (Tao Fu), 278, 281, 300¹⁷
Ch'ing-chü Hao-sheng, 198, 224⁴
Ch'ing-hsüan (Vinaya master), 275
Ch'ing-jui (monk), 73
Ching-shan Hung-yen, 111, 124²⁸
Ching-shan Hung-yin, 278, 300¹⁶
Ching-shan Wên-ch'ü, 259
Ching-tê Record of the Transmission of the Lamp, xvi⁵
Ching-yüan (Ch'an center), 4
Chi-tsang, 10, 11, 35⁸
Chiu-fêng Tzu-hui, 187
Chi-yün (dictionary), 224⁵
Ch'u (monk), 61
Chuan Chou, 73, 178²²
Chuang-tzu, 178²²

Ch'uan-t'an (monk), 266, 279–80
Ch'üan-wei, 238
Chung-hua Dictionary, 224⁵
Chung-hua Ta-ts'ang Ching, see Chinese Buddhist Canon
Chung-i, King, 251
Chü-shih, 49
Chu-yü, 67–8
Collected Works of Ch'an Master Yung-chia Hsüan-chio, 10, 28–30, 35⁷
Collection and Classification of Ch'an Materials (Ch'an-lin Lei-chu), 141, 193, 268
Commentary on Contemplation of Dharmadhātu (by Kuei-fêng Tsung-mi), 46
contemplation, ten ways of, 30–4
Contemplation on Identification and Unification, 245
creepers, 110, 124²³

daśabhūmi, 284, 301³⁵
deportment, 29
devaputramāra, 37⁴²
Dharma, 3, 59, 80¹⁰
dharmadhātu, 42
dharma-eye, 12, 31, 38⁵⁶
Dharmagahanābhyudgatarāja, 155
Dharmagupta, 178¹⁹
dharmakāya (Body of Essence), 18–19, 38⁶¹, 66, 80²², 124¹⁸,²⁷, 215
dharmaparyāya (fa-men), 36²⁴
Dharmaraksa, 124²⁷
dhūta (begging monk), 224¹⁰
dhūta (prescription of conduct), 36³¹
dhyāna (meditation), 155, 179³³, 241, 254¹⁴
Diagrams of the Twelve Stages of Cow Herding (by Ch'ing-chü Hao-sheng), 198, 224⁴
Dialogue of P'ang Yün, 145
Dialogues and Biography of Ch'an Master Chao-chou Chen-chi, 36¹⁸
Diamond Sūtra, 3, 111, 124²⁵, 175

Doctrine of the Mean, 37[48]
Dōgen, 79[5]
Double Truth on Three Levels, 11, 35[8]
dragon's song, poem on, 44–5, 78
Dvādaśanikāya Śāstra, 35[3], 153, 178[21]

Earth God, 154, 179[28]
eating, rules of, 111, 124[29]
eightfold negation, 7
emptiness, see *śūnyatā*; Void
enlightenment (awakening; *samadhi*), xii, 5, 24, 26, 46, 48–50, 52–7, 89, 93, 101, 130, 138, 158, 169, 187, 191, 193, 203, 217; of Fa-yung, 8; Hsiang-yen, 189–91, 220; Hsuan-tsê, 231; Hsüeh-fêng, 262; Kuei-shan, 201; Liang, 89; Lin-chi, 90; Nan-ch'üan, 153; Pei Hsiu, 88; Po-chang, 132; Tao-chien, 230–1; Ts'ui-yen, 232; Tung-shan, 49, 296; Yang-shan, 197; Yung-chia, 15
Entering the Dharmadhātu, 42
Essay on the Double Truth (by Chi-tsang), 35[8]
Essentials of the Transmission of the Mind (by Huang-po Hsi-yün), 85, 87, 123[6]
everyday-mindedness (*p'ien ch'ang hsin*), 259–62
Extensive Records of Ch'an Master Hung-chih, 52, 54

Fa-ch'ang I-yü, 136, 200
Fa-huei, Abbot, 124[36]
Fa-têng (monk), 236
Fa-tsang, 41, 42, 43, 45
*Fā-yen Wên-i, 238–49; xiii, 195, 229, 235; life, 238–40, 248–9; teachings, 230–34, 236, 239, 240–8
Fa-yen School, 229–30, 234, 236; see also Fa-yen Wên-i

Fa-yung of Niu-t'ou Mountain, see Niu-t'ou Fa-yung
feng (objectivity), 51
Fêng-hsien Shen, 235–6
Feng-lu Monastery, 7
Feng-yang Shan-chao, 193
Fên-yang, 98
Five Aggregates (*skandhas*), 5, 35[5], 36[34]
five commandments, 108, 112, 115, 124[19]
Five Levels of Achievement, 51–2; chart, 53
Five Relations between Particularity and Universality, 41, 46, 50, 78n, 79[1], 230
Five Stages of the Emergence of Thought, 29, 37[53]
flower offerings, 8, 17
foot travel, 299[1]
four alternatives, 10–11, 130, 177[1]
Four-Division Vinaya, 153, 178[19]
Four Graces, 62, 80[15]
four heresies, 303
four modes of birth, 179[35]
Four Processes of Liberation from Subjectivity and Objectivity (*ssu liao chien*), 41, 95, 97–101, 230
Four Treatises (*Shih-lun*), 35[2]
Fourfold Dharmadhātu, 41, 42, 51
Fourfold Relationship Between Questioner and Answerer (*ssu pin chu*), 95–7
fu, character for Buddha, 18
Fu of T'ai-yüan (monk), 279
function (*yung*), 188
fu-tzu (pointer), 121, 125[52], 131, 190, 211, 263, 278, 281, & *passim*

gāthās, 79[3], 166, 300[25], of Hsiang-yen, 189–90, 191, 214–5, 220; Hui-leng, 240; Hui-nêng, 292[2]; Hung-chih, 47; Kiangsi, 149; Kuei-shan, 210; Lin-chi, 56–7, 122; P'ang Yün, 174; Tung-

gāthās (cont.)
　shan, 49, 59, 60, 262, 268–9; about turtle-nosed serpent, 260–1; of Yang-shan, 210, 218; Yun-mên, 293, 295; Yung-ming, 252
Gandavyūha script (of *Avataṁsaka Sūtra*), 42
gati, 23, 37[41]
geese, *kung-an* about, 132
General Records of Buddhas and Patriarchs, 35[11], 123[13]
golden lion, parable about, 43, 45
goose in bottle, *kung-an* about, 136
great action (*ta-yung*), 134, 186, 263–4
great potentiality (*ta-chi*), 186
guna, 58, 80[8]

Ho! (*Kwatz*), 9, 97, 131–2, 269, 304
hossu, see *fu-tzu*
Ho-yü Mountain, 72
Hsi (monk), 277, 300[14]
hsiang, see subjectivity
Hsiang-lin Ch'eng-yüan, 266, 267
*Hsiang-yen Chih-hsien, **219–23**; 44, 77–8, 138, 185, 193, 194–5, 199, 207; *gāthās*, 189–90, 214–5, 220; life, 191, 219; teachings, 220–3
Hsiao-tsung, Emperor, 260
Hsiao Yüan-shan (magistrate), 20, 26
Hsi-chio (Vinaya master), 238
Hsi-feng, Abbot, 114
hsin (mind), 87; see also mind
Hsing-shan Chien-hung (Mu-kou), 125[49]
Hsi-t'ang Chih-tsang, 123[6], 135, 138
Hsiu-shan Chu, see Shao-hsiu of Lung-sh'i
Hsüan-lang of Tso-ch'i, 27
Hsüan-sha Shih-pei, viii, 172, 181[72], 248, 255[24]; and Hsüeh-fêng, 259, 260, 265

Hsüan-tsang (translator), 35[2], 36[20]
Hsüan-ts'ê of Tung-yang, 27, 28, 231
*Hsüeh-fêng I-ts'un, **275–82**; 63–4, 80[18] 140, 172, 254[8], 283, 287; life, 259, 275–6, 282; teachings, 260–6, 276–81
Huai-jang, 131, 148
Hua-lin (monk), 187, 202
*Huang-po Hsi-yün, **102–6**; 9, 85–6, 87–91, 96, 116–20, 179[32]; life, 102–4, 106, 123[5]; teachings, 87–91, 103, 104–5, 132, 133, 142–3, 155–6, 165, 179[32], 269
Hua-yen Ching, see *Avataṁsaka Sūtra*
Hua-yen School, x, 41–6, 51, 178[20], 230, 270
Hui-chi, 204
Hui-chü, 248
Hui-ch'üan, 279
Hui-jan (San-sheng), 125[55]
Hui-k'ê, Second Patriarch, 3
Hui-leng, see Ch'ang-ch'ing Hui-leng
Hui-nêng (Lu Hsing-chê), Sixth Patriarch, 3, 14, 27, 86, 129, 144, 162, 180[45], 226[33], 234, 264, 299[2]
Hui-ssu, 14
Hui-yüan, 260
Hung-chih Cheng-chio, 47, 49, 52–7, 79[5], 197
Hung-chih Ch'an-shih K'uang-lu, see *Extensive Records of Ch'an Master Hung-chih*
Hung Chueh-fan, 79[2]
Hung-jên, Fifth Patriarch, 299[2]
Hu Shih, xvi[8]

I Ching, see *Book of Changes*
identification of events, 30
Identification of Reality and Appearance, 41

INDEX

initial consciousness (*yeh shih*), 135, 192–3, 266
Inscription on Ch'an (by Tung-shan Liang-chieh), 45
Inscription on the Chamber of Bliss in Purity (by Hung-chih Cheng-chio), 54, 55–6
interfusion, 44–6
I-tsung, Emperor, 276

jñeyāvarana (intellectual hindrance), 23, 37[43]
Ju-ching, 23, 79[5]
Jung, C. G., viii, 225[29]

kalpa (aeon), 161, 180[44], 241
kamadhātu (sensuous desire), 36[28]
K'ang-hsi Dictionary, 224[5]
karma, 19, 22, 36[27], 290, 301[36]
Karma of Six Courses, 252, 255[36]
*Kiangsi Tao-i (Ma-tsu), **148–52**; xi, 9, 14, 15, 58, 88, 89, 93, 123[6,12], 130–1; life, 148–9, 152; teachings, 132–4, 138, 149–52, 153, 175, 260
King of Hell, 287, 290
kleśa māra (evil spirit), 37[42]
kleśāvarana (conative hindrance), 37[43]
koan, see *kung-an*
kong kung, 51
Korea, 229, 253; see also Sila
Kuan-yin, 161
Kuang-yün (by Lu Fa-yen; dictionary), 224[5]
Kuei (San-lun master), 36[21]
Kuei-fêng Tsung-mi, 46, 86, 87, 197
*Kuei-shan Ling-yu, **200–8**; 59, 135, 138, 142, 199; life, 200–2; 208; teachings, 185–9, 192–8, 203–7, 209–12, 213, 215, 303–4
Kuei-tsung Chih-chang, 105, 123[12], 157
Kuei-yang School, 185
Kumārajīva, 7, 35[3], 36[20], 179[40], 224[11]

K'u-mu Ch'an, 45
k'ung, see *śunyatā*
kung (non-action), 51
kung-an (*koan*), xi–xii, xiii, 9, 15, 52, 88, 136–7, 138, 144, 186–7, 188, 193, 232–3, 260, 267, 272–3
kung kung, 51
K'uo-an Shih-yuan, 224[4]
Kwatz, see *Ho!*

Laṅkāvatāra Sūtra, 3, 34[1], 36[33], 149, 153
leap, further, 9, 15, 41, 43–4
li (reality, universality), 42–5, 51
Liang (monk), 89, 134, 177[14]
Liang-chieh, see Tung-shan Liang-chieh
liang chiu (keeping silence), 177[11]
Liang-hsin (monk), 161
Li Ao, Governor, 301[48]
Liao-yüan Fu-yin, 267
liberation, 97–101
Li Ching-jang, General, 202
Lien-têng Hui-yao, see *Amalgamation of the Essentials of the Lamps*
Lin Chien Lu (by Hung Chueh-fan), 79[2]
*Lin-chi I-hsüan, **116–23**; 9, 15, 41, 44, 56–7, 85, 86, 90, 131, 132, 133; life, 116–20, 122, 269; teachings, 93–101, 120–2
Lin-chi (Rinzai) School, 4, 41, 52, 57, 230, 267
Ling-chao (daughter of P'ang Yün), 145–6, 176
Ling-mo, 58
Ling-shih Mountain, 71
Ling-shu Jü-min, 193, 283, 301[33]
Ling-yen, 263
Ling-yün Chih-ch'ou, 279, 300[19]
lion roar (*simhānāda*), 23, 37[40]
Liu Yen-chung, 48
Li-yü, prince of Nan-t'ang, 243, 255[19]

327

Index

logic, in attaining enlightenment, 15–16
Lo-han Kuei-ch'en, 239, 254[10]
Lokaraksha, 35[2]
Lo-p'u Yuan-an, 120, 125[48], 170, 287
Lotus Sūtra, 37[46], 236, 250, 253, 255[28]
Lu Fa-yen, 224[5]
Lu Hsing-chê, see Hui-nêng
Lu Hsüan, Governor, 135, 136, 154, 158–9, 160–1
Lung-kuang, 249
Lung-shu, see Nāgārjuna

Ming (monk), 129
mirrors, Fa-tsang and, 45–6
moksa (emancipation), 38[61]
mondō, see wên-ta
mrtyu māra (evil spirit), 37[42]
Mu-ch'i (painter), 141
*Mu-chou Tao-tsung (Chên Tsun-su), 107–15; 85, 91–3, 124[31,-36], 132, 269, 283, 287; life, 107, 115; teachings, 107–14
Mu-kou (Hsing-shan Chien-hung), 120–1
Mumon, Rōshi Yamada, 50, 194
Murti, T. R. V., 4, 35[4]

Mādhyamika (Middle Way) doctrine (San-lun; Sanron), 4, 7, 8, 9, 15, 35[3], 178[21]; see also San-lun School
Mādhyamika Śāstra, 35[3], 153, 178[21]
Mahāparinirvāna Sūtra, see Nirvāna Sūtra
Mahāprajñāpāramitā, 291, 301[40]
Mahāprajñāpāramitā Sūtra, 3, 17, 20, 35[2], 36[20], 224[11]
Mahāprajñāpāramitopadeśa, see Ta-chi-tu Lun
Mahāyāna Buddhism, 22
Mahāyāna Sūtra, 37[47]
Mañjuśrī, 98–99, 143, 154, 179[26], 276, 300[12]
Mao, Mount, 17, 36[21]
māras (devils), 23, 37[42], 301[39]
Ma-tsu, see Kiangsi Tao-i
Matthews, R. H., 224[5]
Maudgalāyana, 159
Ma-yü, 121, 157
meditation, 131
mental attitude (ching), 6, 19, 20–21
Mere Ideation (Vijñāptimātra; Wei-shih), 112, 124[31]
Mere-Ideation School, x, 130
Middle Way, see Mādhyamika doctrine
mind (hsin), 7, 18, 19, 20, 24, 36[33], 87–8, 90, 149–51

Nāgārjuna, 35[3], 224[11]
*Nan-ch'üan P'u-yüan, 153–63; 8, 58, 89, 103, 141, 143, 260; and Chao-chou, 164–5, 261; life, 153–4, 163, 178[19]; teachings, 135–9, 154–63, 178[23]
Nan-yang Hui-chung (National Teacher), 157, 220, 225[33]
Nan-yo (Ch'an center), 4
negation, 5, 6, 9, 177[2], 233
nien-fu (reciting Buddha's name), 236, 237
nirmanakāya (Body of Magical Transformation), 124[18]
nirvāna, 34, 38[64], 224[1]
Nirvāna Sūtra, 75, 111, 124[27], 167, 180[58]
Nishida, Kitarō, ix, xvi[3]
*Niu-t'ou Fa-yung, 17–26; 3–9, 90, 195, 292, 298; life, 3, 8–9, 17–18, 20, 26; teachings, 8–9, 10, 16, 20–26
Niu-t'ou Mountain, 3, 17, 20
no-birth, 28
no-mind, 7, 22, 36[33], 264
non-sentient things, 59

Odes on Enlightenment (by Yung-chia Hsüan-chio), 28, 35[6]
Om-mani-padme-huṁ (Jewel in the Lotus), 124[37]

INDEX

One-Thought, 21, 36[35]
Original Nature, 5
opposites, as method of awakening, 234

Pai-yun, 80[31]
Pan-san, 124[21]
*P'ang Yün, 174–7; 144, 150; life, 174, 177; teachings, 145–7, 174–6
P'ao-an of Ta-hung Shan, 303
Pao-ching San-mei, see *Samādhi as Reflection from the Precious Mirror*
Pao-shou Chao, 165, 180[52]
Pao-tsang Lun, see *Treatise of the Precious Treasury*
Pao-tzu Wên-ch'i, 140
pāramitās (ways to reach the other shore), 34[2]
Pei Hsiu, Prime Minister, 88, 90, 104, 123[7], 124[24], 202
Pê-t'an, 113, 124[36]
p'ien ch'ang hsin, see everyday-mindedness
p'ien chung cheng (universality in particularity), 46, 47–8, 270
p'ien chung chih (enlightenment from particularity), 46, 49, 79[2]
Ping-ting T'ung-tzu (God of Fire), 231
Platform Sūtra (by Hui-nêng), 3, 86
Plato, ix
Po-chang Huai-hai, 89, 93, 103, 123[6], 131, 132, 135, 138, 186, 187, 200, 201
Po-ling, Prince, 20–6
potentiality in action (*ta-chi chih yung*), 186, 187
Prajna (translator), 42
prajñā (wisdom), 4, 6, 9, 10, 16, 17, 31, 34[2], 38[61]
Prajñāpāramitā (non-dual knowledge), 4, 6, 9, 35[2]

Prajñāpāramitā Śāstra, 35[3]
Prajñāpāramitā Sūtra, 3, 4, 6, 35[2]
Prajñāpāramitā-hridaya Sūtra, 5, 35[2], 58
pramudita (joy), 161, 180[42]
Pratyeka, 241, 254[16]
Pratyekabuddhayāna, 38[55], 241
Preface to the Complete Explanation of the Source of Ch'an (by Kuei-fêng Tsung-mi), 86
Pu-shang Tzu-hsia, 238, 254[6]
Pure Land School, xvi[8], 32, 236–7
Purification of Karmas, 29

Radical Intuitionism, viii–ix
Reality, 7, 13, 32; see also Ultimate Reality
Recorded Dialogues of Ch'an Master Kuei-shan Ling-yu of T'an Chou, 189
Recorded Dialogues of Ch'an Master Lin-chi, 36[18], 95, 97, 99, 100, 101
Recorded Dialogues of Ch'an Master Ta-hui P'u-chio, 48
Recorded Dialogues of Ch'an Master Wên-i of the Ch'ing-liang Monastery in Chin-ling, 254[1]
Records of Buddhas and Patriarchs in Various Dynasties, 123
Records of Pointing at the Moon, 80[11], 123[6], 145–6, 232, 234–5, 301[52]
Records of Serenity (Ts'ung-yung Lu), 197, 198, 233, 267
Records of the Source Mirror (Ts'ung-ching Lu), 224[4], 229, 253
repetition, as method of awakening, 231–2
Rinzai School, see Lin-chi School
rūpa (material element), 35[5], 36[32], 43
rūpadhātu (realm of form), 36[28]

329

Index

saindhava, 221, 226[34]
Śākyamuni, 34[1], 80[21], 144, 268; see also Buddha
samādhi (sudden enlightenment), 22, 32, 36[36], 42, 153, 179[33]; see also enlightenment
Samādhi as Reflection from the Precious Mirror (Pao-ching San-mei), 47, 48
Samantabhadra, 143, 154, 179[26]
śamatha (tranquillity of mind), 29, 37[54]
sambhogakāya (Body of Bliss), 124[18]
samjñā (perception), 35[5], 36[34]
samskāra (formative principle), 35[5]
sandals, made by Mu-chou, 91, 107
San-lun (Three Treatises), 7, 35[3]
San-lun School, x, 7, 9, 10, 11, 35[3]; see also Mādhyamika doctrine
San-sheng, 122, 125[54]
Sanron, see San-lun
śastras, 27, 37[50]
Śata Śāstra (One Hundred Verses), 35[3], 153, 178[21]
School of Silent Illumination, 52
Self, 95–7, 179[31,32]
self-nature, 129
self-pride, 29, 32
Sêng-chao, 135, 160, 179[40], 245, 255[21]
Sêng-ts'an, Third Patriarch, 20
Shan-shan, 156
Shao-hsiu of Lung-shi (Hsiu-shan Chu), 231, 246, 255[23]
Shên-shan, 157
shih (event, appearance, particularity), 42–5, 51
Shih-lin, 147
Shih-lun (Four Treatises), 35[3]
shih shih yuan yung wu ai, 46
Shih-shih Shan-tao, 210, 255[23]
Shih-shuang Hsing-k'ung, 44, 78, 192, 207
Shih-t'ao, 245
Shih-t'ou Hsi-ch'ien, 145, 151, 174, 181[77]

shou-chi (vyākarana), 239, 254[11]
Shuang-fêng (monk), 215
Shui-liao, 134
Shu-shan K'uang-jen, 221, 222, 226[37]
Śikṣānanda, 42, 178[20]
Sila (Korea), 229, 235–6, 292
silent illumination, 52, 54–7, 188, 196
simhanāda, see lion roar
six levels of reincarnation, 179[35]
six phenomena, 230
Six Procedures for Achieving Śamatha, 29, 37[54]
Skandhas, see Five Aggregates
skandha māra (evil spirit), 37[42]
slap, see striking
Sogen, Asahina, 57
Soothill, W. E., 255[28]
Sōtō School, see Ts'ao-tung School
Śrāvaka, 241, 254[15]
Śravakayāna, 38[55], 241
ssu liao chien, see Four Processes for Liberation from Subjectivity and Objectivity
Ssu-ma, Dhūta, 201
ssu pih chu, see Fourfold Relationship between Questioner and Answerer
striking (for enlightenment), 77, 86, 89–90, 93, 96, 99, 101, 103, 106, 109, 114, 117, 119, 121–2, 133, 262, 263, 277, 278, 279, 280
subjectivity, 51
substance (*ti*), 188
suchness, see tathatā
śūnyatā (emptiness; Void), 4–5, 6, 7, 9, 10, 16, 22, 36[20], 37[44], 38[57], 43, 147; see also Void
Supplement to the Transmission of the Lamp, 260
Supreme Enlightenment, 4, 5
Sūtra of Nirvāna, The, see *Nirvāna Sūtra*
sūtras, 3, 27, 37[50], 300[25]
Su T'ung-p'o, 267, 302

330

INDEX

Suzuki, Daisetz T., xi–xii, xvi[8], 14, 192, 194; works: *Eastern Buddhist Journal*, art. in, 303; *Essays in Zen Buddhism*, Series I, xvi[7], 36[16], 38[64], 254[14]; —, Series II, xvi[6], 194, 224[2], 300[4]; *An Introduction to Zen Buddhism*, foreword by C. G. Jung, viii, xvi[1]; *Laṅkāvatāra Sūtra* (tr.), 34[1]; *Zen Buddhism*, intro. by W. Barrett, viii, ix
swordplay, 196, 199

ta-chi, *see* great potentiality
ta-chi chih yung, *see* potentiality in action
Ta-chih-tu Lun, 224[11]
Ta-chio, *see* Wei-fu Ta-chio
Ta-chu Hui-hai, xi
Ta-hui Tsung-kao, xii, 48, 51, 52, 153
ta yung, *see* great action
T'ai-ch'in, 249
Tai-ming, 7
T'ai-tsung, Emperor, 34, 38[65], 253
Ta-mei, 79
T'ang, 148
T'ang Ching (script/trans. of *Avataṁsaka Sūtra*), 42, 178[20]
Tan-hsia T'ien-jan, 145, 146, 174, 181[77]
Ta-ning Tao-kuan, 13
Tan-yüan Chen-ying, 192, 209, 212
Tao, 6, 13, 18, 19, 29, 31, 34, 44, 100, 130, 165, & *passim*
Tao-fen Hui-chu, 229
Tao-fu, *see* Ching-ch'ing Shun-tê
Tao-hsin, Fourth Patriarch, 5, 8, 17–20
Tao-wu, 137–8
Tao-yüan, xiii
Taoism, 61
tathāgata, 189, 224[1]
Tathāgatagarbha (Mind-Only), 34[1]
tathatā (suchness), 13, 31, 80[13], 130, 302
Ta-yü, 96, 97, 117, 133

Tê-chao, *see* T'ien-t'ai Te-chao
Tendai School, *see* T'ien-t'ai School
Teng Yin-fêng, 151
Ten Pictures of Cow Herding (by K'uo-an Shih-yuan), 224[4]
Tê-shan, 287
Te-shan Hsüan-chien, 65, 93, 133, 259, 275
Tê-shan Yuan-mi, 266
Three Existences, 62, 80[16]
three greatnesses, of Aśvaghosa, 188
Three Realms, *see* Triple World
Three Treatises, *see* San-lun
three truths, 31, 38[59]
Three Vehicles, 30, 38[55], 241, 280, 300[25]
Threefold Body, 300[10]
Threefold Contemplation, 12, 23, 37[39]
threefold truth, 12
ti, *see* substance
T'ien-kung Hui-wei, 11, 35[11]
T'ien-lung, 269
T'ien-t'ai School, 7, 11–14, 27, 80[18]
T'ien-t'ai Tê-chao, 229, 248, 251, 255[33]
T'ien-tung Chen-chio, 233
tiger's roar, of Huang-po, 90, 103
Tin Tu (lexicographer), 224[5]
T'ou-chih Ta-t'ung, 259
Tou-pa, 298
T'ou-tzu Ta-t'ung, 15
Trailokya (Triloka), *see* Triple World
tranquillity (*śamatha*), 24, 29, 198
Transmission of the Lamp, The, xiii, 3, 4, 8, 14, 15, 85, 86, & *passim*
transmission of the mind, 85, 86, 87
Treatise on the Golden Lion (by Fa-tsang), 43
Treatise of the Precious Treasury, The (by Sêng-chao), 225[2]
Treatises of Sêng-chao, 245
Trikāya, *see* Triple Bodies
Triple Bodies (Trikāya), 108, 124[18]
Triple World (Trailokya; Triloka), 19, 36[28], 112, 289

Index

Triratna, 301[44]
Ts'an Tung Ch'i, 245
Ts'ao Mountain, 72
*Ts'ao-shan Pên-chi, 71–79; 41, 50; life, 71–2, 79; teachings, 44–5, 46–7, 72–8
Ts'ao-tung (Sōtō) School, 4, 41, 47, 51–2, 54, 57, 79, 267[5]
Tso-ch'i Fa-lang, 11, 35[18]
Ts'ui-yen K'ê-chen, 232
Ts'ui-yen Ling-ts'an, 250, 255[30]
Ts'ui-yen Yung-ming, 252, 259
Ts'ung-ching Lu, see *Records of the Source Mirror*
Ts'ung-yung, 37[48]
Ts'ung-yung Lu, see *Records of Serenity*
Tung-ch'an Ch'i, 232–3
Tung-shan Hsiao-ts'ung, 268
*Tung-shan Liang-chieh, 58–70; xii, 8, 41, 43, 44, 46, 49, 71, 90, 259; life, 58–9, 69–70; teachings, 50–1, 53, 60–9, 161
*Tung-shan Shou-ch'u, 296–9; 49, 132, 133, 236, 266–7; teachings, 271–3
turtle-nosed serpent, parable, 260–1
Twelve Divisions (of Buddhist Canon), 281, 300[25]
Tzü-fang (monk), 240
Tz'u-ming, 232

Uda, King of, 42
Ultimate Essence, 5
Ultimate Reality (Absolute beyond Reason), 4, 5, 9, 10, 11, 17, 25, 30, 71, 147, 241
Unimpeded perfect mutual solution between particularity and particularity, 42, 46
upekṣā (equilibrium), 29

vairocana, 68, 80[26], 172
vajra (guardian spirit), 109, 113, 124[20]
vāsanā (force of habit), 224[12]

Vasubandhu, 125[54], 290, 301[38]
vedanā (sensation), 35[5], 36[84]
vijñāna (consciousness), 35[5]
Vijñāptimātra (Wei-shih), see Mere Ideation
Vimalakīrti, 144, 177, 276, 300[12]
Vimalakīrti-nirdeśa Sūtra, 65, 80[21]
Vinaya-Pitaka, 210, 225[20]
vinayas, 27, 37[50]
vipaśyanā (perfect insight), 29
Void, 6, 7, 8, 12, 13, 17, 20, 21, 25, 46, 47, 87, 224[1], 230–1; see also *śūnyatā*
vyākarana, see *shou-chi*

Wang-sung, 233
Wang Wei, 144–5
Wan-ju T'ung-chê, 52
Wan-ling Records of Ch'an Master Huang-po, 123[5]
wei, 46–50, 79[1]
Wei-chien, Abbot, 124[36]
Wei-chou, 210
Wei-fu Ta-chio, 121, 125[51]
Wei-ma Chi Ching, see *Vimalakīrti-nirdeśa Sūtra*
Wei-shih, see Mere Ideation
Wên-mo, King of Wu-yüeh, 250
Wên-sui, 248
wên-ta, 9
wisdom-eye, 12, 31, 38[57]
wu, 48, 49, 52
Wu-chu Wen-hsi, 122, 125[54]
Wu-k'ung, 246
wu wei kung hsin, see Five Levels of Achievement
wu wei p'ien chêng, see Five Relations between Particularity and Universality

*Yang-shan Hui-chi, 209–18; 89, 142, 185–6, 188, 195–7, 203, 204, 206–9; life, 209–10, 218; teachings, 188–99, 203–7, 210–18, 303–4

INDEX

yeh-shih, see initial consciousness
Yen-kuan Ch'i-an, 7, 89, 166, 180[53]
Yen-t'ou Ch'üan-huo, 210, 225[21], 259
Yen-yen Tzu-yu, 238, 254[6]
yin, see Skandhas
Yogācāra School, 124[31], 125[54], 301[38], see also Mere-Ideation School
Yo-shan Wei-yen, 301[48]
Yüan of Yü-chou (Vinaya master), 148
Yüan-ching (monk), 261
Yüan-wu K'ê-ch'in, xii, 273
Yüeh-shan, 50, 76–7, 90, 137
Yün-chu Tao-ying, 62, 64, 69, 169–70, 180[60]
yung, see function

*Yung-chia Hsüan-chio, 27–34; 7; life, 27–8, 34; teachings, 10, 11, 14, 15, 29–33
Yung-ming Tao-chien, 230–1
Yung-ming Yen-shou, 250–3; xvi[8], 229–30; life, 250, 253; teachings, 234–5, 236–7, 251–3
*Yün-mên Wên-yen, 283–95; 49, 91, 132, 135, 246, 259, 260; life, 283; teachings, 235, 236, 266–71, 272, 284–95
Yün-yen, 50, 59–60, 61, 62, 137–8, 206

Zen Teaching of Huang-po on the Transmission of the Mind, 123[5]

333

禪

作　　者／張中原　CHANG CHUNG-YUAN
發 行 人／徐國樑
出版發行／護幼社文化事業有限公司
地址：台北市中山北路三段二六號七〇三室
電話：（〇二）五九四一一八三一四
　　　　五九七〇八〇三一四
傳眞：（〇二）五九一〇八七四
印　　刷／百杰電腦排版印刷有限公司
出版登記／局版臺業字第四二八〇號
初版日期／一九六九年
初版二刷／一九九三年十二月
本書定價／美金貳拾肆點玖伍元
ISBN 957-9561-67-2

ISBN 957-9561-67-2
REPRINT 1993